Tolley's
Flexible Benefits:

A Practical Guide

By Philip Hutchinson, Jardine Lloyd Thompson

Tolley
LexisNexis™

Members of the LexisNexis Group worldwide

United Kingdom	LexisNexis Butterworths Tolley, a Division of Reed Elsevier (UK) Ltd, 2 Addiscombe Road, CROYDON CR9 5AF
Argentina	LexisNexis Argentina, BUENOS AIRES
Australia	LexisNexis Butterworths, CHATSWOOD, New South Wales
Austria	LexisNexis Verlag ARD Orac GmbH & Co KG, VIENNA
Canada	LexisNexis Butterworths, MARKHAM, Ontario
Chile	LexisNexis Chile Ltda, SANTIAGO DE CHILE
Czech Republic	Nakladatelství Orac sro, PRAGUE
France	Editions du Juris-Classeur SA, PARIS
Hong Kong	LexisNexis Butterworths, HONG KONG
Hungary	HVG-Orac, BUDAPEST
India	LexisNexis Butterworths, NEW DELHI
Ireland	Butterworths (Ireland) Ltd, DUBLIN
Italy	Giuffrè Editore, MILAN
Malaysia	Malayan Law Journal Sdn Bhd, KUALA LUMPUR
New Zealand	Butterworths of New Zealand, WELLINGTON
Poland	Wydawnictwo Prawnicze LexisNexis, WARSAW
Singapore	LexisNexis Butterworths, SINGAPORE
South Africa	Butterworths SA, DURBAN
Switzerland	Stämpfli Verlag AG, BERNE
USA	LexisNexis, DAYTON, Ohio

A CIP Catalogue record for this book is available from the British Library.

ISBN 0 7545 1966 X

Typeset by Letterpart Ltd, Reigate, Surrey

Printed and bound in Great Britain by Hobbs the Printers Ltd, Totton, Hampshire

Visit Butterworths LexisNexis *direct* at www.butterworths.com

Preface

The aim of this book is to introduce the reader to the issues associated with the design, development, implementation and administration of flexible benefits. The challenge of this book is that each of the areas it covers (feasibility, strategy, design, product selection, pensions, tax, employment law, communication, administration and outsourcing) is a specialism in its own right, with its own unique issues and challenges. With flexible benefits it is a case of the sum of the parts being greater than the whole. The mix of benefits is the key unique feature.

Assuming no prior knowledge of flexible benefits or its constituent parts, the reader is introduced to the challenges of developing, implementing and administering a flexible benefits strategy.

When first introduced into the UK market schemes were over engineered and expensive and based on product selection rather than strategy and solution. This meant that they were difficult to assess in terms of delivering added value to an organisation.

Today flexible benefits are more of a strategic policy than an arrangement of advantageous products. With the introduction of new technology, there has also been a reduction in costs due to simpler and more effective administration.

There have been several market surveys carried out to determine future demand for flexible benefits which suggest a large proportion (about 70%) of UK organisations believe flexible benefits would be a valuable vehicle for managing cultural change. A smaller amount (about 40%) is actively looking at implementing new schemes.

This book begins by looking at the flexible benefits marketplace and how they are being used to respond to the changing world of work. It then addresses the issue of establishing the feasibility of such a scheme and developing a business case for its introduction.

The chapter on strategy and design process includes product selection, rules and regulations and statutory requirements. Because it is a specialist area, there is a separate chapter on pensions in the UK and how to included them in a flexible benefits scheme.

The tax implications for flexible benefits is crucial to the success of any such scheme and this book concentrates on the effect of mixing different types of benefits and funding options. Employment law issues are also important, especially terms and conditions of employment, current legislation and business transfers.

With the growing array of media available, the chapter on documentation looks at what is required and alternative methods of delivering them, including a review of e-communication and total reward statements. Scheme launch and communication, has a particular emphasis on education and managing expectations and includes a review on the use of technology.

The different options available to manage and administer a flexible benefits scheme along with the various options available are covered in a separate chapter, which also includes a review of web-based systems. There is also a separate chapter on outsourcing flexible benefits, including guidance on selecting and managing outsourcers. There is also a review of generic site offerings, a new form of outsourcing being developed for this market.

There is a step by step guide to installing and implementing a flexible benefits scheme which contains hints on timing and fault finding as well as a look at the *Data Protection Act*.

As it is an important part of managing such a scheme, there is a summary of the costs, savings and risks associated with flexible benefits, including a variety of useful suggestions on how to manage them effectively and profitably.

The book concludes with a summary of the major points, along with the key criteria for success for the design, development, implementation and administration of a flexible benefits scheme.

The appendix contains a variety of useful reference materials and examples referred to throughout the book along with a list of the author's preferred product providers.

For those of us who have been involved in flexible benefits throughout the last decade, it has been difficult enough to keep up with developments. For anyone trying to understand how the various issues come together, the complications must appear daunting. That, I hope, is where this book will provide a useful support.

The book is not meant for those who are experts on the areas listed above. It is meant for anyone who, whilst he or she may have knowledge in one or two of these fields, is a newcomer to the others and needs to understand how the various issues relate to each other.

There are a number of people I wish to thank for their support and advice in helping me to write this book. The first is my colleagues at Jardine Lloyd Thompson: June McIntosh, Phil Wadswoth and Chris Doukaki, who advised on the chapters covering pensions and employment law. Next, Jean Knowles and Carol Hutchinson for their hard work and patience in preparing and proofreading the various script. And finally my family, Carol, Patrick and Isabelle, for their understanding and encouragement.

Philip Hutchinson BSc. M Inst. D.
Head of Reward Consulting
Jardine Lloyd Thompson

Contents

Table of Statutes

Table of Statutory Instruments

Abbreviations

ASP	Application Service Providers
AVC	Additional Voluntary Contributions
CPA	Compulsory Purchase Annuity
DPA 1998	Data Protection Act 1998
DWP	Department for Work and Pensions
EPP	Executive Pension Plan
ESOP	Employee Share Ownership Plan
ET	Earnings Threshold
ETO	Economic, technical or organisational reason
FSAVC	Free Standing Additional Voluntary Contribution
FURBS	Funded Unapproved Retirement Benefits Scheme
GOQ	Genuine occupational qualification
GSO	Generic site outsourcing
GPP	Group Personal Pension
IPR	Intellectual property
ISP	Internet Service Provider
ITT	Invitations to Tender
LV	Luncheon Voucher
MA	Maternity Allowance
NHS	National Health Service
NICs	National Insurance contributions
PAYE	Pay As You Earn
PI	Procedural Instruction
PIA	Personal Investment Authority
PLP	Personal Lease Plan
PMI	Private Medical Insurance
PP	Personal Pension

PRP	Profit Related Pay
RAP	Retirement Annuities Plan
RFIs	Requests for information
RPI	Retail Prices Index
S2P	State Second Pension
SAP	Statutory Adoption Pay
SASS	Small Self-Administered Scheme
SERPS	State Earnings Related Pension Scheme
SIB	Securities and Investments Board
SLA	Service level agreement
SMP	Statutory Maternity Pay
SPP	Statutory Paternity Pay
SSL	Secure socket layer (technology)
TPA	Third Party Administrator
TUPE	Transfer of Undertakings (Protection of Employment) Regulations 1981 (SI 1981 No 1794)
UURBS	Unfunded Unapproved Retirement Benefits Scheme
VPN	Virtual private network

1 — Introduction

This chapter covers the following:

- How to use this book
- Flexible benefits market place

How to use this book   1.1

This book is intended to be both a basic overview of the whole subject of flexible benefits and also a textbook that can be referred to for information on a specific subject. It will be most appreciate by professionals who are new to the subject or looking for an alternative perspective on the design, development, implementation and administration of a flexible benefits scheme.

As with similar complex and intregral projects the main challenge of flexible benefits is knowing where to start and how to best project manage the different elements of the scheme. This book is designed to give both a quick overview of the key elements together with detailed step-by-step guide to each of the key areas. There is also a project brief in **APPENDIX 1** which readers can refer to as a particle example of a flexible benefits project.

The book is not intended to be an exhaustive review of the whole subject. It covers mainly the key points and the most commonly asked questions and, as such, is more of a practical guide to the subject.

Tolley's Flexible Benefits is so designed that you can read the whole book if you want a quick review, or refer to various sections if you want information on a specific subject using the contents section and/or the index.

Outline of subjects covered 1.2

The book covers a wide range of subjects outlined below:

- Chapter 1: Introduction and the flexible benefits market place.

- Chapter 2: The changing world of work and the resultant business and HR issues that are shaping reward strategies.

- Chapter 3: An introduction to flexible benefits, how they work and where they are used.

- Chapter 4: Establishing the feasibility of a flexible benefits scheme and developing a business case for its introduction.

- Chapter 5: The strategy and design process including product selection. Rules and regulations and statutory requirements are also covered.

- Chapter 6: A basic introduction to pensions in the UK and how to include them in a flexible benefits scheme. The advantages and disadvantages of the options available.

- Chapter 7: Tax implications and considerations for flexible benefit schemes. The effect of mixing different types of benefits and funding options.

- Chapter 8: Employment law issues concerning flexible benefits schemes, including terms and conditions of employment, current legislation and business transfers.

- Chapter 9: The documentation required and alternative methods of delivering them. This chapter also includes a review of e-communication and total reward statements.

- Chapter 10: Scheme launch and communication, with particular emphasis on education and managing expectations. This chapter also includes a review on the use of technology.

- Chapter 11: The different options available to manage and administer a flexible benefits scheme along with the various options available. Includes web-based systems.

- Chapter 12: A practical review of outsourcing flexible benefits, including guidance on selecting and managing outsourcers. Includes a review of generic site offerings.

- Chapter 13: Step-by-step guide to installing and implementing a flexible benefits scheme. This chapter also contains hints on timing, fault finding as well as looking at the *Data Protection Act 1998.*

- Chapter 14: This chapter contains a summary by section, of the cost, savings and risks associated with flexible benefits. Includes a variety of useful suggestions on how to manage them effectively and profitably.

- Chapter 15: This chapter contains a summary of the major points of the book along with the key criteria for success of the design, development, implementation and administration of a flexible benefits scheme.

- Appendix 1: This contains a variety of useful reference material and examples referred to through out the book.

- Appendix 2: This section contains a list of the author's choice of providers.

Flexible benefits market place   1.3

Although there has recently been much interest shown in flexible benefits by the trade press, the fact remains that since 1996 only a hundred or so schemes have been set up. These have tended to be large schemes and part of a larger reward strategy.

When first introduced into the UK, schemes were over-engineered and expensive and based on pure products rather than addressing key issues. This meant they were difficult to assess in terms of delivering added value to the organisation. Nowadays flexible benefits are more of a strategic policy than an arrangement of advantageous products. There has also been a shift to more realistic costings and planning with improved and effective administration.

There have been several market surveys carried out to determine future demand for flexible benefits, which suggest a large proportion (about 70%) of UK organisations believe flexible benefits would be a valuable vehicle for managing cultural change. A smaller amount (about 40%) is actively looking at implementing new schemes.

The main reason for the high interest in flexible benefits is the increasing pace of change. Organisations are looking for flexible and adaptable mechanisms for dealing with a multitude of variables that do not require continuous re-engineering.

A changing workforce   1.4

Higher expectations, productivity and HR returns have forced modern management to re-evaluate their pay and benefits policies to ensure best value for money and lower risks. As the workplace dynamics are in continuous motion, so too are demanding reward structures that can change with them.

Our workforce is increasingly diverse and ageing. This is leading to a tightening labour market. Old benefits structures no longer work and simply modernising them is not good enough. To keep up with the demand for more competitive schemes to improve recruitment, retention and motivation requires a continuously evolving mechanism that offers choice, flexibility and adaptability.

The emergence of the virtual society has now changed the workplace to one that mirrors the fast moving and perceptive world we live in. Improved communication and managing expectations is important and one of the most popular reasons for introducing flexible benefits.

There are, however, perceived barriers to adopting this new concept. These are based mainly on concerns about administration complexity, obtaining effective software and design and installation costs. Later on in this book we will consider these in more detail and look at alternative ways of dealing with them.

Cultural change 1.5

Currently, there are several main uses for flexible benefits and the first is as a vehicle and catalyst for cultural change. The communications of flexible benefits schemes are being used to deliver powerful messages in a way that suits our virtual society. For instance, the creation of a single benefits 'brand' encompassing two different schemes.

With a continuous dynamic of mergers, acquisitions and disposals, organisations have started to use flexible benefits as a mechanism for consolidating and harmonising dissimilar pay and benefit structures. Its advantage is that it can cope with continual modification without having to 're-invent the wheel'.

The first part of designing and implementing a flexible scheme is research. It is not surprising, therefore, that they are also used as a vehicle for the analysis and development of reward policies and strategies.

One of the main reward issues facing organisations today is improving the perceived value of total reward packages, in particular benefits. This is becoming more important as the competition for talent increases.

Giving employees a choice over how they receive their reward and then enhancing it is the ultimate form of maximising perceived value.

Flexible retirement planning 1.6

There is an increasing concern with the level of retirement in the UK now that it is no longer a pre-requisite to reach the age of 60/65. There is a need to retain high skills, experience and maturity, as this is the demographic group where the bulk of an organisation's intellectual and emotional wealth is. As a result, flexible retirement planning is becoming more important in flexible benefits schemes along with the inclusion of pensions.

Costs 1.7

Improved control and reduction in long-term costs of employee benefits and better targeting is the final important reason why flexible benefits are becoming more popular. By giving employees a choice over where their money is spent, the organisation ensures the best choice at all times.

Note the use of the word 'control' and not 'savings'. In the short run, flexible benefits do not save money, as was the claim when first introduced into the UK. These claims were based on direct costs only and did not take into consideration indirect costs such as improving infrastructure, increased resources to run the scheme etc. In the long run flexible benefits do reduce risk and overall costs because they generate better efficiency and utilisation.

Most organisations that have put in flexible benefits have done so to address all of the objectives above. As a consequence they have obtained stepped improvements in addressing the key short- and long-term issues facing businesses today.

2 — The Changing World of Work

This chapter covers the following:

- The forces of change
- Individual response to change
- Corporate response to change
- Group response to change
- Key influences of business performance
- Organisational response to change
- Thriving in the new work place
- Key cultural issues
- Key HR issues
- Key reward Issues
- Key reward strategies

The forces of change   2.1

To fully understand and appreciate the advantages and disadvantages of flexible benefits one must have a clear understanding of the changing world of work and the forces that are creating it.

Today, database society is based on the concept of managing perceptions. Power and influence now lies with those who can successfully gather, manipulate and use information on groups of people and individuals. It is now commonplace, for instance, for HR departments to have and use powerful and sophisticated IT systems to record and manage their employees.

Flexible benefits is suited to a database society continuously re-organising individual information to match up employee benefits with personal preferences. Also, by offering choice, value is improved.

Changing demographics 2.2

Demographics are changing and most developed countries are seeing an increasingly ageing, diversifying and diminishing population. Over the next few years, in the UK, the retired population will outnumber the working population.

Attitudes are changing too. The concept of a job for life is now moribund and so too is the ideals of long-term loyalty. New initiatives are being introduced such as flexible working, employability, and life/work balance. The emphasis is on shorter-term returns and loyalty for both employer and employee.

In the UK these demographic and attitude changes are leading to severe shortages of skilled employees for a large variety of industries. Because of the shift in approach to loyalty, organisations have to rethink how they recruit, motivate and retain key staff.

The unpredictability that a global economy brings, forces both employer and employee to prepare for the unknown. A balance is required between longer-term desires of growth and prosperity and shorter-term needs of survivability and sustainability.

Globalisation is not only a major catalyst for change but, for many organisations, is the main reason for change. Multi-national organisations with multi-cultural teams need a common benefits platform with the ability to provide local variations. The need for global communication is increasing.

One of the consequences of improved technology is the increasing demand for 'real time' information to manage our lives and finances. We no longer tolerate waiting for days for a quote for insurance. We automatically database these quotes and compare them with others to ensure the best buy. This is a major reason why flexible benefits have traditionally been designed around internets, intranets and web sites.

Databases also allow the user to manage the perceptions of others by understanding their preferences and habitual patterns. By using database information they can re-model individual and group reactions to change.

Along with the continuing evolution of our society has come an increase in social responsibility. The last few years have seen the introduction of stakeholder pensions, fixed time directive, part-timers rights and more. Over the next few years we can look forward to FRS 17 and directors pay disclosure to name but a few. Along with this increase in corporate activity an increase in personal litigation and claims has also emerged.

Individual response to change 2.3

Humans by their very nature are complex and how they respond to change is a subject worthy of a book in its own right. However, for the purpose of this document, we shall use the diagram below to consider how we maintain a balance in the management of work and lives.

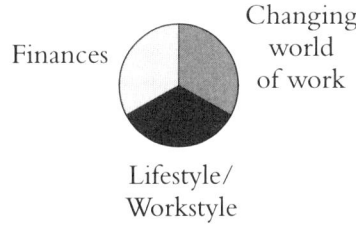

Figure 1: Individual response to forces of change

Most employees go to work to earn money to fuel their lifestyles. For some this requires very little money; for others a lot. Whichever, it is a major determining factor in what careers they choose and how they are motivated in them.

So, if finances and work style / lifestyle can be 'balanced', what happens when the third variable (the changing world of work) changes? To maintain equilibrium they must either change their work style / lifestyle aspirations, financial or both.

Corporate response to change 2.4

The corporate response to forces of change is not too dissimilar to the individual response except the variables are changed. For finances substitute stakeholder expectations and for workstyle/lifestyle substitute vision/capabilities.

When there is a shift in the market place (changing world of work) the two other variables need to change to return to the equilibrium. So if the market for the company's product dives, it would be advisable to either accept a drop in profit or redefine the company's vision/capabilities and move into new areas or both.

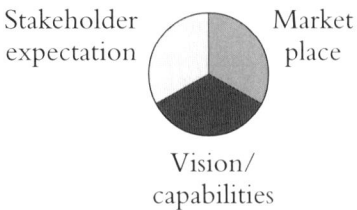

Stakeholder expectation

Market place

Vision/capabilities

Figure 2: Corporate response to forces of change

Group response to change 2.5

For groups of companies, this equilibrium is a balance between acquiring new companies, disposing of companies that no longer fit the core business and re-engineering those that do. The key is the mix of businesses where the sum of the parts is greater than the whole.

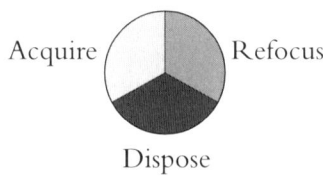

Acquire

Refocus

Dispose

Figure 3: Group response to forces of change

Key influences on business performance 2.6

The diagram in Figure 2 below is a simple representation of the key influences on business performance.

The first and most important influence is from the top of the organisation where the shareholders and senior management have set out their expectations for the company. This may include share value, profitability, compliance, ethical conduct, corporate image etc.

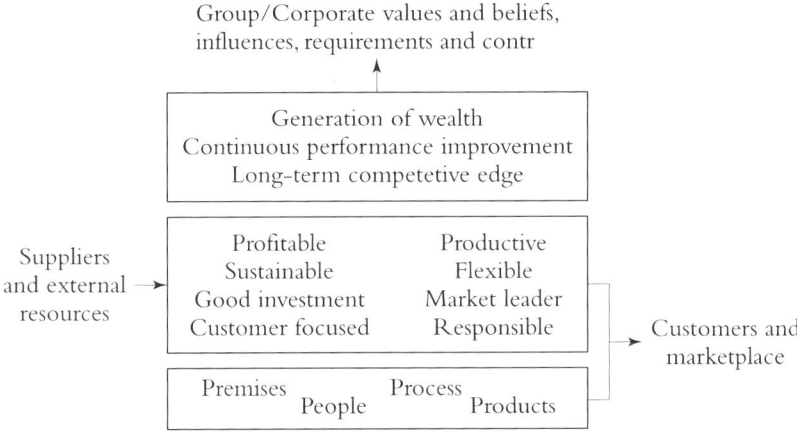

Figure 4: Key influences on business performance

In setting out their vision for the organisation they may decide that the company exists to fulfil the objectives outlined in the box in Figure 2 above, ie generation of wealth, long term competitive edge etc. To achieve this the company needs to be profitable, flexible, a market leader etc.

Customers and the market place dictate the direction the company takes. This not only relates to sales but resources too. Suppliers and external resources also influence the make up and behaviour of an organisation.

The foundation of any organisation is the products (services) required to meet market demand, the process required to make (deliver) them, the people required to run those processes and the premises to house them in. The most important of these is the people, without which none of the other components would be possible. In today's world it is also the last bastion of productivity having exhausted most other forms of rationalisation, such as business process re-engineering.

Organisational response to change 2.7

By its very nature, an organisation is affected by the corporate, group and individual responses to change. These create the circumstances and determine the solution. As with any community, all organisations are unique and there is no standard response, but there are some common denominators:

- a continual redefining of the organisation vision, mission, objective and strategies;

- a process of continuous re-engineering of products, process, people and premises;

- continuously re-engineering the organisation – a mix of self-managed, cross-functional and multicultural teams;

- a rise in part time and contract workers;

- a new breed of manager.

All of the above activities require a continual replenishment of new skills, values, beliefs and behaviours. Some of this will be achieved through re-training and some through recruitment. Inevitably there will be those that cannot or will not change and they will be made redundant.

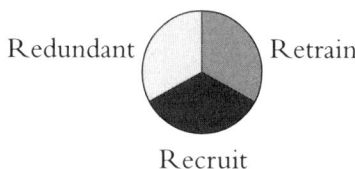

Redundant   Retrain

Recruit

Figure 5: Organisational response to forces of change

Thriving in the new workplace   2.8

In this brave new world that we live in, survival on its own is no longer desirable. Both individuals and organisations now expect to thrive whatever the situation is and to improve year by year.

To capitalise on the areas outlined above, organisations need to re-focus on appropriate skills and behaviours required to develop sustainable growth, such as:

- systems thinking;

- the ability for individuals to work in a variety of changing teams;

- teamwork based on the ability to work individually towards a common achievement;

- focus on productivity;

- focus on research and information management;

- expert communication;

- managing expectations;

- able to manage change and deal with all the ambiguities that it creates.

Key cultural issues   2.9

In order to best respond to the changing world of work, the modern organisational culture is more likely to be driven by learning, empowering, flexibility and teamwork than by competition and marketplace.

Organisational culture has changed over the last few years as it has re-engineered itself to enhance and support the new objectives, skills, values, beliefs and behaviours developed above.

There is a pronounced shift from market to people driven attributes. The culture of today is about blending product, processes, people and premises to take best advantage of the current situation. It is also about anticipating, adapting to and taking advantage of future change.

Key HR issues   2.10

The diminishing working population coupled with a continuing healthy economy is leading to severe shortages in skilled employees. Companies are increasingly turning to 'poaching' staff as a means of filling vacancies traditionally recruited for in other ways.

Although salaries may not have increased at a rate expected, benefits have increased as organisations capitalise on the improved perceived value that they offer over cash. Recruitment difficulties are further exasperated by problems with retaining key staff fuelled by a breakdown in old practices and loyalties.

Changes in loyalty are causing a decline in the long-term aspirations of working for the same employer. Without this employees are less likely to go the extra mile without some form of additional incentive. Motivation is an important part of productivity and creativity and whatever initiatives can be used to improve and enhance them can only be for the best.

Managing performance is also now high on the company strategic agenda. Performance is related to productivity, which in turn is linked to profitability and long-term sustainability. The key to improving this is to understand, appreciate and effectively manage employee expectations. The more closely they are aligned with the organisation expectations the better the result.

Improving communication along with timely and effective response to changes in opinions is the key to managing expectations. Other important initiatives, such as responding to changes in employee demographics, enhance the organisations ability to pre-empt and respond to change also.

HR accountability is increasingly being measured in financial 'returns', in particular, the cost of benefits and return on payroll. Pay and benefits can account for up to 50% of a company cost base, and in some cases a lot more, and organisations are now looking for ways of making this investment work harder for them and with less risk.

Key reward issues 2.10

The management of reward (pay and benefits, compensation) is a major key task for all modern companies today. The key objectives are to control future costs and maximum return on monies invested. This means careful management of change and resultant adjustment of reward strategies to minimise future risks.

The most prominent example of this at the moment is the shift from defined benefit to defined contribution schemes. On the face of it, the defined benefit scheme offers the best for the employee but is costly and risky for the employer. The best way forward would appear to be to change from defined benefit to defined contribution. However, it may be the one unique feature the company offers over and above its competition and in doing so may lead to a fall in recruitment, retention and motivation.

Control of future costs, improving perceived value, linking reward to performance and improving flexibility will be among the key reward issues that will help to shape pay and benefits packages of the future.

Other key reward issues include:

● Improving the perceived value of pay and, in particular, benefits offered to employees.

● A new mix of benefits designed to suit different groups of employees at different times of their lives.

14

- A reward structure that can be easily modified. It also needs to blend in with other new and old companies in the group that are also changing on a regular basis.

- Linking reward to performance.

- Particular focus on employee benefits.

- Improving value for money spent on pay and benefits.

- Use of reward to manage cash flow more effectively.

- Making rewards more attractive.

- Simplifying administration, infrastructure and IT costs.

- Developing long-term advantages from short-term initiatives.

Key reward strategies 2.12

The main measure of success for any reward strategy will be its positive impact on both individual lifestyle and organisational culture. Developing and designing reward policies and strategies must ensure that whatever initiatives are developed, can be translated into tangible results for all stakeholders. They must not only support, but also enhance the company's recruitment, retention and motivation strategy.

The design, development and implementation of reward strategies must be based on competitive advantage and must complement and enhance business objectives and strategies. They must meet the needs of an increasingly diverse and ageing workforce. The resultant strategies must enable pay and benefits to become more adaptable and effective

Employees must understand and appreciate the pay and benefits provided. Where choice is available, they must also take responsibility for the consequences of decisions made.

3 — An Introduction to Flexible Benefits

This chapter covers the following:

- Standard reward package
- Definition of flexible benefits
- Basic structure
- Basic principles
- Basic process
- Harmonising different reward systems
- Total reward
- Reasons for introducing flexible benefits
- Assessing suitability
- Cost and risks
- Pensions
- The added value of flexible benefits
- Design and implementation
- Criteria for success

Introduction   3.1

The number of flexible benefits schemes in the UK have doubled over the last few years and are set to increase over the next decade. But what are flexible benefits, how do they benefit organisations and what are the considerations in designing and implementing them?

This chapter is designed to give an introduction to and an overview of flexible benefits. Because of the holistically and integrated nature of such schemes, it would be difficult to understand individual chapters on their own without this basic understanding.

As we have seen in the previous chapter, organisations are increasingly re-evaluating their employee benefits strategy, in particular:

- ensuring that the way they reward their employees fits in with their business strategy;

- making sure rewards match the needs of an increasingly diverse and ageing workforce;

- changes to their business in the future, enabling pay and benefits structures to be adapted easily and effectively.

As employment patterns and lifestyles are changing so too is the traditional reward structure of a basic salary and fixed benefits. Most existing benefit schemes are unlikely to match the needs of the future workforce.

Standard reward package   3.2

A standard reward package can be broken down into four basic components; basic pay (including holidays and leave), variable pay, allowances and benefits (including compulsory benefits, variable benefits, other benefits). The diagram in Figure 1 below splits these into five areas.

The main characteristic in this package is that you cannot exchange cash, leave or benefits in one category for another. For instance, employees cannot trade holidays for extra pay. Although inflexible, this arrangement is relatively easy to administer and has been in wide use in the UK for decades.

It is possible to have benefits that are flexible in this type of arrangement but this does not constitute flexible benefits.

Definition of flexible benefits   3.3

The words 'flexible benefits' are misused and cover an infinite variety of benefit schemes. A true scheme is one that offers a 'common benefits trading platform', which gives employees a choice over the mix of cash and benefits they receive. At its simplest, it might be the choice between a car and additional cash. More sophisticated programmes give

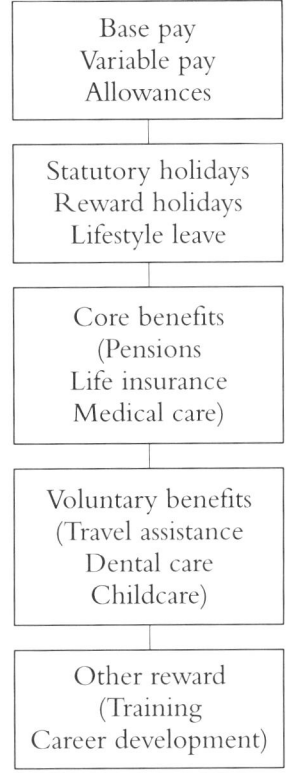

Figure 1: Standard reward package

employees choice between different benefits, or offer a range of options within one benefit category such as the choice of self or family medical insurance.

Basic structure   3.4

In its simplest form a flexible benefits scheme is a standard reward package with a 'bolt-on' facility that allows employees to trade between each of the six areas. In the diagram in Figure 2 below it is possible to trade, for instance, holidays to buy extra pension. In practice, however, there may be some items that the organisation does not want to be traded, such as core and statutory benefits.

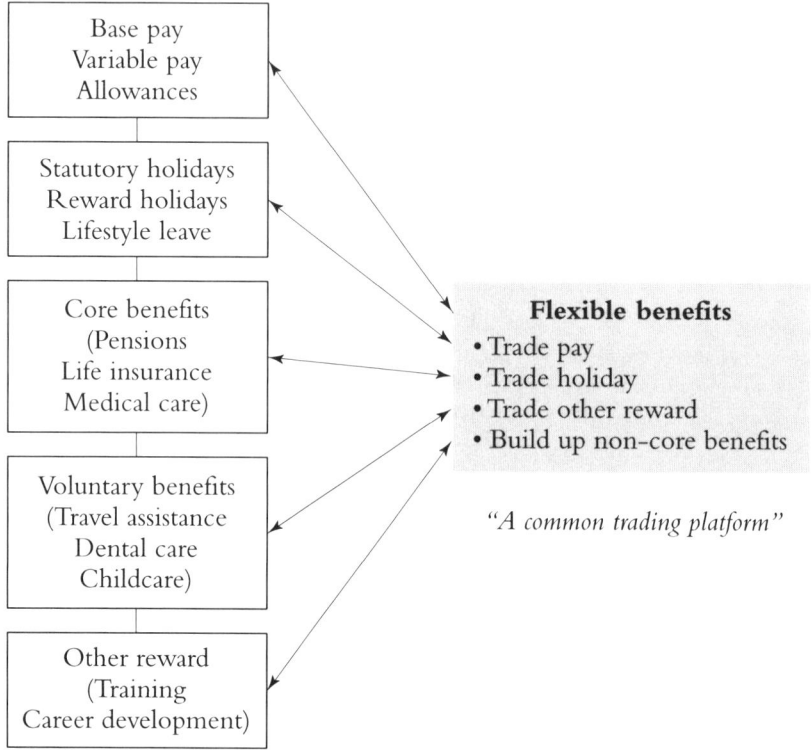

Figure 2: Standard reward package with flexible benefits

Basic principles 3.5

The basic principle of a flexible benefits scheme is that a cash price is placed on existing benefits and employees can then exchange these benefits for cash, or conversely, cash can be exchanged for benefits. Because employees are able to choose the mix of cash and benefits which best meets their needs; the perceived value of their rewards is enhanced.

The only limiting factor, other than costs and administrative constraints, on whether a benefit can be included in such a scheme is that it has to have a finite value that can be annualised. This does not rule out benefits such as concierge services or discount vouchers; it just makes them more difficult to manage.

The chart in Figure 3 below is a typical example of products that can be found in a flexible benefits scheme.

Figure 3: Examples of benefits in a flexible scheme

● Private medical insurance	● Employee share schemes
● Company cars	● Additional Voluntary Contributions (AVCs)
● Holidays	● Defined contribution pension
● Dental and optical care	● Health screening
● Critical illness insurance	● Leisure/retail vouchers
● Permanent health insurance	● Annual travel insurance
● Child-care vouchers	● Health clubs
● Personal accident insurance	● Private lease plan

Flexible benefits are not only about process and products but branding and communication. Both can combine to create a scheme that has a much higher perceived value than the benefits they contain. The nature of flexible benefits lends itself more towards the modern way. That is, the way we assess, select and obtain our desired services and products at home.

Basic process   3.6

There is no such thing as a standard flexible benefit process. Each is dependent on the organisation and its unique situation. However, most follow a similar process to the four steps discussed below.

The first step is that the employer designs and presents a menu of benefits, which includes prices. These are usually illustrated in an employee handbook, which also contains the rules and regulations governing the scheme, the options available, a short description on each of the products in the menu and the tax effect on them. Also included in the handbook will be an explanation of whether and how employees can use some of their salary, bonuses or holidays to trade for flexible benefits.

Prices are usually included in a preference form, which is used by the individual to calculate and select the mix of benefits that they want. The reason being the preference form is usually in an electronic or paper form, which is relatively easier and cheaper to change than the employee handbook.

Traditional schemes allow employees to make their selection once a year. There are, however, an increasing number of schemes that allow quarterly changes and have an additional range of products that can be selected at any time. There are special circumstances – mainly changes in lifestyle – where employees may be able to make their change outside of these fixed dates.

The next step is where employees select their preferred combination of cash and benefits to match their needs. This need to be double-checked by the administrative department to ensure that no limits have been exceeded and the correct information has been supplied.

Once this is completed the employer approves the employee's preferences and the information is processed. This approval may also extend to the line manager's approval for buying and selling holidays to ensure proper management of respective teams.

Following selection, the employer notifies all the providers and suitable arrangements are made for transfer of money to them from employer and employee. A benefit statement is also issued to employees as a record of what they have chosen.

It is important to note that this is a short summary of the flexible benefits process and there are many other items that have to be considered, which are covered in **CHAPTER 5.**

Harmonising different reward systems 3.7

If this basic concept is placed between two dissimilar reward schemes, it can be used as a vehicle to replace the dysfunctional sets of benefits with one unified scheme and a common identity.

In the example illustrated in Figure 4 below, Company B offers 24 days' holiday a year and company A offers 25 days. Company A has been acquired by Company B under TUPE (*Transfer of Undertakings (Protection of Employment) Regulations 1981 (SI 1981 No 1794)* as amended) and its holiday allowance cannot be changed.

By linking both companies with a common flexible benefits scheme, both company employees can buy and sell holidays. Those who consider it important to have 25 days holidays in Company A can trade other benefits to top up their entitlement, whilst those in company B can choose to trade down. The net perceived effect is a single benefits scheme in which everyone can have 25 days if they wish. The cost of harmonisation is reduced, as the company has not had to grant all employees an increase of one day's holiday across the board. This, of course, is a simplistic analogy.

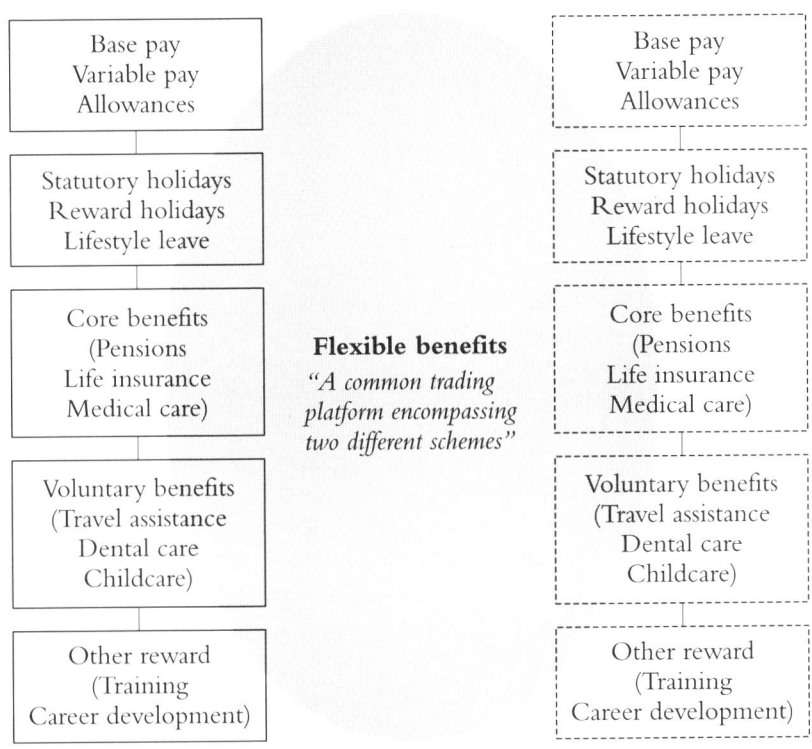

Figure 4: Harmonising with flexible benefits

Total reward   3.8

The ultimate form of flexibility and choice is total reward, sometimes referred to as flexible reward. This is where employees have complete choice over how they receive their pay and benefits. It can be done on an annual basis and they are not restricted to fixed product rules and regulations. Although popular in the United States this concept has yet to emerge in the UK.

The use of total reward statements is becoming more popular in the UK, mainly as a means of improving the overall perceived value of the employee's reward package. It is important not to confuse the two, as total reward statements mainly record the employee's mix of reward package as opposed to offering choice.

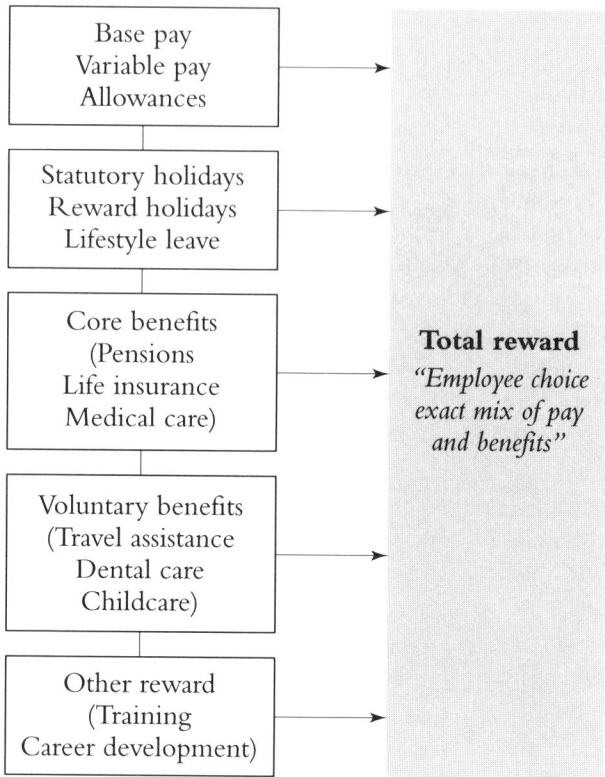

Figure 5: Total (flexible) reward package

The diagram in Figure 5 is a very simple representation of total reward, concentrating on the pay and benefits elements only. It is important to understand that total reward also includes work environment and quality of life considerations, the opportunity for advancement and recognition and training and flexible working.

One of the reasons why this concept will become more popular in the UK is the pressure of an ever-tightening labour market. As covered in the previous chapter, the labour market is not only affected by an ageing population but by changes in attitude to lifestyle. It will become increasingly necessary to attract workers back into the labour market from areas such as retirement as well as those with young families.

Reasons for introducing flexible benefit schemes 3.9

There are very good reasons for having a flexible benefits scheme. These include harmonisation, improving the perceived value of benefits and improving communication generally. Flexible benefits can bring great advantages to organisations if they can identify and meet employee needs and expectations. At the same time, it can form a valuable part of gathering information.

In the UK, the most popular reason for introducing flexible benefits into an organisation has been the integration of incompatible terms and conditions for reward and benefits after mergers and acquisitions. The example illustrated in Figure 5 is a typical model for such an exercise and not only allows the organisation to harmonise benefit products but also to rationalise different sets of benefits, processes and administration. For groups who are aggressively acquisitive, flexible benefits offer a one-off simple solution to the integration of a different organisation into the group on a regular basis.

The second most popular reason has been the use as a vehicle and catalyst for cultural change. For the majority of employees in the UK the main incentive to work is to earn money to fuel their lifestyle. Because of this, any interventions that effect pay and benefits create an immediate and decisive response. Flexible benefits achieve this and is a powerful catalyst for change and its communication process.

Flexible benefits can also enable businesses to make reward more attractive, without increasing costs, because employees are able to choose the mix of cash and benefits which best meet their needs. This is particularly relevant in today's market situation where organisations are trying to steer away from entering into a wages war with their competitors, by choosing to concentrate on improving perceived value.

Because the process of setting up a flexible benefits scheme involves research, analysis, development, strategy, communication and administration, they are often used as a vehicle for the analysis and development of reward policies and strategies.

Flexible benefits have been introduced by organisations looking to improve recruitment retention and motivation of staff. Unfortunately, there are very few statistics to quantify their success, but in the majority of cases there has been qualitative improvement.

As well as improved communication, flexible benefits offer better targeting of money spent. For example, an organisation offering single cover private medical insurance may also offer the option to trade up (as part and parcel of a flexible benefits), as opposed to full family medical cover. Particularly if only a minority perceives the benefit to be of any value because the majority do not have a family.

In the long run this improved control, better targeting and reduction in risk of the money spent on employee benefits leads to an increase in the return on money invested.

Pensions have been subject to great interest in the press for a few years. The continuing trend of a move from money purchase schemes to defined contribution is also acting as a catalyst for the introduction of flexible benefit schemes. By including other retirement packages, such as employee share schemes, individual saving vehicles and AVCs in the flexible benefits scheme, the company can offset the perceived loss by offering alternative vehicles.

The Government has made clear its intentions to reduce the use of company car schemes through its new 'green levy'. The perception is that an individual will never be able to afford the company car through their own financing and there is a risk that if made redundant they will not be able to continue payments. Flexible benefits can help to reverse this image by introducing products such as personal lease plans, which almost duplicate the company car scheme, but with reduced risk. This is covered in **CHAPTER 5** and **CHAPTER 7**.

As well as reinforcing change, flexible benefits has also been introduced to help manage the introduction of broad banding. The move to broad banding basic pay and benefits has also been accompanied by a change in the way people are categorised in the workplace. Traditional pay bands used to be based on levels of pay and department, whereas today they are based on job clusters and rates of market pay. The migration from one system to the other is not an easy one and flexible benefits have been used effectively to smooth the path.

Assessing suitability 3.10

An extensive feasibility study is advisable as a flexible benefits scheme is not always the right choice for an organisation. For example, if it cannot build a substantial business case to support it or if the culture is not ready for such a change or there is no easy way of communicating such a concept.

The subject of a feasibility study is covered in **CHAPTER 4** but in summary the following questions need to be asked to establish whether a flexible benefit is suitable for the organisation is as follows:

- Will flexible benefits improve HR competitive edge?

- Can they build a substantial business case for this introduction?

- What is the return that they expect on the money that they are going to invest in this new venture?

- Is their culture ready for such a concept?

- Will the flexible benefits scheme support and enhance their existing reward and motivation policy?

- How easy will it be to communicate?

- How easy will it be to administer?

- What will be the total costs of the new scheme?

Cost and risks   3.11

In the short run, flexible benefits do not generate direct cost savings but in the long run they do. By targeting benefits to where they are needed by employees, it is possible to save the cost of providing unwanted benefits. National Insurance, income tax and VAT savings can be achieved through more efficient payment structures. Further savings can be made through the additional buying power which employers and their employee benefit advisers have.

Businesses can be protected from the risks of the rising costs of benefits. Within a flexible benefit scheme each employee takes responsibility for choosing his or her own mix of benefits, taking into account any cost increases.

It is easier for a business to make continuous improvements to its pay and benefits structures. If new and attractive benefits come onto the market these can be offered to employees. Conversely, if benefits become more costly this is reflected in the pricing.

Pensions   3.12

There is a growing recognition amongst employees of the importance of pensions and the need to provide for their own retirement. This increase in 'pension awareness' may prompt many individuals to find ways of improving their company or private pension, and a flexible benefits package, with pensions as one of the menu items, can help them do this.

Components of pension schemes, such as Additional Voluntary Contributions (AVCs) and death benefits, are already relatively prevalent in flexible benefit schemes. Pensions themselves figure less prominently, but they are a feature of some schemes and their importance, as part of the flexible benefits menu, is growing.

One reason that pensions may not be included in a flexible benefit scheme is that, particularly in the case of final salary schemes, their inclusion can be complex. However, this complexity, which can be more apparent than real, is not insurmountable. There are ways of 'flexing' pensions without complexity before deciding if and how to include pensions in the scheme. However, there are some ethical tax and legal implications that need to be understood by employers and employees.

The added value of flexible benefits   3.13

Flexible benefits have many advantages for the employer:

- better targeting of employer costs to save unnecessary over-provision;

- a workforce in which all individuals feel that they are being looked after; and

- a modern image in the recruitment market and elsewhere.

However, there are further added values. They can be used to communicate the true cost of pay and benefits. A cash price is placed on existing benefits; employees can then exchange these benefits for cash and conversely cash can be exchanged to benefits.

Companies can be protected from the risks of the rising costs of benefits. Within a flexible benefit scheme each employee takes responsibility for choosing his or her own mix of benefits, taking into account any cost increases.

It is easier for an organisation to make continuous improvements to its pay and benefits structures. If new and attractive benefits come onto the market these can be offered to employees; conversely if benefits become more costly this is reflected in the pricing.

Design and implementation 3.14

If a decision is made to introduce a flexible benefit scheme into a company, the main measure of success will be its positive impact on both the individual and organisation. It is important, therefore, to ensure that the 'new' flex scheme can deliver tangible HR results. Benefit design must be complementary with reward policies and must not only support but also enhance the company's pay and motivation strategy.

The key to successful implementation begins with identifying the most appropriate mix of flexible benefits required and the true cost of the various options. This needs to be benchmarked against competitors in the same 'labour' market.

Establishing the right administration structure and processes (in particular IT systems) required to support the new scheme is vital. The simplest way forward is to use existing processes and incorporate the new scheme. However, this may not be feasible in which case budgeting for a new system may be required or consider outsourcing.

Communication of the scheme must be unique in brand and style. It needs to be proactive, based on internal marketing rather than just issuing information. The process should establish what needs communicating, who it needs to be communicated to, what media will be used, who will be the communicators and the timing of each individual event.

Employee counselling on a structured basis is becoming increasingly important. The increase in choice of benefits available to the employee means that it is vital to ensure individuals make informed decisions. As well as enhancing the perception that the employer is behaving ethically and responsibly, employee counselling also reinforces the communication process.

Criteria for a successful flexible benefits scheme 3.15

The key to the successful choice and implementation of a flexible benefits scheme is to establish a clear strategy linked to the overall objectives of the business. Once the strategy is determined, there must be a structured framework for its implementation. This must be based on clear communication, not just the benefits themselves, but also the message which management wishes to send to employees.

The following is a summary of the top six criteria for success.

- Establish a clear strategy linked to the overall business objectives.
- Ensure a structured framework for implementation.
- Base strategy and implementation on clear communication.
- Build solid management and administration processes.
- Deal with infrastructure issues as soon as possible.
- Introduce the initiative at an even pace.

4 — Establishing the Feasibility of a Flexible Benefits Scheme

This chapter covers the following:

- Supporting and enhancing reward strategy
- Flexible benefits scheme principles
- Market driven issues
- HR issues
- Product selection and mix
- Administration and outsourcing
- IT and infrastructure
- Project management
- Research
- Financial benefits, costs and risks

Introduction   4.1

An extensive feasibility study is usually undertaken to ensure that the introduction of a flexible benefits scheme is the right choice for the organisation. The main objective is to build a substantial business case for its introduction, ensure the culture is ready for such a concept and determine the best way of communicating the new scheme.

In some circumstances, the introduction of such a scheme may actually work against the interest of the organisation. It is important to remember that a flexible benefits scheme is a vehicle and catalyst for managing change. So if the organisation is not ready for change, then this may not be the right time for such an initiative. For instance, when a major telecommunication company de-merged its mobile phone business, they decided to manage out all the inherited legacies within their reward policies first, before looking at flexible benefits. This entailed rationalisation of certain benefits and buying out of others. It was felt that this was necessary to create a more stable base to launch the new flexible benefit scheme.

Other feasibility indicators include assessing whether flexible benefits will improve HR competitive edge and support/enhance the existing reward and motivation policy. The study also needs to establish if the organisation infrastructure should be modified to support the new scheme and what the total cost for the initiative will be.

The output of the feasibility study should be policies and strategies rather than detail. For instance, it should examine the types of products that should be included in the scheme, their basic cost and administration requirements as opposed to the full details of specification and individual/corporate costs.

The amount of money and resources allocated to the feasibility study usually determines how detailed it is. However, this is an important part of the project and is usually used as the foundation stone for the new scheme.

Such is the complex nature of flexible benefits, It is recommend that you return to this chapter again after having read the complete book and, therefore, have more of an understanding and appreciation of the subject.

Supporting and enhancing the reward strategy   4.2

The success of any policy and/or strategy is based on the defining principles that they are built on. Because of the holistical and interactive influence that flexible benefits will have on reward in any organisation, these principles are both pivotal and important.

Reward principles   4.3

There are five main principles that underpin the success of any reward strategy. The first part of the feasibility study should assess if the introduction of the flexible benefit scheme will enhance and support them.

- Reward policies, strategies and key performance indicators must support and enhance future business development of the organisation by aligning expectations of performance with reward.

- Any resultant strategy needs to blend the expectations of the company with individuals, teams, departments and the external relations they influence. It must have a positive impact on both individual lifestyle and organisational culture.

- Proposed solutions should be uniquely branded. Their vision and mission must be meaningful and based on desired outcomes relevant to the organisation. They must be clearly communicated, articulated, understood and inter-linked.

- As reward policies and strategies are influenced by and influence the culture of the organisation; their design and implementation should be based on managing behaviour. They are both a vehicle and catalyst for change.

- Each element of the proposed solution should have a purpose and have quantifiable measures of performance. Strategy should identify to whom it applies, when it should apply and the desired performance it should achieve. It must be translated into tangible results for all stakeholders.

Reward components 4.4

These principles are usually supported by a selection of reward key management components, within which the new scheme should fit comfortably. For example:

- An over-arching reward strategy, which links to other HR sub-strategies (ie resourcing, development and employee relations) and which is positively positioned to gain the required organisational commitment.

- A revised pay architecture to include review of the suitability of the grade structure and design and implementation of a framework, which will meet the organisation's future needs.

- A revised job evaluation system. Review of relevance of existing points factor approach in relation to future needs, identifying future factors to be applied and selection of an appropriate system to meet future needs.

- A new approach to pay progression. Review of success of contribution related pay for staff and managers and identify future changes – also consider extension of the bonus scheme to other staff groups.

- Comprehensive benefits review to ensure appropriate attraction and retention within a framework of organisational affordability. To review the company car policy and realign it with the new reward strategy and modify/add new benefits, where appropriate.

Benefits review 4.5

The last component, comprehensive benefits review, needs to identify key assumptions about the desired benefits strategy, which in turn will influence the feasibility of the proposed flexible benefits scheme. For example:

- The need to both support their developing performance management culture and to attract and retain the required staff has necessitated a comprehensive review of the organisation's approach to employee benefits.

- They have identified a poor fit between current policies and changing needs during the recent restructuring programme. Staff and managers alike may be dissatisfied by the current policies and systems, which have been in operation for some time and appear to no longer meet current and future organisational needs.

- The ability to measure and incentivise the performance and behaviours that they wish to encourage amongst various staff groups will be essential, if they are to achieve their corporate objectives.

Benefit scheme objectives 4.6

From this review the key benefits scheme objectives can be set. Now the organisation can consider if a flexible benefits scheme is the best vehicle to deliver these objectives and whether other incentives are required to support it. Examples include:

- Review, design and implement a benefits strategy, which is designed to meet the future needs of the organisation.

- Be key to attracting and retaining the people needed to deliver the new business strategy – delivering skills needed, when needed and in the locations where needed.

- Be key to driving individual, team and organisational performance.

- Underpin and support the development of the desired culture and behaviours needed to achieve corporate objectives.

- Be an integrated resolution to a range of urgent business-driven reward issues, which have resulted from the need to review and update reward strategy in line with recent and planned changes.

Flexible benefits scheme principles 4.7

Once the key benefit scheme objectives have been established it should now be possible to define the flexible benefit scheme principles in terms of supporting and enhancing both the organisation's mission statements and key priorities.

This will also help to start the process of establishing the cost benefits of the scheme. For instance, underpinning the business needs relating to recruitment and retention using a reduction in the recruitment budget in order to offset the cost of the flexible benefit scheme. Examples include:

- Movement from passive pay and benefits administration to active reward management aligned with strategic goals.

- To support changes in working methods, traditions and attitudes.

- To ensure coherent direction to benefits management avoiding mixed messages and one-off, uncoordinated initiatives.

- To create the conditions for greater staff motivation.

- To underpin the business needs relating to recruitment and retention.

- To provide value for money and prescribed value. Better targeting of benefits. Counteract continual erosion of the benefits that are being provided.

- Improve perceived fairness.

- Improve flexibility.

The above example is one based on improving recruitment and retention, however, the process applies equally to harmonisation, rationalisation and modernisation.

Most organisations in the UK are looking for a better link between contribution and reward. One of the most important and influential parts will be employee benefits, particularly in improving the perceived value of the overall reward scheme.

It can be clearly seen how flexible benefits may be the most effective way to package and deliver employee benefits, but there are other points that need to be considered as part of the feasibility study.

Market issues 4.8

Whatever the driver is in considering a flexible benefits scheme, there must be clearly defined market reasons for introducing it. Even in the case of harmonisation, where there is no immediate link, without such consideration, the new scheme could work against the company's interests in the marketplace.

The ever-increasing pace of change in our world today is a major reason for the use of flexible benefits. However, it is also a major influence on its design and development. When considering the feasibility of such a scheme, the organisation must ensure that it is robust and flexible enough to adapt to the forces of change detailed previously.

For example, a predominately UK based company may be expanding into Europe through a programme of acquisition. The scheme should therefore be capable of handling European transactions in the future and/or employees wishing to take advantage of 'local' products and tax regimes.

Productivity and added value 4.9

As the company grows and its market share increases, so will the expectations of productivity and HR returns. As flexible benefits are a 'growing' entity (new products are added and the obsolete are removed), it too will be expected to contribute more each year.

As well as defining what returns the new flexible benefits scheme will bring in the first year, the longer-term added value is also important. Defining this also helps to justify the expense of designing and implementing the new scheme. This is covered later in this chapter (see **4.38** below).

Changing demographics 4.10

Most organisations today consist of a mix of two distinct groups of employees: those who have been with the company for less than five years and those who are looking forward to retirement. This diverse mix does not lend itself to a traditional benefit structure. However, the feasibility study should qualify and quantify how a flexible benefits scheme could improve the situation for both at the same time.

An increasingly diverse and ageing workforce may be one of the driving forces for the new scheme. The feasibility study should qualify and quantify what effect this is having on the organisation and the resultant loss in productivity and market share. There are many examples in the work place today of companies that have purposely targeted sectors of the labour market to outsmart the competition.

Diversity and work/life balance 4.11

Diversity is a key initiative in the Government's aims to create a more inclusive society, encouraging a more equal balance of age, gender and ethnic background. Some companies have used flexible benefits as a vehicle for encouraging this balance. Also high on the list of both Government and companies is the healthy balance between work and home life. Again the feasibility of the new scheme may depend on its ability to address theses issues.

Recruitment, retention and motivation 4.12

As outlined previously, the tightening labour market is a major concern for companies in the UK. Retention, motivation and recruitment may be the primary reason for introducing a flexible benefits scheme but the advantages they bring should be quantified. For instance, by how much can the recruitment budget be reduced if the new scheme works and can this cost saving be used to offset some of the costs of its design and implementation?

HR issues 4.13

The first and most important part of examining the HR issues for introducing a new scheme is to decided whether the main reason for considering the scheme is because of the employer or employee. The employer would use the flexible benefits scheme to harmonise two sets of benefits, as apposed to the employee's reason for improving choice. This will make it easier to develop definable outcomes for each of the issues identified and the appropriate measures.

Employer-driven issues 4.14

Consolidating and harmonising reward structures are one of the more popular reasons for introducing the flexible pension scheme. The feasibility study should identify the current status quo and the desired harmonised structure. For instance, the use of buying and selling holidays to harmonise dissimilar levels of holiday entitlement.

Consolidation and harmonising different structures is not only about the technical complexities of creating a single status scheme, but also the communication and cultural aspects. If the decision were to create a totally new culture from the combination of the old, as opposed to establishing a dominant culture, then the way the flexible benefit scheme is introduced would be just as important as its make-up. Quite often a flexible benefit scheme is used to speed up cultural change.

Cultural change may be required regardless of whether there is a need for consolidation or harmonising, for instance the installation of a high-performance work environment. The same principles as above apply and the feasibility study should be able to map out what the key change objectives are and how each of the different elements of the flexible benefit scheme will enhance and support them.

Employee-driven issues 4.15

The above examples are change driven by the needs of the employer, however, there may be changes that have been driven by the employee. The most common of these is the need to design and implement benefit structures that can cater for a wide and varied workforce.

In the first instance, a simple democratic analysis will highlight where the peaks and troughs are in the organisation in terms of age, gender and length of stay. This analysis may need to go one stage further and examine how may people in the workforce have dependants, as this will be a major influence on their lifestyle. If from the analysis, for example, the organisation finds the peak of age at 35 with less than five years service and 60% of them have young dependants, then there is a strong possibility that the introduction of childcare vouchers would help to improve retention and motivation.

Employee questionnaires and focus groups are used to find out what employee preferences are – see Research at **4.37** below. It is also an ideal way of finding out which method of communication employees prefer. The use of the word preference suggests some form of prioritisation, as it will be unreasonable to expect the organisation to provide every single benefit that employees are looking for.

Employment law issues 4.16

The final stage of examining the HR issues of introducing a new scheme is to consider the impact on and of employment law. This is covered in more detail in a **CHAPTER 8** but for the purposes of the feasibility study the four main areas to consider are:

- The consequences of any direct or indirect change to the terms and conditions of employment.

- The effect of new and current legislation such as the Employment Bill.

- The effect of/on the *Transfer of Undertakings (Protection of Employment) Regulations 1981 (TUPE) (SI 1981 No 1794)*, where relevant.

- The possibilities of inadvertently building in discrimination by the structure of the new scheme.

Communications issues 4.17

The management of expectation and perception is the most important aspect of communicating effectively. It ensures a consistent and accurate message about the different elements of a package and their perceived value, especially where choice affects levels of pay and benefits.

Effective communication is more an art form than a science. Organisational culture is made up of individuals, so there can never be a 'one size fits all' solution. The feasibility study sets out to develop a framework and define alternative steps to implement an effective strategy.

A communication audit is the most appropriate way of carrying out this part of the feasibility study and covers the areas discussed below.

Unique brand and style 4.18

There is very little difference between the way individuals respond to being sold a car and being sold an employee benefit. They will respond better if that product has a name. The study needs to ensure that this concept can be developed and will be well received by potential scheme members.

It is important to note that communication is a two-way process and is based above all on education. The study should establish that employees will not only be encouraged to 'buy into' the benefit scheme, but will clearly understand, be aware of and take responsibility for, any decisions that they make.

Proactive 4.19

The most effective form of communication is two-way dialogue. Reactive communications is not two-way dialogue because it does not encourage discussion or debate. The communication strategy should be based on internal marketing, not just issuing information. It should be proactive and deliver a mutually beneficial message.

The study should establish the feasibility of the two main elements of proactive communication;

● the management of the process – which entails endorsement and commitment from the top; and

● employee communication – based on two-way educational and responsive dialogue.

What needs communicating? 4.20

The organisation needs to ensure that as well as technical and legal requirements of communication, individuals know what their benefit options are and the implications of their personal choice. These will include tax, contracts etc.

Branding is an important part of communication, and the organisation needs to ensure that it has reinforced this. For instance, if through a merger or acquisition, two or more organisations have been brought together under a new cultural identity, this can be reinforced, not only by creating a unique combined set of benefits, but by using a style and language that is different and unique to the new organisation.

Who are you communicating to? 4.21

There will be many people affected by the introduction of the feasible scheme.

- The executive committee (top team) will need to be convinced and assured that the new scheme will bring about the desired culture changes that they are seeking, within the budget that has been set out.

- The management team will need to understand how best to manage the communication process for their individual departments and the best way to plan for such an exercise.

- Existing employees or those that will be directly affected by the introduction or modification of the new scheme will need to understand exactly what the implications are and how they will benefit from them.

- Potential employees will need to appreciate how their overall benefits package will be enhanced by the benefits scheme. In the current economic climate of pressure on recruitment and retention, this will be a vital part of the communication strategy.

What media do you need to use? 4.22

The most important point about the choice of media is to ensure that the message that you are delivering dictates choice of media, not the availability of technology.

The first consideration is the internal marketing literature required. These include items such as announcement letters, scheme handbook, in-house magazine, employee benefits statement, total reward statement, etc. Cost and resources required to put these together will obviously be an important factor.

The organisation needs to consider how it intends to launch the new scheme. Choices range from interactive websites and videos to simple presentation and discussion/focus groups. The most effective form of launching a product is via one-to-one meetings, however, these are usually too costly and time consuming to consider. The ideal compromise lies between effectiveness, affordability and practicality. This may overlap with considerations for outsourcing and IT.

Who will be the communicator? 4.23

Just as we are affected by the perception of the events and messages that surround us, the character of the people that create them also affects us. The communicators chosen need to embody the whole ethos of the communication strategy that has been developed for the benefits scheme.

They need to be the most respected and the most positive in the organisation. They also need to be diplomatic and able to enter into constructive debate and dialogue on the scheme. The organisation may choose to have different communicators for different stages of the scheme launch and/or levels of the organisation. The right mix is the one that reinforces the brand and strategy developed for the scheme.

Timing 4.24

Timing is all-important to any communication, as it will affect the perception of those involved. It must fit into the company strategy but at the same time, not be diluted by any other initiatives that have been carried out. For instance, introducing a new benefits scheme at the same time as announcing major restructuring of the business may not have the desired effect.

The feasibility study needs to consider when the pre-launch meetings should take place, taking into account pay rises, holiday periods, etc. As communication is a two-way process, thought also needs to be given to monitoring feedback adaptation of whatever communication strategy is used.

Product selection and mix 4.25

At this stage of the project, the feasibility study needs to define the policy and strategy for the scheme and the basic structure of the products and how they mix together. The organisation also needs to decide the costing structure for the products, whether the company or the individual will pay, as well as the rules and regulations that will bind them all together.

Product selection 4.26

The choice of products for the scheme will be driven by employee preferences and corporate requirements. To begin with the initial selection of products will probably be too many to administrate effectively and a process of elimination will be required to develop a more manageable portfolio. Considering the priority each individual product has, compared to its ease of administration and cost, does this best.

As well as these criteria the organisation will continually ensure that each individual product meets the desired requirements already outlined in previous sections of this chapter. For instance, will the selection of childcare vouchers improve the perceived value of benefits offered to employees? Will it be cost effective as well as easy to administer? The selection of products is covered in more detail in **CHAPTER 5**.

Non-standard products   4.27

It is also important at this stage to consider those products that do not fit in to such a scheme, for instance, those that cannot be defined on an annual cost basis.

For these products the organisation could consider setting up an additional part of the flexible benefits scheme based solely on introducing products to employees rather than selling. This could be, for instance, discount vouchers for Christmas shopping, where the flexible benefits scheme could be used merely as a point of advertising and individuals will be left to deal directly with the provider. This is becoming an increasingly popular addition to flexible benefits as it keeps the scheme active beyond the annual selection date.

Tax implications   4.28

Flexible benefits products fall into four basic tax categories:

- benefit in kind;
- voluntary benefit;
- 'tax free/advantaged' benefit;
- holidays.

The tax considerations of each one of them are covered in more detail in **CHAPTER 7**. However, for the feasibility study it will be important to ensure that the product mix will be giving the best possible tax advantage for both individual and employee. For example, where a company provides a final salary scheme care must be taken to ensure that individuals are aware that a trade of a taxable benefit for a non-taxable benefit could effect the final salary calculation.

Restructuring existing benefits   4.29

As well as considering the consequences of introducing new products the feasibility study also needs to consider the consequences and costs of restructuring existing products. The most complex are those products based on underwriting, for instance, private medical insurance where premiums are based on claims history. The organisation may wish to switch to a core provision of single cover allowing employees to trade up. However, the underwriter may feel the risk of such an exercise and a possible reduction in overall fees would require an extra premium.

Ethical considerations   4.30

As well as putting together a portfolio of products that have the best tax, National Insurance (NI) and cost advantages, the organisation also needs to consider what ethical stance it will take on flexing certain benefits. The most sensitive area in the flexible benefits scheme is the provision of retirement planning schemes such as pensions, AVCs and share schemes. These are covered in more detail in CHAPTER 6, however, for the feasibility study some basic principles need to be established. For instance, deciding whether or not pensions should be an integral part of the flexible benefits scheme.

Contractual considerations   4.31

Finally the study needs to consider the contractual situation regarding existing benefits and entitlements. It may be that for some existing benefits the organisation has to negotiate a change in the Terms of Conditions of Employment, if it intends to withdraw or reduce core entitlement. For instance, replacing full family medical cover with core single cover and the option to trade up

Administration and outsourcing   4.32

In essence, the administration of a flexible benefits scheme consists of inputs, process and outputs. It needs to be accessed by two main groups of people – administrators and employees. It also needs to send information to other parts of the organisation such as payroll and HR as well as product providers.

Administrators need access to the system to be able to correspond with employees and generate reports. They also need to be able to add joiners and delete leavers as well as making mid-term adjustments for lifestyle changes.

Before choosing which option, the employer needs to consider the administration functions that need to be performed. These include:

- producing personalised enrolment forms;

- processing employees' choices;

- producing statements confirming benefit choices;

- providing member details to benefit providers;

- providing details of leavers to benefit providers;

- liasing with payroll department/external payroll bureau;

- providing P11D details;

- liasing with product providers.

One of the main concerns of establishing the feasibility of new scheme is administration and/or outsourcing. As well as establishing affordability and ease of managing, the study should ensure the systems and processes provide security, service and good value.

Web-based technology is now playing a major role in scheme administration and member communication. The organisation should determine whether the schemes management services would add value to the overall reward and benefits strategy through innovative communication solutions.

Outsourcing 4.33

The first consideration for this part of the feasibility study is to establish whether to administer the scheme in-house or to outsource. Whichever option is preferred, the company needs to ensure that the service achieves maximum possible integration with their Human Resources and Payroll systems.

With the day-to-day administration outsourced, the organisation can more readily focus on reward, benefits and communications policies without the worry of maintaining computer systems or resolving staff issues. The quality and frequency of reporting to management can also be enhanced. In most cases, outsourcing is considerably more effective and can offer improved budgetary control of the scheme administration expense.

However, if the organisation is outsourcing they will need to be aware that, while ultimately beneficial, this is a complex process and needs careful management. Time is needed to select the service provider – an experienced administrator will make the process easier and provide much needed assurance – and to identify any potential difficulties so that they are fully discussed and resolved before implementation.

Depending on the scheme's needs, the feasibility study needs to ensure that the external provider will work as their flexible benefits department dealing directly with employees and members via dedicated scheme help-lines. Alternatively, they may operate behind the scenes, providing back office support while the organisation continues to be the main point of contact.

Web-based technology 4.34

Internet and Intranet solutions are playing an increasingly dominant role in the provision of administration services and the feasibility study needs to determine whether these new technologies will be to their advantage. Modern web-based services can meet the challenges faced by organisations looking to provide first class administration to scheme members. However these need to be combined with rapid access to benefits information.

IT and infrastructure 4.35

If the decision is made to use the organisation's in-house systems, there will be a need to assess the infrastructure required to process the various transactions created.

Every scheme is unique, and so, there are no fixed formulas for designing the required IT infrastructure. However, experience dictates that simplicity and modification of existing process is by far the best option.

For the feasibility study, it is important to understand, in basic terms, what the organisation's existing systems are. This can be compared to the requirements of the new scheme. The following questions cover the majority of areas that need to be assessed:

- Is there an integrated IT system/database for HR, pensions, PAYE/P11D/NI and payroll? If so, who is the provider and what is the system?

- If the above are all separate; who are the providers and what are the systems?

- If the above are all separate; how are they linked?

- Are there any future plans for replacement or modification of any of the above?

- Can your payroll database cope with shadow (contractual as opposed to actual) salary calculations? (Perhaps you may have had a Profit Related Pay (PRP) or similar bonus scheme in the past).

- Is there a facility in your database(s) for electronic transactions with external providers?

- Do you issue any form or benefit statements?

- Do you show/refer to employee benefits on your payslips?

- What type of management reports do you prepare, relating to the above and enclosed flow chart?

- Are there any special requirements with regard to the *Data Protection Act 1998* for any of the above?

- Do you have/what are the general service standards for the above?

The above questions are a selection of some main areas the organisation needs to look at in terms of designing and building its own IT process. They are not exhaustive and will probably create more questions as the feasibility study progresses.

The main objective, however, is to be aware of logistics required to manage such a system and the resultant costs in any modifications required. Costing should also look at additional resources such as software writers and administrators to run the systems once they are installed.

In quite a few instances flexible benefits have been used for the prime reason of modernising the administration of employee benefits. It may be that the plans for installing a new IT system to manage the proposed flexible benefit scheme ends up as a smaller part of an overall initiative to upgrade the whole of the HR and payroll system. This is sometimes a major determinant factor in whether to outsource the whole of the process or keep it in-house.

Project management   4.36

Flexible benefits are in their very nature complex and holistic. Management of such projects requires a special approach based on key tasks and timescales.

The feasibility study should establish from the outset how much of this project management will be carried out within the organisation and what, if any, there will be on external providers and consultants.

It has already been shown that the development of a flexible benefit scheme involves nearly every single aspect of an organisations management. It also will involve external providers and possibly a third-party administration to administer the scheme, all of whom will have to be managed in an effective and focused way.

Most external consultants provide a wide range of support varying from advice only to design and implementation of complete turnkey projects. Whichever route is chosen by the organisation, ownership and control must be retained as well as minimising costs to ensure successful implementation. Any use of external consultants must be clearly defined in terms of expectations and outcomes to ensure these objectives are met.

Project management will be covered in more detail in **Chapter 5**, however, for the feasibility study a partnership approach to project management is recommended using a mix of existing personnel, complemented by specialist managerial skills and flexible benefit advice from external providers.

Setting up a typical partnership/project team usually follows the following steps:

- Establish expectations for the successful project.
- Establish key outcomes to be measured and milestones.
- Produce a project model/blueprint.

- Evaluate the required expertise and experience to successfully complete the project.

- Assess organisations resources against requirements identified.

- Select the right mix of external consultants and organisational personnel.

- Decide key areas of responsibility for each team member.

The use of external consultants for up front scheme design has traditionally accounted for the highest proportion of the cost of the design and implementation of a flexible benefits scheme, along with a lack of control. However, this can be avoided by using existing generic models to build around a scheme or by outsourcing.

Research   4.37

The quality of the feasibility study for a flexible benefits scheme will depend on the quality of information and statistics gathered at the commencement of the project. The objective is to research each one of the influences on business performance relevant to the new scheme.

There are a variety of tools and techniques that can be used to gather this information from key areas of influence and, at the same time, contribute to the communication process of the organisation. These are discussed below.

- *Internal fact find* – Ensure IT, infrastructure and resources can support any new initiatives developed. Also any policy or strategy developed is both effective and practical. Carrying out internal research on an organisation, looking at areas such as company culture and structure, is vital to ensure that the initiative can be implemented with the minimal disruption. (See further **APPENDIX 1**.)

- *Competitive benchmarking* – Determine how competitive each pivotal job role is against industry and local norms. Measuring individual reward against market norms, looking at both direct competition and similar process industries. This allows employers to design more competitive packages and thus improve recruitment and retention. (See further **APPENDIX 1**.)

- *Benefit audits* – Identify all benefits provided, their respective costs, take-up and effectiveness/competitiveness. This form of research is usually undertaken by organisations that are looking to regain management control of benefit costs, as a tool to help manage change, or in response to the changing needs of their employees. ((See further **APPENDIX 1**.)

- *Employee preferences* – Identify the true picture of the benefits offered by the organisation, their perceived value and realisation by employees. Using a variety of techniques, including satisfaction surveys and focus groups, this measures the perceived value and level of appreciation of reward by employees. This also allows more effective targeting of money spent, by identifying which benefits are most important by employees and where communication needs improving. (See further **APPENDIX 1**.)

- *Administration process and IT infrastructure* – Carry out a risk audit covering all functions relating to the administration of the flexible benefits scheme. Assessing the impact on the organisations ability to maximise efficiency and cost effectiveness. Reviewing compliance, quality controls and service standards. Assessing cost impact of any changes required. (See further **APPENDIX 1**.)

- *Communications audit* – Identify preferences, key concerns and communication issues from the perspective of employees. Identify current strategy, policies and structure to determine key issues and how best to manage communication of new initiatives developed. (See further **APPENDIX 1**.)

- *Evaluation against best practice* – Measure overall performance against industry norms. By taking a look at similar process organisations and industries, the developed strategy can be both tested and refined, by comparing it to the experiences of others.

Financial benefits, costs and risks analysis   4.38

The ultimate objective of considering the feasibility of a flexible benefit scheme is to determine whether the benefits and advantages it forms for the organisation is worth the investment and the risk. This measure of worth does not necessarily have to be directly linked to the bottom line, although it does need to be shown to have at least has some impact on the bottom line.

Potential costs for a flexible benefits scheme are covered in more detail in **CHAPTER 14**.

Financial benefits   4.39

For the purposes of a feasibility study the following are examples of financial benefits that need to be considered:

- Better targeting of money spent on unwanted benefits could be used to subsidise the new scheme.

- The introduction of flexible benefits could allow the organisation to reduce spending elsewhere in the reward budget.

- The new IT systems and procedures introduced could streamline and reduce the running cost of the existing administration systems.

- Outsourcing may reduce this further.

- The increased preserved value of benefits offered could improve retention and reduce the recruitment budget.

- The flexible benefits may, indirectly, lead to improved performance and efficiency.

- Introduction of new benefits such as personal lease plans for cars could reduce the company's risk and dependence on high capital expenditures such as company car fleet.

- The engineering or introduction of certain benefits could reduce the company's tax and National Insurance bill.

Costs   4.40

For the purposes of a feasibility study the following costs should be considered:

- The cost of the feasibility study itself. This should be in proportion to the total anticipated spend on the total scheme and structured in such a way that it forms the first part of the design and strategy stage of the project.

- Use of external consultants and support for project management and/or specialist advice.

- Total cost and/or risk analysis of outsourcing all or part of the new scheme.

- IT structure and infrastructure to run new system.

- Resources required to run new scheme.

- Cost of communicating the new scheme including employee handbooks, preference forms and use of independent financial advisors. Cost of launching the scheme including road shows and 'clinics'.

- Additional costs of administration for the voluntary products which are deducted from pay.

- Administration costs if the scheme is not outsourced.

Risks 4.41

For the purposes of a feasibility study the following risks should be considered:

- Risk of flexing holidays, ie more employees decide to sell than buy.

- Risk of including pensions, which in turn could lead to an increase in pension members and therefore company contribution costs — particularly if additional contributions are matched.

- Effects if any, on salary increases on triggered benefits such as pensions and other entitlements.

5 — Strategy and Design

This chapter covers the following:

- Project management
- Analysis of feasibility study and research
- Basic design and framework
- Product selection
- Trading salary and bonuses
- Rules, regulations and limits
- Inland Revenue considerations
- Employment law considerations
- Administration, IT structure and infrastructure considerations.
- Communication and launch consideration
- Due diligence
- Options to review
- Quality procedures and control
- Time scales

Project management   5.1

Reward and Human Resources initiatives are in their very nature complex and holistic. Management of such projects requires a special approach in order for the organisation to maintain ownership and control of the flexible benefits scheme and to minimise costs.

It is advisable that a joint project team is formed to manage, coordinate and drive through the various key tasks required. The best way forward is a partnership approach to project management, which balances specialist management skills and advice with local knowledge and resources.

The process should be diagnostic, rather than prescriptive, with the aim to balance the visionary characteristics required for developing concepts, with the pragmatism needed for planning and implementation. External advice and support should be, wherever possible, based on using specialist expertise and experience to facilitate, rather than control, the process.

Setting up the project team 5.2

The first stage of setting up this project team is to evaluate the required expertise and experience to complete the project by concentrating on a good mix of personnel. These will include not only the organisation's employees but also external advisors and third-party providers. Dependant on how may people will be involved in various elements of the design, development and implementation of the scheme, the company may choose to set up a smaller steering/management group to oversee the planning and progress of the individual key tasks and objectives.

Selecting external advisors 5.3

As part of the feasibility study the decision would have been taken whether or not to use external advisors to manage with all or some of the design and implementation of the new scheme. On their appointment an agreement needs to be drawn up defining their contribution and output to the scheme along with anticipated timescales and costings. It is also important to re establish the following:

- What is it that the organisation wants the consultants to achieve?

- Is the contract tight enough to ensure that consultants do not complete extra work not anticipated without authorisation?

- If they do, is there is a clearly defined procedure for work outside the scope of their contract?

- Are they committed to work to the set-up that delivers the most from their service?

The above points also apply to third-party providers. If a decision has been taken to outsource all or part of the scheme, then the emphasis and roll of the project management team will, of course, change.

Managing and co-ordinating the project team   5.4

Once the chosen personnel are in place, each then needs to be assigned areas of responsibility to manage and co-ordinate. As with any other such project they should be required to report back to the steering management team on a regular basis and be empowered to implement whatever plans are necessary to ensure their part of the project is completed on time.

Establishing expectations   5.5

The next step is to establish the expectations from the organisational directors and key staff for the success of this project. Hopefully, this will agree with the results of the feasibility study, however, some situations may have changed and need to be redefined. For instance, resources to support design and development of the new scheme, which may have been agreed at the time of the feasibility study, are no longer available. These expectations are also important, as the success of the project will eventually be measured against them.

Key tasks and timescales   5.6

The next stage is to establish the key tasks and outcomes to be measured and their respective milestones. Examples of both are included in **APPENDIX 1** and, as in any such project, form the framework required to plan the project.

The final stage is to produce a project model/blueprint from the results of the feasibility study so that the project team has a concept that they can visualise. This model should also include the anticipated timescales, budget and resources etc.

Analysis of feasibility study and research   5.7

Most of the groundwork will have been covered in the feasibility study allowing the organisation to develop the basic concept and framework for the flexible benefit scheme. However, further information may have been gathered as part of the research process, which can be used to design the new scheme.

Principles for the flexible benefits scheme   5.8

The principles previously developed should provide the basis for integrating the new scheme into the company's reward strategy. For instance, if one of the principles was to generate a move from passive pay and benefits administration to active reward management, then the communication of the new scheme needs to reflect this. This may also affect the choice of product and the administration systems.

Existing employee benefits   5.9

The benefits audit carried out on the feasibility study will be able to provide the company with up to date information on benefits in situ, including their cost realisation and appreciation by employees. This information may, for instance, highlight that an old established benefit such as subsidised travel is still highly appreciated, even though it may not be considered 'modern' in terms of flexible benefit design.

The benefits audit should also allow the project team to assess whether the current providers are capable of adding value to their services if their products are included in the flexible benefits scheme. Although it is recommended that where possible to remain with the company's existing provider (an established relationship and tract record) there are circumstances where a change would be beneficial, for instance poor service or exceptionally high costs.

Competitive information   5.10

From the information gathered on the organisation's competitors, through competitive benchmarking, a clear indication of the types of benefits provided will have been gained. Analysis will allow the design team to decide whether or not the products that they have chosen are competitive and offer a unique edge to the employee's reward package. For instance, the competition may offer a flexible benefit scheme but not the ability to buy and sell holidays and this may be considered a competitive advantage if included in the design of the new scheme.

Competitive benchmarking will also help to establish total reward offered by competitors. This is a more accurate way of comparing different reward packages.

Employee preferences   5.11

One of the most important areas or research carried out in the feasibility study will have been employee preferences. Whether through questionnaire or focus groups or through one-to-one meetings, the project team should now have a very clear picture of what is, and what is not, important to employees and the best way to communicate this. Further enhancement may include demographic information, exit interviews, entry interviews etc.

The best way to deal with this vast amount of information is on a statistical basis. For instance, how many people in the organisation have young dependants and what age group do they tend to fall into? How many people are in the pension scheme and how close to retirement are they?

Very often the employee survey produces the key selling point for the scheme. It could be something as simple as saving money for individuals, or more complex, such as style of communication.

Employment law issues   5.12

Employer-driven issues and employment law will also have been analysed as part of the feasibility study. These will help to highlight some of the technical requirements for the scheme such as harmonising different benefits and required changes to the terms and conditions of employment. It is important at this stage to double check that the information gathered from the feasibility study for these areas is up to date, as it may have been some time since the study was carried out.

Communications audit   5.13

The communications audit will have highlighted what strategy needs to be applied to the scheme. In addition, the information gathered from the feasibility study, which looked at communication issues, now needs to be assessed in order to decide how to brand and style the new scheme. Consideration should be given to how the various elements will fit together in such a way that they can be proactively communicated. The basic framework of the communication strategy will start to highlight what needs communicating, who the organisation is communicating to, what media is going to be used and who the communicators will be.

It is important to develop this framework now, as it will save time later if the organisation develops the communication strategy alongside all the other various elements of the scheme. For instance, later in this chapter (see **5.21** below) we deal with product selection. The way these are communicated to prospective employees will, of course, affect the communication strategy. The nature of flexible benefits is very much integral and holistic which is why the development of the scheme needs to be based on several initiatives running side by side.

Administration and IT   5.14

The most complex and time consuming part of the design and implementation of benefits schemes is the administration, outsourcing and IT required to run the processes. The feasibility study will have established basic assumptions and criteria for the new scheme and may have even suggested outsourcing as the best alternative. Whatever the recommendation, this now needs to be translated in to a workable plan where the assumptions have been tested and verified. This is particularly relevant to the organisation's ability to maximise efficiency and cost effectiveness.

As with communication the information gathered in the feasibility study and research needs to be organised in such a way that it can be easily accessed during the design and development stage of the project, as well as the administration, outsourcing and IT. For instance, the feasibility study may have highlighted an apparent weakness in the ability of the current systems to electronically communicate with outside bodies, such as providers. Therefore, in the selection of the products and their systems, the organisation needs to ensure that whatever is selected is compatible or, alternatively, upgrades the IT capability.

Costs, savings and risks   5.15

The final part of the feasibility study will have determined the financial benefit, cost and risk for the project. These will be at the forefront of the strategy and the design needs to ensure that the set targets are met.

The best way of analysing the financial information gathered by the report is to organise them into a set of budgets and associated objectives. For instance, the feasibility study may have highlighted the possibilities of reducing the recruitment budget by 10%, as well as other financial advantages and cost savings. So if the basic premise of the scheme is not to incur any net cost, any subsequent costs must be less than this. Again this is covered in more detail later on in the book.

It is recommended that all the various research material is put together in an easily accessible format so that it can be used as a (continuous) point of reference for the project.

Basic design and framework   5.16

The design of the scheme needs to be innovative to mirror the developing culture of the organisation and create a set of benefits above and beyond those offered by the organisation's competitors.

Eligibility to join the scheme needs carefully thought. Care must be taken to ensure that choice is based on clearly defined groups of employees rather than individuals, for instance, in the case of a pilot scheme, senior managers.

Discrimination is a key issue in this type of selection process and organisations need to ensure fair treatment, within the group(s) selected. This is particularly relevant when dealing with part-time and contract workers (see **CHAPTER 8**).

Other criteria to consider in terms of eligibility are: probationary period; leaving the organisation; statutory leave and absence (see also **5.38** below).

Flexible benefits, by their very nature, are voluntary. The scheme design should contain certain provisions for those who do not want to exercise any choice or enrol. A typical default for those who do not wish to enrol is to maintain their benefits package as before. This can be communicated 'globally' by stating the consequences of such a decision (ie 'your benefits will remain unchanged and you will not be entitled to change your decision until the next enrolment date'), or by adding a tick box on the preference form indicating 'no change' in existing benefits.

The basic design of the framework concerns what type of product will be included in the flexible benefits scheme, how they will be linked together in terms of trading, what the basic rules and regulations will be covering each one and how the individual calculations of funding and costs will all be linked together.

From the feasibility study and other work the organisation will have already drawn up a list of potential products and services for inclusion in any scheme. This is covered in more detail at **5.21** below. Once this list of products have been consolidated to produce an easily manageable portfolio they need to be segregated into three categories:

- *Core benefits* – these benefits cannot be flexed due to ethical reasons set by the company or for administrative reasons set by the provider. Employees cannot receive cash in place of these benefits and they cannot be traded for any other benefits.

- *Flexible Benefits* – these benefits can be flexed and employees may also be able to receive a cash salary in place of them.

- *Source of funding* – these are elements of reward, including trading benefits, which can be used to pay for employee selection. They also include salary, bonus, cash for car allowance etc.

Each one of these categories will require its own set of rules and regulations common to all of the products within them.

Core benefits 5.17

Core benefits are usually included in the flexible benefit scheme even though they cannot be flexed. For instance the company may feel ethically obliged to ensure that all employees have adequate provision for retirement and, therefore, should not be able to alter their pension contributions in any way. Employees may of course top up their pension provision through Additional Voluntary Contributions (AVCs) or a similar vehicle.

There may be strategic reasons why some benefits have to be core, ie the minimum amount of holidays allowable in the UK is 20 days. For any organisation that offers 25 days as a contractual entitlement, employees would not be able to sell more than five days, as this would take them below the statutory requirement. In organisations where there is a high usage of VDUs, eye testing is usually a core benefit because of statutory health and safety requirements.

The final reason why the benefit may be a core provision is that their provider is not willing to offer them as a flexible option. Permanent health insurance is a good example of this where, because it is usually provided as insurance for the pension scheme, providers do not allow any flexibility at all.

Flexible benefits   5.18

For those products that are not core, the only requirements for them to be included in a flexible benefit scheme is that they can be valued on an annual basis, for instance critical illness, which is based on an annual premium and has definable benefits. Where the benefit has a variable contribution rate, such as leisure vouchers, the organisation needs to decide whether to offer them on an annual fixed-price package or to include them in a separate facility of the flexible benefits scheme which allows employees to purchase them on an ad hoc basis.

It is usual for organisations to take the annualised contribution rate for flexible benefits and ask employees to pay for them on a monthly basis. Because of this, it is worth checking at an early stage that the provider will allow this to happen and will not charge any extra premiums for doing so.

Funding choices   5.19

The simplest way of funding a choice in the flexible benefits scheme is to trade one benefit for another. For instance, an employee may choose single cover private medical insurance (PMI) and take the additional premium paid for family cover (offered by the company before the flexible benefits scheme was introduced) to top up their pension scheme via an AVC.

The second most popular way of funding the flexible benefits choice is by trading salary. (Organisations should take care to use the word 'trading' rather than 'salary sacrifice' as both have completely different tax treatments.) It is usual in the first year of a flexible benefits scheme to put a maximum percentage of salary level that can be traded, to ensure that employees retain enough cash to pay for their day-to-day commitments.

Similarly, cash bonuses and cash allowances can also be included in a flexible benefits plan but usually do not have the same limitations as trading salary.

The final way of paying for benefits selected is to sell holidays. Holidays also are a core and purchasable benefit. Careful guidelines need to be drawn up to ensure the proper management of this facility and this is discussed at **5.26** below.

At this stage of the design, the organisation needs to decide if it will be adding any extra money towards the purchasing of benefits or whether this is going to be offered on a cost-nil basis.

This consideration may not be as simple as it seems, for example, there are whole range of benefits including life assurance, health care and defined benefit pension schemes that become more expensive to provide as employees get older. The decision at this stage is whether they should be offered on the basis whereby younger employees subsidise older employees, or whether the cost of the extra premium should be borne out by the individual. Perhaps the option may be for the company to subsidise these particular benefits allowing a similar contribution rate regardless of age.

Flexible benefit fund   5.20

The final part of the basic design and framework is to agree how each individual's flexible benefit fund (flex fund) will be calculated. The fund can include all benefits, just flexible benefits or the complete reward package. The flex fund can also be made up of trading salary holidays and allowances along with any top up the company wishes to put in to the new scheme. Before doing so however, the organisation needs to decide on whether it will be contributing any extra money towards these funds or not. If it is not, then any additional selection will have to be funded from the employee's reward package. On the other hand, the organisation may wish to contribute extra to the employee's benefits package because it has identified, through benchmarking, that they offer below the market norm and wish to make their pay and benefits more attractive.

The simplest type of flexible benefits fund is one that can only be spent on flexible benefits. This assumes that the individual's basic pay and core benefits are not included in the scheme — flexible benefits are totally separate and in addition to them. The basic design and structure, including elements such as selection and cost, is based solely on those products that can be traded. The advantage of this is simplistic administration, however, the main disadvantage is that it does not really help to promote the overall perceived value of the employees reward package.

The second option is to base the flexible benefits scheme on all employee benefits offered, both flexible and core. In this case, the employees' flexible benefits fund will have an automatic deduction at the commencement of the scheme year to pay for their core products. For instance, if their total flexible benefits fund is £2,000 and their core benefits amount to £500 then their first payment would be £500 (automatically) leaving them with £1,500 left to trade.

The final type of flexible benefits fund is based on the concept of total reward. Here the employees can choose exactly how they receive their pay and benefits. However they will still need to reserve money to pay for core benefits, statutory holidays etc.

Product selection   5.21

As mentioned in the introduction to flexible benefits there is no real limit to the type and amounts of products used and included in the flexible benefit scheme. However, in order to administer the scheme effectively and not to dilute the preserved value that it offers, most schemes limit the choice to about a dozen, particular in the first year. Once the scheme starts to evolve, more products can be added, however, to ensure that the overall impact is not diluted, obsolete benefits are removed before new ones are added.

Flexible benefits fall into one of four categories:

- lifestyle (holidays, childcare etc);

- financial (pension, loans etc);

- professional (personal development, business equipment etc);

- insurance/assurance (life, medical etc).

Product providers   5.22

As with traditional benefit provision it is recommended that several alternative suppliers for each product is evaluated to determine who offers the best of the following:

- the most cost effective alternative;

- the benefits offered are superior to those found in equivalent products on the high street;

- their communication processes enhance the flexible benefit scheme;

- their administration services and support are complementary;

- their after sales service will enhance the overall image of the flexible benefit scheme;

- they can provide up-to-date technology such as online modelling to allow employees to see not only the cost, but also the benefits of their selection, using IT technology;

- they will contribute as a valuable member of the project team.

Typical flexible benefit products   5.23

In several recent surveys the most common benefits offered in a flexible benefits plan were identified as follows:

• Season ticket loan	• Group personal pension
• Dental insurance	• Additional death-in-service insurance
• Home Insurance	• Buying/selling holidays
• Long-term care insurance	• Pension
• Legal advice counselling	• Childcare vouchers
• Company cars	• Gym membership
• Critical illness insurance	• Subsided loans
• Share or share option plan	• Pet insurance
• Luncheon arrangement vouchers	• Private fuel

Each one of the above has unique features and benefits as well as requirements in terms of administration.

The following paragraphs summarise those products that would be included in a typical flexible benefit scheme. There is a copy of an employee handbook with more detail on each of the products in **APPENDIX 1**.

Pensions   5.24

By including Additional Voluntary Contributions (AVCs) and pensions in a flexible benefit scheme, the company is providing a tax efficient and flexible vehicle for retirement planning. Because employees have different needs and affordability at different stages of their lives, this option allows them to manage and tailor their investments to their own unique circumstances.

The provision of pensions is often the highest costing benefit that the organisation provides. The two main considerations when deciding whether or not to flex this benefit are:

- cost and ease of actuarial valuation and administration; and

- ethical considerations in ensuring employees provide for future retirement.

A defined benefit pension scheme is a lot more difficult to flex than a defined contribution because of its intrinsic complexities. The scheme may for example offer a core actuarial rate of 1/60th with the option to trade up to 1/55th 1/50th or 1/45th. Care needs to be taken though to ensure that Inland Revenue limits are not breached for reasons including high potential service, significant retained benefits and the impositions of the earnings cap.

For a defined contribution scheme the formula is much simpler with the organisation setting a core contribution value of, say, 5% allowing individuals to trade up, usually at fixed percentage levels (eg 5%, 6%, 7%) which the company may choose to match.

A more common way of allowing individuals to top up their pension schemes, being a defined contribution or defined benefit, is the use of AVCs.

AVCs are a tax-effective means for employees to save an extra amount towards their pension. There are many reasons why they may wish to consider an AVC including:

- they may simply wish to have a large income when they retire;

- they may wish to take further advantage of the tax relief available when saving for retirement through approved pension funds;

- AVCs allow them to use bonuses for pension saving up to Inland Revenue limits;

- if they began saving for retirement late they may wish to use AVCs to 'catch-up';

- They may wish to use AVCs to save for early retirement.

Because of their complexity **CHAPTER 6** is devoted entirely to pensions and their inclusion in flexible benefit schemes.

Life assurance 5.25

Many larger employers cover their employees for life assurance. The levels of cover is usually linked to employees' earnings (eg up to four times salary for life cover). The cost of providing these on a group basis is kept relatively low providing the majority of staff are members, and as a result, they are often kept as core benefits within a flexible benefit scheme.

There are, however, opportunities to introduce some flexibility with such benefits. This can be achieved by including a reduced core level of benefits (for example from four times to two times salary in cover) with staff having the options to buy back up to the previous level.

Whether an existing group scheme is being adapted or an insured risk benefit is being introduced for the first time, one of the major issues of concern to the insurer is the principle of 'adverse selection'. The worry is that allowing employees choice will cause those more likely to claim to elect to receive higher benefits, whilst those less likely to claim will opt out. The result could range from a significant increase in premiums, to a requirement for greater disclosure of medical evidence by members and possible restrictions or exclusions in cover.

Example: Life assurance product

The company already provides employees with life cover of four times basic salary, which cannot be reduced. They believe that this is an important benefit and should therefore remain a core benefit. The company has, however, negotiated the ability to:

- select additional life cover for employees up to a limit of £250,000 in increments of £25,000;

- select life cover for employee's spouse/partner up to a limit of £250,000 in increments of £25,000.

In both cases additional cover is subject to underwriting approval. ➤

Tax information:

Any additional life cover employees choose to buy will be paid out of their net pay which normally does not give rise to any income tax and National Insurance liabilities as employees are paying the cost out of their pay that has already incurred tax.

Buying and selling holidays 5.26

The option to trade up or trade down holidays is usually included in a flexible benefits scheme. It is often an important way of releasing money to spend on new benefits. A minimum core limit is usually placed on the amount of holidays that staff must take – usually 20 days – which is the statutory minimum requirement in the UK.

There is also a limit placed on how much additional holidays staff can buy, usually 2–5 days. This is to ensure that the company is not left short staffed. Choice is usually made on the scheme renewal date and holiday entitlement has to be signed off on a holiday agreement form by the employee's manager. This is to allow the usual planning of resources required from when people have time off.

The monetary figure usually used to calculate the element of payroll gross pay used to trade up or trade down holidays is 1/260th of contractual pay per day.

On the assumption that the flexible benefits scheme does not allow any benefits to be cashed in, the main risk to the employer of offering holidays in a flexible benefits scheme is trading down. In the main, most schemes balance out the amount of days traded down against trading up, resulting in a near zero balance.

This type of flexible benefits has a major advantage, when trying to harmonise different sets of benefits schemes, where holiday entitlement is uneven. It offers those employees with a lower level of holiday entitlement, to trade up to a similar level to those with a higher level and at the same time, those employees with a high level of holiday entitlement, to trade down where they are not using their full entitlement.

Even if the trading of holidays does not balance, it is usually a lower cost to the organisation than increasing holiday entitlement of all the employees on the low level to the high level. This is particularly effective in dealing with the constraints imposed by the *Transfer of*

Undertakings (Protection of Employment) Regulations 1981 (SI 1981 No 1794) (TUPE) for mergers and acquisitions.

The above can also be used for changing company policy on holidays, for instance, bringing in a new holiday entitlement for new starters of 20 days as opposed to 25 days for those already in employment. Charging an administrative fee for buying extra holidays can reduce the risk of buying and selling holidays. This may be justified on the premise of covering the cost of employing temporary staff or paying other workers overtime.

Example: Buying and selling holidays

To help get the right balance between work and private life the company lets employees vary the amount of holiday they may take:

- they can reduce their holiday entitlement by up to two days in order to increase other benefits of their payable salary; or

- they can increase their holiday entitlement by up to three days by reducing their payable salary or other benefits.

Holidays can only be changed at the start of the plan year and cannot be amended during the scheme year in the event of a lifestyle change (see **5.39** below).

The holiday year runs from 1 April to 31 March each year (all other terms relating to holidays are unaffected).

Tax information:

The tax implication of trading up or trading down holidays is that taxable pay is reduced/increased. This may have implications on final salary and AVC calculations. Employee's National Insurance contributions are based on the resultant payroll gross pay. The tax implication is such that is more advantageous for an employee to trade up holidays rather than trade down.

Private medical insurance   5.27

Private medical insurance (PMI) is often included as the number of options available makes it easy to be flexible. A common way of approaching this benefit is for a core benefit of 'employee only' cover to be provided. Employees can use their flex fund to extend cover to their partners and family or select a higher hospital band. Alternatively, they might be able to increase their flex fund by selecting a higher excess.

Some schemes allow employees to opt out of private medical insurance and have the cost available as part of their flex fund. However, employers considering this option need to take into account the consequences, for example, on premium rates. If a larger number of employees opt out, the underwriter may reduce the group rate discount or even refuse to offer cover. An employee who wishes to rejoin later may also need to provide medical evidence and face possible exclusion from cover as underwriting may be required.

Although PMI is a benefit for the employee, the employer has a vested interest, particularly for key staff. By enabling the majority of major medical conditions to be dealt with at a convenient time and without delay, insurance keeps the disruption to the business at a minimum. It may, therefore, be good business practice to restrict the availability of opting out. More flexibility is available where employers support the cost of full family cover as allowing this to be reduced to a minimum of 'employee only' cover provides staff with the opportunity to boost their flex fund to spend on alternatives.

Most PMI providers insist on at least single cover as a core benefit, to make the scheme viable. As with life insurance, the major concern to the insurer is adverse selection. Allowing employees choice may cause those more likely to claim to elect to receive higher benefits, whilst those less likely to claim will opt out. The result of single cover remain a core benefit with the option to trade up to higher levels of cover could lead to a significant increase in premiums. It may also lead to a requirement for greater disclosure of medical evidence by members and possible restrictions or exclusions in cover.

Example: Private medical insurance

The company has two PMI schemes: one is for senior staff, and the other scheme is for employees with over two years' service.

The senior scheme provides medical insurance for members and their families (where appropriate). It covers the cost of outpatient and inpatient treatment received as private care, up to defined limits. No excess fee is charged to the member.

If employees are in the senior scheme they must retain single cover, they may however, use the difference between the value of ⟩

---

the single cover and their current level of cover to buy other benefits. They can, choose to keep, their existing benefit.

The other scheme provides single basic cover for those with over two years' service. This is a core benefit. There is an excess fee chargeable or £100.

There is a range of options in terms of whom the cover may apply to. These are cover for:

- employees and their partner;

- employees, the employee's partner and children; or

- employees and their children.

Options:

- There are a range of options and terms of cover available and they are not dependant on age or state of health.

- They can put the single basic cover with the £100 excess.

- Once they have selected the level of cover, and the company has accepted this, they would normally only be able to change at the annual review. For a lifestyle change (see **5.39** below), cover would be reassessed.

- If employees do decide to leave the scheme at any time, and then want to rejoin, they may be asked to supply evidence of good health. In this case, treatment for any pre-existing conditions, diagnosed within the last five years, will not be covered.

Tax information:

PMI is treated as a benefit in kind – so employees' PAYE tax coding will be affected.

Health screening 5.28

For a number of years employers have provided health screening for senior employees. This is to ensure that key staff are able to identify health issues before they become major problems and hence, affect job performance. A growing culture of health awareness has led to a demand for screening to be made available to a wider range of employees.

Various options can be made available from a basic 'Well Woman/Well Man' check to more comprehensive tests including exercise electro cardio-graphs. The screening process usually involves completion of a health and lifestyle questionnaire, prior to the appointment, during which various tests and assessments are carried out. Following a consultation with a doctor, a confidential report is provided with the test results and appropriate recommendations for improving and maintaining health.

Example: Health screening

The health screening programme is designed to educate and help employees to detect a range of health problems at an early stage when it is often much easier for appropriate action to be taken to prevent them becoming more serious.

Health screening is already offered to certain employees, but is now available to all employees through this scheme.

Options:

- If they have this benefit they cannot opt out but can also select a health screen for their spouse/partner.

- If they currently do not have this benefit they can select this benefit for them and/or their spouse/partner.

Important notes if employees purchase a health screen for them or their spouse/partner.

1. Health screens can only be purchased at the start of the scheme year.

2. A minimum of two clear working days (Monday to Friday) notice is required to cancel or move an appointment; otherwise it is possible that a fee will be charged.

3. Health screens booked through the scheme are at significantly reduced rates with selected hospitals.

4. Health screens not taken in the year in which they are purchased will be lost and no refund will be given.

Tax information:

Note that the company agreed with the Inland Revenue that employees would not be taxed upon the value of their health

---

> screens. However, this agreement cannot extend to health screens for their spouse/partner and so, if selected, they will be taxed upon the value.

Dental insurance 5.29

Although the majority of people continue to receive dental treatment under the National Health Service (NHS), around 40% of treatment is now carried out privately. With charges becoming increasingly expensive, dental insurance is a common choice within flexible benefits programmes.

A number of specialist insurers offer a range of schemes designed to reimburse members for a variety of treatments, including check-ups. Different levels of reimbursement are provided for each treatment depending on whether NHS or private treatment is required. Dental insurance often proves to be popular with employees as it can be provided at relatively little cost and there is a strong likelihood of deriving some financial benefits from selecting it.

Example: Dental insurance

Whilst the dental insurance providers' cover levels have increase year on year they have also been able to offer lower annual premiums. Employees are being offered the facility to buy dental insurance at the company-negotiated rates for themselves, their spouse/partner and/or their family.

Option 1:

Reimburses most NHS charges up to an annual maximum of £550 for routine treatment and £550 for accident/sports injury treatment.

Option 2:

Suitable for those who attend a private dentist, with an annual limit of £1,250.

Option 3:

More appropriate for those who attend a more expensive private dentist, with an annual limit of £1,550.

Policy terms and conditions:

Cover is up to the age of 65 with children being covered up to the age of 21 or up to 24 if in full-time education.

Tax information:

This benefit is taxable and, if chosen, income tax calculated in the value of the benefit will normally be deducted each month via the payroll from employee's salary.

Critical illness insurance 5.30

Critical illness cover provides a tax-free cash sum if individuals are diagnosed as suffering from a specified critical illness, while an employee of the company. Benefits are provided through an insurance policy, and they may specify the level of cover, which they require.

Example: Critical illness insurance

Flexible benefit options are available in units of £10,000, up to a maximum benefit of £250,000 (or four times annual salary).

- They may increase their cover by up to two units of £10,000 at each annual review date and if they experience a 'lifestyle' change within that period, without certification of health.

- There is a pre-existing condition exclusion that applies from the date that cover or increase in cover is put into effect. If they choose to take cover of £100,000 or more, they will need to complete a medical declaration.

- Cover may be extended to include spouse or partner. The level of this cover mush not exceed their own, or £50,000 if less. The same table of premium rates would apply for their partner as themselves, with the cost being based on the appropriate age and sex.

- They may not be required to provide any medical evidence. However, if they are not actively at work on the day in which they take out the cover, it will only become effective on their return to work (with the consent of the company doctor or medical adviser).

- No benefit will be paid for any pre-existing condition that they have suffered prior to start of cover, or increase in cover. The benefit will be payable after the diagnosis of a critical illness for the first time.

Tax information:

Critical illness cover is deducted from an employee's net pay; therefore they pay no additional tax.

Personal accident insurance 5.31

Accidents do happen. Indeed, they are the fourth leading cause of death for people in all age groups. Personal accident insurance protects employees' families from economic loss due to accidental death or permanent serious injury.

Example: Personal accident insurance

For £100,000 of cover, employees may have the following options.

Options:

- They can retain the cover they have been given.

- They can also select £100,000 of cover for their spouse/partner and/or family.

- They can choose to opt out and use the value of this benefit toward another or to increase their payable salary.

If the employees wish to upgrade or downgrade the level of cover for themselves, spouse/partner and/or family they can participate in the voluntary personal accident scheme instead.

Tax information:

This benefit is taxable and, if chosen, income tax calculated on the value of the benefit will normally be deducted each month via the payroll from the employee's salary.

Travel insurance 5.32

This is an annual travel insurance, which provides cover for employees' own leisure travel.

Example: Travel insurance

Options:

- They can choose to retain the cover they have been given.

- They can take out cover for their spouse/partner and/or family.

- They can chose to opt out and use the value of this benefit toward another or to increase their Payable Salary.

Key features:

- Annual cover

- Comprehensive worldwide cover

- Children under three years old are free on family annual travel cover

- Winter sports cover for up to 17 days

- Covers trips of up to 31 days

Tax information:

This benefit is taxable and, if chosen, income tax calculated on the value of the benefit will normally be deducted each month via the payroll from employee's salary.

Childcare vouchers 5.33

Demographic and social changes over the last few decades mean there has been an increase in families with two working parents and hence a significant rise in demand for childcare services, either on a full-time basis or during school holidays. Major employers with large numbers of staff on a single site have gone as far as providing crèches and other facilities. However this is not practical for most companies.

A number of specialist providers have emerged who can provide assistance to employees and from whom vouchers can be purchased. These can be redeemed with recognised providers of childcare such as nurseries and registered nannies. Employees are often asked to nominate at the start of the scheme year the value of the vouchers for the whole year that they wish to purchase from their flex fund.

Childcare vouchers are exempt from employee and employer NI and some schemes may also be corporation tax deductible. This saving could be passed on to employees or used to offset the scheme cost.

The specialist providers also offer helplines to provide advice on a wide range of childcare issues. They are usually able to provide practical help in finding local facilities, which most closely meet individual employee's needs.

Example: Childcare vouchers

The childcare voucher scheme is very simple to operate and administrate.

- Employees complete a voucher order form and the amount is deducted from their salary on a monthly basis.

- A spreadsheet indicating the total amount of vouchers required is sent to the provider who then distributes the vouchers direct to the employee's home address.

To give employees full flexibility when choosing their childcare, childcare vouchers, which can be used for children up to the age of 14 are accepted at a wide range of childcare providers, which include:

- registered childminders;

- day nurseries;

- close family members;

- holiday provision.

Tax information:

The childcare voucher scheme provides a very simple and cost effective way for employers and employees to obtain valuable National Insurance savings through their childcare costs.

This benefit is taxable and, if chosen, income tax calculated on the value of the benefit will normally be deducted each month via the payroll from employee's salary.

Company cars 5.34

From 6 April 2002, the benefit in kind company car tax has meant that drivers of company cars registered after 1 January 1998 are taxed according to a calculation based on the price of the vehicle and its CO_2 emissions. This makes a company car far more attractive for 'perk' drivers as they are no longer penalised for driving relatively few business miles – the basis of the previous tax structure.

However, for essential business users, the new tax means that they could end up with a higher tax bill for driving the same car.

As many employers seek to implement alternative schemes to avoid the new taxation minefield, a common option has been cash-for-car often within a flexible benefits scheme.

As with benefits such as private medical insurance, the operational requirements of the business need to be balanced with a desire to provide genuine choice. This is relevant for staff who need a car for their job, where the employer may wish to retain more control over the choice of car to ensure that the right image is projected. This is sometimes achieved by not allowing essential business users to opt for a cash allowance, but to be able to trade up or down by one grade of car.

One way for the employer to have at least a little control over what their employees are driving around in, is a personal lease plan (PLP). It must be pointed out that PLPs will not help employees avoid the new tax unless they enter a credit sale agreement so that the car ownership transfers to them immediately.

Example: Personal lease plan

The company acts as an 'introducer' to a personal car leases plan provider. The provision and contract of this service is independent (ie a private arrangement between employee and the car lease plan company). The company will not act as guarantor or pick up the cost of any default.

The Personal Lease Plan allows employees to finance a new car for themselves or a member of their family, and they are not tied to a specific dealer, make or model of vehicle. They are able to lease the car at an agreed guaranteed purchase price, and enjoy the security and peace of mind of owning a fully maintained and serviced vehicle. ➤

Options:

- Unlike various plans from specific dealers, this scheme allows employees to take advantage of a competitive reliable finance scheme to purchase any make or model of car.

- Employees choose the make and model of the car that they or their family member wants. Next decide whether they want to keep the car for two or three years, taking into account the annual mileage they are likely to do. The monthly repayments are then calculated to cover the difference between the 'on the road' price (minus any deposit they choose to pay), and the 'option to purchase' price.

- They can use their current car as part exchange. Its value can be used as all, or part, of a deposit.

- At the end of the agreement they would have a variety of options to choose from: They can return the car, choose another one, and start another agreement. They could purchase the car outright – this would be at the 'option to purchase' price previously agreed. Finally, they can simply return the car and walk away.

Tax information:

There are no tax considerations, as this will not be deducted from payroll or other company benefits.

Additional voluntary benefits   5.35

As mentioned before it is possible to enhance the brand of the flexible benefits scheme by offering an additional range of products that are not directly linked to flexible benefits. These are usually based on special terms negotiated with providers but rely on the direct contract with the employees. This means that the company acts merely as an introducer and that there is no payroll deduction or any administration involved: employees pay for it direct from their bank account.

Products here may include:

- concierge services (more information in appendix);
- break down rescue;
- high street stores;
- entertainment and leisure centres;

- book clubs; and

- banking services.

Trading salary and bonuses 5.36

The size of the available flex fund will often depend on how far core benefits have been reduced to create additional spending power, or how generous the employer has been in providing additional funding. Some flex funds will be relatively modest and, therefore, restrict the additional benefits an employee will be able to purchase.

As a result, many schemes allow members to spend a proportion of their salary or benefits. In some cases this is restricted to a percentage of their salary, often 10% or 20%, although some employers do not put any restrictions in place.

Companies have different approaches to allowing employees to take the flex fund as cash. Some do not allow this as part of the scheme rules, as the intention is to offer flexibility over benefit choice rather than additional pay instead of benefits. Others take a more relaxed view, although they may reduce the amount taken as cash to cover the cost of employer's National Insurance contributions.

It is becoming more common, in flexible benefit schemes, for employees to be able to supplement their 'flexible fund' by trading a proportion of their salary for benefits. This reflects the fact that, in some circumstances, the size of the benefits allowance, on its own, does not offer an attractive range of options.

Shadow salary 5.37

Where employees choose to 'trade' a proportion of their salary to acquire additional benefits or opt to increases their salary by reducing the amount of benefits, their 'resultant' basic salary ceases to act as a fixed 'trigger' for calculating salary related items such as:

- terms and conditions of employment;

- sick and maternity pay;

- redundancy and retirement;

- overtime and holidays;

- annual pay rewards and bonuses;

- performance related pay;

- pension contributions;

- death in service life assurance;

- permanent health insurance;

- critical health insurance;

- PAYE and NI.

A shadow salary is an 'artificial' salary, set up along side the basic salary, that allows the above (except PAYE and NI) to continue to be calculated, without loss to the individual, once deductions from basic salary have been made for payment towards additional benefits (or increasing salary).

The shadow salary cannot be used for PAYE and NI calculations as these are directly effected by the combination of remaining basic pay (after sacrifice) and additional benefits bought (that may attract P11D, tax exception etc).

With flexible benefits, the shadow salary is set/adjusted once a year or for lifestyle changes. Once set it does not change. Therefore, there is no need for continual adjustments and calculations.

Voluntary benefits and profit related pay (PLP), where funds are deducted from net salary, need separate analysis to ensure they are not mixed up with salary sacrifice/core benefits and that there is no double accounting.

Where benefits are converted into cash (ie salary addition), a nominal charge of 10% is levied to cover administration costs.

Each flexible benefit scheme has its own unique administration system. Some convert to a 'total reward' value as the base for all calculations, others simply insert the shadow salary into their payroll process at the point of calculating gross pay. Each situation should be analysed to ensure the right balance of ease of calculation and processing

Product mix   5.38

Having selected the products that will form the flexible benefits scheme, the next step is to decide how to mix them together to obtain the best advantage for both employer and employee. At the same time the company needs to ensure compliance with Inland Revenue requirements and the other scheme rules and regulations.

The grid below is a typical example of product mix. It restricts the amount of salary that can be traded, ensures holidays traded fall within statutory requirements and pensions are provided as core, on an ethical basis. It also caters for the core single cover requirements imposed by the PMI provider and company eye testing required by health and safety.

Flexible benefits – typical product grid		
Benefit	*Core*	*Flexible*
Salary	80%	20%
Holidays	25 Days	Buy or sell up to a maximum of 5 days.
Pension	Final salary and defined contribution	AVC.
Spouse/ Dependants Pension	50/50	—
Life Insurance	1 x DIS	Additional cover up to 3 x DIS.
PHI	Up to 75% salary. Pension contributions payable to retirement	—
Critical Illness	—	Several fixed levels, voluntary benefit.
PMI	Single cover	Dependants cover. Single parent cover.
Personal accident	—	Several fixed levels, voluntary benefit.
Medical screening	—	Executive programme. 'Well person' programme.
Eye test	VDU eye test/2 years	

Flexible benefits – typical product grid		
Benefit	*Core*	*Flexible*
Cars	Required for job – contract purchase	Required for job – trade up/down. Not required for job – personal lease plan.
Childcarev-Vouchers	—	Several fixed levels, voluntary benefit.
Dental plan	—	Basic plan. Extensive plan.

Rules, regulations and limits 5.39

In order for the new flexible benefit scheme to meet Inland Revenue and legal requirements as well as allowing structured and easy administration, a set of rules and regulations and limits are usually drawn up as part of the design of the scheme. Each product and service within the scheme will have its own rules and regulations, however, there may be some common to all.

The following are the major rules, regulations and limits that should be applied to a flexible benefit scheme.

- For new permanent staff there will be a two-week period, immediately following their start date, in which they may opt into the scheme.

- There will be a fixed date for registration at the commencement of the scheme.

- The date for annual review of the scheme will be 1 January.

- Wherever relevant, the financial value of a flexible option will be based on annual shadow gross salary.

- Employees can forego up to 20% of their annual shadow salary in order to provide flexible benefits.

- There is no option to 'cash in' unused benefits at the end of the scheme period.

- All options exercised must fall within statutory limits imposed from time to time by the Government.

- The company will set core benefits from time to time.

- Participants will not be able to exchange core benefits, as defined in the employee handbook, for additional salary.

- Each option will have its own individual specifications, cost and rules and regulations.

- Employees wishing to participate in the scheme mush sign a preference form indicating the benefits that they would like the company to consider providing for them for the duration of the scheme year and that they acknowledge that certain benefits (indicated in the handbook) will involve deductions for income tax and National Insurance contributions.

- Flexible benefits, and any subsequent changes to them, will only be accepted on an authorised preference form obtainable from the HR department. Qualified personnel ensure that the choices fall within the scheme rules and are acceptable to the company.

- Options may only be altered annually, on the annual review date, except in the case of 'lifestyle changes'.

- All choices and/or changes will be confirmed to the employee by means of a signed acknowledgement. This could include changes brought about by changes in Government legislation.

- If an employee takes maternity leave, their return to work will constitute a lifestyle change.

- Terms such as 'partner', 'dependant', 'family' etc, are clearly defined in the section on lifestyle changes (see **5.39** below), and must be strictly adhered to.

- Unless otherwise specified all flexible benefits will cease immediately an employee leaves the company.

- There will be no refund for unused benefits once selected and approved.

Lifestyle changes 5.40

During the course of employee's employment with the company there may well be changes in their personal or family circumstances. The circumstances, which would constitute 'lifestyle changes', are marriage; birth or adoption of a child; death or a partner or dependant; divorce or permanent separation.

It is recognised that these events may result in changes to their benefit requirements. Therefore, if they do experience a lifestyle change between annual scheme review dates, they are usually permitted to make appropriate changes to their benefit package.

'Partner' is the person with whom the employee cohabitates, at the same permanent address. 'Family' includes their partner and any immediate dependants. Either they, or their partner, must be the parent or legal guardian of any dependants. Dependants must be under the age of 18.

When an employee returns from maternity/paternity leave they should be given the opportunity to revise their chosen benefits on the birth of their baby. If an employee is on maternity leave at the annual enrolment date they will be eligible to enrol when they return to work. The same applies to paternal and adoption leave.

Inland Revenue consideration   5.41

Employees must be aware of the tax and National Insurance implications when they make their decision about their flexible benefit. CHAPTER 7 covers this subject in more detail, but a summary is given below.

- *Non-taxable benefit* – Some core and flexible benefits are non-taxable, and therefore, particularly cost effective, eg AVCs and medical screening.

- *Taxable benefits in kind* – Some benefits within the scheme are treated as 'benefits in kind', for tax purposes. This means a taxable value is assigned to the benefit purchased on the employee's behalf by the company, which may then reduce their PAYE tax coding, eg medical insurance and company car.

- *Voluntary benefits* – Voluntary benefits deducted from net salary after tax are not taxable. Basically, employees have already paid tax on their salary, and so will not have to pay again on any voluntary benefits that they may choose, eg personal accident insurance, critical illness insurance and the dental care plan.

- *Introduced products* – These benefits are based on a private contract between the employees and the provider with no payroll deductions, and so will not affect their PAYE tax and National Insurance,eg personal lease plans.

When considering the choice between a benefit in kind and a voluntary benefit, employees must weigh up the different tax implications. The benefit in kind option would reduce their PAYE tax coding, and thereby increase the amount of income tax payable, whereas the voluntary benefit is deducted from their net salary without affecting their tax position.

Although there is no legal requirement for a flexible benefit scheme to be approved by the Inland Revenue, it is common practice to obtain endorsement from the local Inland Revenue office. The earlier in the project this can be done, the easier it will be to manage any changes required by them to the scheme.

The tax treatment of the various products that make up a flexible benefits scheme are fairly straightforward and other than negotiation on individual benefits, the Inland Revenue's main concern is how the tax and NI situation is communicated to employees, in particular, the effect of mixing the benefits and the ability to use holiday and basic pay to fund them.

Employment law considerations 5.42

Employment law issues are covered in more detail in **CHAPTER 8** but in summary the five main areas that need to be reviewed during the design stage are:

- *Terms and conditions of employment* – identify those benefits and contractual arrangements that will be affected or changed to buy individual choice and selection. Next, agree how to affect any changes in the contract required.

- *Discrimination* – ensure that the rules and regulations governing entitlement and choice of benefits do not indirectly discriminate against an employee. For instance, exclusion of part-time workers for those benefits which require full-time employment (in this case an alternative value of benefits needs to be offered).

- *Employment Act* – ensure that all statutory entitlement and pay is included in the scheme and not affected by it. The rights of fixed-term workers are not affected or discriminated against in terms of product selection and mix.

- *Equal opportunities* – ensure the choice of products and mix do not contradict the *Sex Discrimination Act 1975*, the *Race Relations Act 1976* and the *Disability Discrimination Act 1995*. Also, that they do not indirectly contradict the proposed part-time workers regulations, which is in the process of being introduced into the UK.

- Business transfers. The choice and mix of products do not contradict the transfer of undertakings regulations (TUPE) if requiring an other organisation and using this scheme to harmonise different sets of pay and benefits.

Administration, IT structure and infrastructure consideration   5.43

The administration, IT structure and infrastructure considerations are covered in more detail in **CHAPTER 11**, **CHAPTER 12** and **CHAPTER 13**.

In summary the main considerations are:

- Decide on in-house administration and/or outsourcing some or all of the scheme.

- Set up the basic administration of the scheme.

- Agree inputs, processing and outputs.

- Evaluate and confirm organisational requirements.

- Ensure integration with other systems (HR, payroll, P11D etc).

- Set up management and administration system.

- Agree system options (eg web based systems etc).

- Evaluate impact of outsourcing contracts on the overall design of the scheme.

- Set up any IT software and hardware required for the scheme.

Communication and launch consideration   5.44

This is covered in more details in **CHAPTER 9** and **CHAPTER 10** but in summary the considerations are:

- Ensure the scheme is uniquely branded and has its own style.

- Base the communication on proactive internal marketing, not just issuing information.

- Decide what needs communicating.

- Decide who the organisation is communicating to.

- Decide what media will be used.

- Choose the right communicators.

- Ensure the timing of the various communications are chosen for maximum effect.

- Pre-empt any foreseeable communication difficulties.

Due diligence   5.45

Once the plan and design of the flexible benefit scheme has been completed it needs to be double tested to ensure credibility and viability.

Systems design tests are needed to prove that the individual product calculations work and that the links between the flexible benefits scheme and other parts of the organisations infrastructures are sound. These links could include those to payroll, P11D, PAYE etc.

The other main aspect of due diligence is to make sure that the scheme really is offering the advantages set out in the feasibility study. For instance, the organisation needs to ensure that those on a lower pay band can actually afford the products that have been offered in the scheme. They also need to make sure that if individuals go down the route of trading salary or other cash bonuses as entitlements, they are not left short of cash required for day-to-day expenses.

The due-diligence stage should also check that the safe guards put in to ensure, for instance, employees do not exceed their Inland Revenue entitlement to topping up pension schemes, are working correctly. It should also ensure that other procedures established, eg approval of buying and selling holidays, actually work in practice.

Because of the integral nature of flexible benefits, due diligence is best achieved on an ongoing basis. Every time a change is made to the scheme it is highly likely to have an effect on several other areas of the scheme, which in turn will have a cascading effect on other parts.

Options to review   5.46

A flexible benefit scheme is a live entity. It needs to cope with the current situation and grow in terms of the advantages offered to both employer and employee. The initial design stage of a flexible benefit scheme should ensure that new products can be added at a later stage and obsolete products be removed easily.

This is not just a simple case of changing the product selection but making sure that all the other parts of the scheme, such as communication, are designed to cope easily with this type of change. This means that the research phase of the feasibility study also needs to be continued on an annual basis to assess the effectiveness of current products and identify new preferences.

Quality procedures and control   5.47

Quality control and customer care is the hallmark of any good benefit scheme, and flexible benefits are no different. Because of the multitude of variables involved, a quality control and code of practice needs to be developed. This includes the development of the quality control manual and associated policy.

It may be that some of the products provided are regulated under the *Financial Services Act 1986* and could be subject to the rules of the personal investment authority. If this is the case then the scheme needs to emulate this and ensure that where appropriate that it complies with it.

There are other quality control policy and procedures that the company may have implemented such as ISO 9001 and investors in people and the new scheme needs to be linked into these. For instance a quality control audit trail may be required in order to ensure compliance.

As in any project of this nature, there are bound to be times when complaints arise and the scheme must have its own set of policies and procedures to deal with this. If these are clearly identified and published it will add credibility to the scheme and reassurance to employees that in the event of misunderstanding their rights are protected.

There are examples of a customer care policy and quality management policy in the back of the project brief included in **APPENDIX 1**.

Timescales   5.48

The average time scale for the design and implementation of a flexible benefits scheme is typically six to nine months from initial concept to going live. It is possible to achieve a launch date in a shorter period of time, but this usually necessitates an element of compromise in the design of the scheme.

The initial strategy and design of the flexible benefits scheme should consider when best to launch the scheme. Most schemes are launched on the same day of the annual pay review so that they are mutually supportive. However, this may be too much of an administrative burden for the company or may aggravate the current situation, for instance, if there is a dispute around levels of pay being offered.

An alternative time to launch a scheme is halfway during the reward year. However, this is more difficult and time consuming, as it will involve changes to the scheme six months later as new pay levels and entitlement are introduced.

The final areas to consider in terms of timing are other events that are happening within the organisation. For instance, the company could be going through a major relocation exercise and feel that the new scheme would add to the general confusion caused. On the other hand it could offset the general feeling of disruption by offering perceived improvement in their reward package.

6 — Pensions and Flexible Benefits

This chapter covers the following:

- Introduction
- Stakeholder and personal pensions
- Defined contribution pension schemes
- Occupational defined benefit pension schemes
- Executive pensions
- Small self-administered schemes
- Unapproved pension schemes
- Contracting out of SERPS
- Death-in-service benefits
- Additional Voluntary Contributions
- Topping up of pensions via flexible benefits
- Salary sacrifice
- Earnings Cap
- Legal issues

Introduction   6.1

To fully understand and appreciate the advantages and disadvantages of including pension in a flexible benefit scheme, organisations must first have a basic understanding of the various types of pensions available. They also need to appreciate the tax implications such as the 'Earnings Cap', salary and bonus sacrifices etc. This chapter outlines the key features of the main types of pension schemes in the UK and how they may be flexed.

About half of the employed workforce in the UK are currently active members of occupational pension schemes. This proportion has changed very little in the last 20 years although, with the abolition in 1988 of the practice whereby an employer could make joining, and staying in, the company scheme a condition of employment, around one-fifth of eligible new employees have declined the offer of membership.

Expenditure on pensions is one of the largest elements of non-cash reward for an organisation. By including pension in a flexible benefits plan either as a core benefit, flexible benefit – or a mix of both – the organisation can provide a better understanding of the perceived value of this benefit for employees.

The continuing trend of organisations switching pension provision from defined benefit to defined contribution is another main reason why pensions are also being included.

Flexibility 6.2

The inclusion of pensions greatly increases the success of a flexible benefit plan. It allows individuals easy access to additional contributions for those looking to top up their retirement planning and affordability for those who have greater priority for other benefits. This in turn allows pension planning to respond more effectively to the changing needs of the work force and to facilitate harmonisation of different pension arrangement schemes, rationalisation and the transition from a defined benefits to defined contributions.

Flexing pensions can also reduce HR and payroll administration, as some transaction activity can be provided through the flexible benefits delivery mechanisms. These include:

- inter-scheme transfers;
- more efficient and proactive distribution of materials;
- more efficient capture of information;
- more effective handling of employee queries.

Historically, few flexible benefit schemes have included pensions within the available flexing choice, in particular, the core retirement income element of a typical pension scheme. Other elements of the typical pension scheme are already popular flexing choices such as Life Assurance Benefits, and Additional Voluntary Contributions (AVCs) (see **6.40** below).

The two main perceived difficulties for including pensions in a flexible benefit scheme were:

● Some companies take a paternalistic approach to pensions, holding the view that the pension promise should be part of the 'core' benefit package.

● Pensions, particularly defined benefit, are seen as complex, difficult to administer and to value within the total compensation package.

There is some evidence, however, that employers who established flexible benefit schemes some years ago are now considering including pensions as a flexing option having satisfactorily incorporated other benefits.

Stakeholders and personal pensions   6.3

Stakeholders in their original form as PPs were originally designed as a vehicle for the self-employed and employees who were not members of occupational pension schemes. The tax changes introduced in the wake of the launch of stakeholder pensions have considerably extended the numbers and categories of people eligible to contribute to PPs and effectively created two different personal pension tax regimes – PPs and retirement annuities plans (RAPs).

From 1988 the Government encouraged pension provision through PPs, introducing the concept of contracting out on a money purchase basis.

Together with the complexity of administration, occupational deferred contribution schemes for few employees, groupare now being offered to fewer employees. Group personal pensions (GPP) have increased rapidly such that they now form a major part of the pension scheme.

Tax   6.4

The tax position of personal pensions is as follows:

- Legislation governing the approval and tax treatment of personal pension schemes is to be found in the *Income and Corporation Taxes Act 1988* and the *Finance Act 2000*.

- Personal pensions are the successors to retirement annuity plans (RAP). While no new RAPs have been available since July 1988, many of the then existing contracts remain in force and can generally receive additional contributions.

- The earliest date on which a personal pensions could start was 1 July 1988 (some could be backdated to April 1997).

- Stakeholder personal pensions first became available on 6 April 2001. They share the same tax regime as non-stakeholder personal pensions.

- Personal pensions may receive transfers from other personal pensions and other approved pension arrangements, eg occupational pension schemes.

- All personal contributions are paid net of basic rate tax, which is reclaimed by the provider. Higher rate tax relief is provided by adjustment to employees tax code. Employer contributions are paid gross.

- Contributions are invested in funds that are free of UK tax on non-dividend investment income, and capital gains tax. Pension schemes have been unable to reclaim the tax credits on UK dividends since 2 July 1997.

Contractual basis   6.5

Personal pensions are usually established by issuing contracts, which are subject to personal pension scheme rules adopted by the provider, for example an insurance company or authorised unit trust manager.

Personal pensions can also be established as trust-based schemes, although in practice this approach is likely to be used mainly for stakeholder personal pension schemes, sponsored by employers, affinity groups and trade unions. All forms of personal pension operate on a money purchase basis.

The primary difference between ordinary personal pensions and the stakeholder version of personal pensions is that the stakeholder plans are subject to an additional layer of DSS regulations, covering such areas as maximum charges and employer access.

Pension benefits are based on the amount of funds accumulated and annuity rates applicable at the time benefits are taken from an arrangement. All pension benefits are taxable as earned income. Lump sum payments are generally tax-free, although the lump sum is restricted to broadly 25% of the fund. Death benefits may be liable to inheritance tax in some circumstances.

It has been common to segment personal pensions into a number of arrangements, each of which can be dealt with separately, thereby allowing the policyholder to draw benefits in stages. In theory, this has not been necessary for new policies since October 2000, as the *Finance Act 2000* permits partial vesting of policies.

General eligibility rules – non-member of occupational schemes   6.6

Individuals who are not members of an occupational scheme are eligible to join a stakeholder (or personal pension scheme) provided they are aged less than 75 and/either:

- resident and ordinarily resident in the UK at some time in the year the contribution is made; or

- a Crown servant or the spouse of a Crown servant.

The effect of this wide eligibility is that a person who is not a member of an occupational scheme can become a member of a stakeholder or personal pension scheme if they have non-pensionable employed earnings or no earnings whatsoever.

Members of occupational schemes   6.7

Members of occupational schemes may also become members of a personal pension scheme with respect to the same employment (a process known as 'concurrency') in the following circumstances:

- at some time in the year, the individual is either resident and ordinarily resident in the UK, or is overseas as a Crown servant or as the spouse of a Crown servant; and

- the individual is not, and has not been a Controlling Director at any time in the year or in any of the five tax years preceding it (tax years before 2000/01 do not count); and

- the individual has taxable remuneration not exceeding the remuneration limit (£30,000 in 2001/02) for the year of contribution or has remuneration less than the limit in at least one of the previous five tax years (again, tax years before 2000/01 do not count).

There are three other circumstances in which an occupational scheme member is eligible to become a member of a personal pension scheme:

• the occupational pension scheme offers only death-in-service benefits; or

• the occupational scheme is unapproved; or

• the personal pension scheme is used solely for the purpose of contracting out of S2P (State second pension).

Contributions to personal pensions 6.8

Contributions of up to the earnings threshold (£3,600 gross a year in 2001/02)2002/03) may be paid to a personal pension for anyone who satisfies the eligibility criteria, regardless of their level of earnings. If contributions of more than £3,600 pa are to be made, these are based on net relevant earnings. The £3,600 earnings threshold places a premium on eligibility, as in certain circumstances a very small amount of non-pensionable income will allow an otherwise ineligible individual to contribute up to £3,600 to a personal pension.

Maximum contributions to personal pensions are calculated as a percentage of net relevant earnings, according to age, but:

• regardless of net relevant earnings, a personal pension for any eligible member may receive contributions of up to £3,600 gross every tax year;

• net relevant earnings are subject to the Earnings Cap (see **6.54** below);

• net relevant earnings used as a basis for contributions do not have to be those for the tax year to which the contribution is related.

Tax relief on personal pension contributions 6.9

A key advantage of personal pensions, compared with most non-pension investments to provide income in retirement, is the tax relief on contributions.

Individual contributions   **6.10**

The general principle is that an individual's personal pension contributions qualify for tax relief at their marginal rate(s) of income tax, as they count against total income.

All personal pension contributions made on or after 6 April 2001 benefit from tax relief at basic rate by deduction from the contributions. The provider will gross up the contribution to allow for basic rate relief, which is reclaimed from the Inland Revenue. Before 2001/02, the self-employed had to make all pension contributions gross and reclaim tax through their self-assessment return.

Even if the individual is non-resident, a non-taxpayer or a starting rate taxpayer, basic rate relief is given at source and not reclaimed by the Inland Revenue.

Any higher rate tax relief is given separately, either through the PAYE coding system or the self-assessment return. The additional relief is given by extending the basic rate band by the amount of the gross contribution. The pension contribution does not count as a deduction against income for calculating total income, eg for age allowance purposes.

The basic rate relief is that given for the tax year in which the contribution is made. However, under the carry-back rules, an individual can choose to have the contribution treated as if it had been made in the previous tax year. Where a contribution is carried back, tax relief is given at the rate for the tax year to which it is carried back.

If a contribution is made in 2001/02 and carried back to 2000/01, basic rate relief is given at source, regardless of employment status in 2000/01.

Employer contributions   **6.11**

An employer may pay personal pension contributions to an employee's personal pension in respect of the net relevant earnings for the employee's basic year.

Alternatively, where the employee is a member of the employer's occupational scheme and is also eligible to be a member of a personal pension scheme under the concurrency rules, the employer may also contribute.

The employee is not liable to tax on the benefit of the contributions paid to the personal pension.

National Insurance contributions (NICs) are not chargeable on the contributions.

Employer contributions are aggregated when assessing whether maximum contributions have been breached.

Employer contributions are paid gross.

Personal pensions and flexible benefits are discussed at **6.19** below.

Occupational defined contribution (money purchase) pension schemes

6.12

Defined contribution members receive pensions based on the investment performance of funds paid into their scheme. Until 1988, money purchase occupational schemes were the only practical means whereby an employer could provide pension for a workforce which was too small to sustain funded final salary benefits. They were rejuvenated in 1988 when changes in legislation meant they could take advantage of the contracting-out option for the first time. Even before then, because of growing legislative demands and the open-ended commitment, many employers had become increasingly disenchanted with final salary schemes.

As a result, first-time pension schemes were, and still are, predominately money purchase. Some existing final salary schemes have been converted to money purchase, while others are seriously considering following their example. With money purchase schemes, the position is broadly that the scheme benefits for a member are dependent on the amount and timing of contributions paid by, and in respect of, them and annuity rates prevalent at the time benefits are required.

At the smaller end of the money purchase market, the occupational version is via group personal pension.

Money purchase occupational pension schemes have much in common with final salary occupational pension schemes. Until April 2001, they both automatically operated under the same laws and broadly the same tax regime. Under this regime, Inland Revenue rules apply to contributions.

From April 2001 a money purchase occupational scheme can choose to operate under the new defined contribution regime. This regime covers all personal pensions, both group and individual and stakeholder pensions, but not retirement annuities. This is testing the maximum under Inland Revenue rules and it is the benefit that is measured.

Principal personal benefits

Retirement age   **6.13**

The scheme must set out a normal retirement age for each member or class of member. Retirement may be before, on or after normal retirement age (see **6.22** below).

All members' benefits must be taken at retirement, with the exception of the residual pension taken by pre-89 member (those who joined the scheme before 1989), after he or she has taken any tax-free cash at, or after, normal retirement date. The concept of phased or staggered retirement is, therefore, effectively ruled out by this requirement.

Pension drawdown   **6.14**

The Inland Revenue has introduced a system of pension drawdown for contracted-in money purchase occupational schemes. The chief features for this are:

- the scheme's trustees may choose to offer drawdown as an alternative to annuity purchase at the time the pension starts;

- if the member is offered this facility and accepts it, the maximum benefits regime still applies. Thus, for example, the member's maximum lump sum death benefit during drawdown is the balance of the first five years' pension instalments;

- deferral of annuity purchase cannot currently extend beyond age 75.

Benefits on normal retirement   **6.15**

Benefits can normally be taken in the form of tax-free cash and pension.

Tax-free cash   **6.16**

Tax-free cash is usually available except where either:

- the scheme consists of pure protected rights (when the only contributions are contracted-out contributions); or

- there is no scope in the scheme's rules for any of the proceeds to be paid out as tax-free cash.

Normally, anyone who has the chance to take tax-free cash selects the maximum available, unless there is a reason to believe there may be future discretionary enhancement in retirement – which is highly unlikely under a defined contribution scheme.

Taking maximum tax-free cash is an option for members, even if their objective is income rather than capital. Tax-free cash could be applied to income-producing investments in a tax-efficient manner. For those prepared to tie up their capital, a purchase life annuity may be an option. (NB: proper investment advice should always be sought before considering these types of options.)

The entire pension from an occupational pension scheme is treated for income tax purposes as earned income subject to deduction of tax under PAYE.

For post-89 members, the maximum tax-free cash is the greater of 3/80ths for each year of service and 2.25 times the initial pension. This initial pension is calculated before commutation and allocation to provide a spouse's and/or dependant's pension.

An important issue for flexible benefits is that the assets from any AVC or Free Standing AVC (FSAVC) started on or after 8 April 1987 cannot be commuted for cash.

However, where tax-free cash is calculated on the basis of 2.25 times the initial pension, any pension arising from the AVC or FSAVC, may be included, thus indirectly boosting the member's tax-free cash sum.

Pension   **6.17**

The pension is the amount the individual's money purchase assets will buy after tax-free cash has been provided, subject to the maximum benefits check. For an insured money purchase scheme, it is determined by current Compulsory Purchase Annuity (CPA) (defined or in full) costs.

The same method might apply to a directly-invested money purchase scheme, but the scheme might instead contain alternative provisions, for example, a rate of conversion from cash to pension which is fixed in the scheme rules. (This is not money purchase and is very unusual nowadays other than in a scheme which has converted from final salary.)

This could be a well-intentioned attempt to shield the retiring members from stock market fluctuations, but it creates an annuity option against the scheme.

This means that the member can take his pension from the scheme when CPA rates are worse than those in the scheme rules, but when CPA rates are better, the member takes a transfer shortly before retirement.

Personal benefits on early retirement   **6.18**

Early retirement may occur because of the employee's incapacity, or it may be prompted by other reasons.

If an employee, particularly a director, is seeking to take early retirement benefits but is to retain a service contract (even unpaid) with the same employer, it is strongly suggested that prior approval to this move is obtained from the Inland Revenue, however, it is rarely granted. This policy is being reviewed by the Government.

Defined contribution pension and flexible benefits   **6.19**

These fit into a flexible benefits arrangement more comfortably than defined benefit pensions because the cost for each member is readily ascertainable; and constant.

The 'vehicle' for a defined contribution pensions can be an occupational scheme, a group personal pension plan or even, since April 2001, a stakeholder pension scheme.

By the nature of the scheme, the employer's contribution is fixed, although it may vary depending on staff category, grade or other factors such as length of service.

A simple way of lowering the employer contribution is by reducing the core contribution to an amount below the current level and providing the balance as part of the flex fund. This enables employees to 'buy-back' pension contributions or trade the money purchase alternative benefits.

Whilst this is effectively cost neutral for employees, the danger for the employer is the possibility of a significant increase to their National Insurance (NI) bill. (Note also that most defined contribution schemes are contracted-in which means higher NI needs to be budgeted for this.) If a large number of employees opt to spend the balance on other benefits, these may attract employer's NICs, whereas pension contributions do not.

Usually there will be a 'core' employer and employee contribution (for those who elect to join the scheme), as well as an option for additional contributions.

For instance, the basic employer/employee contribution could be 2% of basic pay. Employees would then be given the option to make extra contributions, by using their benefit allowance or by deduction from salary, and the company will match them up to a specified level, say, 5%.

Sometimes, to reflect the fact that the cost of providing benefits increases as employees get older, an age-related contribution approach is used. For instance, instead of a core contribution of 2% 'across the board', employer/employee basic contributions could be based on an age-related table as illustrated in Figure 1 below.

Figure 1: Age-related table

Age	*Employer contribution*	*Employee contribution*
20–29	2%	2%
30–39	3%	3%

Age	Employer contribution	Employee contribution
40–49	4%	4%
50 and above	5%	5%

Defined benefit pension schemes

6.20

Defined benefit scheme members receive pensions based on their final salary at, or close to, their retirement age. These schemes (or final salary schemes as they are sometimes referred to) are a crucial element in pension planning in their own right because, in practice, they tend to deliver not just larger benefits but also a wider range of benefits than other types of schemes.

The cost of funding a defined benefit scheme is agreed by the company and trustees (based on a recommendation by the scheme's actuary) and is expressed as a percentage of pensionable salaries. Apart from mortality experience there are, however, a number of cross subsidies:

- younger members subsidise older members;

- early leavers subsidise members that stay in the scheme until retirement;

- members with lower salary increases subsidise those with higher salary increases.

When defined benefit occupational schemes were first sponsored by private sector employers, they were intended to perform the simple functions of paying a pension to a retiring employer or paying a lump sum to the family on death before retirement.

Over time, further benefits were added to answer particular needs, sometimes by voluntary action on the employer's part. Frequently, they arose as a result of legislation and, more recently, European Court of Justice requirements.

Because of this there has been increased focus on a variety of other benefits including survivor incomes, early leaver benefits and options, generous treatment for ill-health early retirement and the general protection of pensions in payment.

The provision of these benefits has varied widely from scheme to scheme, according to such factors as the scheme's professional advisers' own ideas for improvement, representations from the members (sometimes through their trade unions) and the employer's own priorities, duly influenced by how much extra outlay could be afforded.

Historically, employers have almost always paid for improvements, although their cost was often allowed for in the annual pay round. Employees' average contributions have generally stayed at around 4% to 6% of earnings.

Recent experience has, however, seen pressure on employee contributions and whereas 5% was the norm, 6% is increasingly replacing this.

Personal benefits 6.21

The level of benefits to specific members depends on a number of factors, including years of service, pensionable earnings and whether retirement occurs at 'normal retirement age' – see **6.22** below.

Normal retirement age 6.22

Historically, normal retirement age has usually been 65 for men and 60 for women to mirror the pre-equalisation State pension age, although some employers have used 60 or, on a few cases, 62 for both sexes.

The Inland Revenue states that the normal retirement age is between 60 and 75. A lower age can be allowed if the Inland Revenue accepts it is customary in a particular employment.

Any difference in normal retirement age between men and women in a scheme is no longer permitted as a result of various rulings from the European Court of Justice. In particular, benefits accrued after 16 May 1990 must be equal for both sexes.

Most schemes have, therefore, equalised their normal retirement age at 65 rather than 60, although some of them allow employees of either sex to retire between 60 and 65 without any reduction in the pension accrued to date, provided the option is offered on sex equal terms. This option will usually be at the employer's discretion.

Eligibility conditions 6.23

In the past, the typical scheme allowed entry after age 25 and up to age 64 (or 59 for women in cases where their normal retirement age was five years earlier), often after a probationary period of one or two years.

Now, entry ages have tended to be much lower – at 21, 18 or in a few cases even 16 – and probationary periods have been shortened to six months or have even been abolished. For stakeholder access this must be from 18 and one year's service.

Employers are free to include or exclude whatever group of employees they choose. Thus, a staff-only scheme does not admit hourly-rated employee, although this exclusion has become less common as employers have harmonised employment conditions.

Many schemes have historically used the formula 'full-time, permanent employees', so excluding part-time, temporary or casual employees. Excluding women, or admitting them on stricter eligibility conditions than for men, has been illegal under equal access law since 1987. As a result of a sequence of European Court of Justice's rulings, indirect discrimination based on sex is also outlawed. As a result, many schemes that had refused membership to part-timers are now admitting them on the same terms as full-timers.

Since July 2000 part-timers have the protection of the *Part-time Workers (Prevention of Less Favourable Treatment)* Regulations 2000 (SI 2000 No 1551). These regulations are designed to ensure part-timers are treated no less favourably than comparable full-timers, regardless of the gender make up of the different categories.

Pension build-up rate 6.24

The large majority of schemes in the private sector build-up pensions at the rate of 1/60th of final pensionable salary for each year of pensionable employment. A few offer 1/80th, but build-up rates lower than 1/80ths are rare due to the contracting out rules on minimum pensions. How this may fit into a flexible pension scheme is explained at **6.25** below.

A scheme may use all the years spent in the employer's service or just those spent since joining the scheme to define pensionable employment. Whole years or, more helpfully, years, months and even days can be used in the final calculation of pension.

Some schemes for executives offer a rate of 1/45th or better, because that produces the maximum allowable pension of two-thirds of final salary after 30 or fewer years of membership.

Final pensionable salary is typically the average of the employee's last three or more consecutive year's pensionable service the last ten years before retirement. However, the last year's salary may be used if preferred. The earnings figure on which the employee's own contributions are based is usually the pensionable salary definition.

The earnings figure for the death-in-service lump sum calculations can be different; for example, any offset for the basic State pension can be ignored.

Defined benefit pensions and flexible benefits   6.25

It is possible to include a defined benefit scheme within flexible benefits, although it may not be a straightforward process because of the intrinsic complexities. Where it is included, employees will typically be given a choice over the accrual rate each year. A scheme may, for example, offer a core accrual rate of 1/60th with the option to trade up to 1/55th, 1/50th or 1/45th. Where this is allowed, it is vital to build in a checking process to ensure that Inland Revenue limits are not breached. This could occur for many reasons, including high potential service, significant retained benefits and imposition of the Earnings Cap (see **6.54** below).

The perceived problems associated with flexing defined benefit pension promises can be summarised as:

- valuing the benefit promise;

- possible selection against the employer/scheme;

- contracting out;

- dealing with benefits which are based on prospective, rather than actual service; and

- funding variations which affect value of benefits (eg some schemes have to cut back benefits due to MFR shortfalls).

The cost of funding a defined benefit pension scheme is typically agreed by the company and the trustees based on a recommendation by the scheme's actuary. The cost is usually expressed as a percentage of all members' pensionable salaries.

If it is considered unacceptably complex to deal with defined benefit flexing on the basis of individual (age-related) cost, one alternative option might be to base the cost on an average of ages or, perhaps, some compromise depending on age bands.

An even simpler alternative would be to operate the flexible pension element on a defined contribution basis in conjunction with the defined benefit core.

Members switching from benefits to cash nearer retirement age can automatically create an additional pension liability (remember, defined benefits are based on final salary at retirement and all reckonable service built up before then). This can be avoided by a very simple restriction in the flexing structure – so that each year's additional 'top up' pension through flexing is based only on that year's salary. Some form of revaluation is applied so that year's top up pension maintains its value in real terms until it comes into payment.

None of these issues should preclude a defined benefit pension from being included in a flexible benefits arrangement, but they must be addressed in advance. If this is too complex to cover at the time a flexible benefit scheme is introduced, it is always possible to 'flex' the pension at a later date, after employees have become more accustomed to flexible benefits.

Executive pensions   6.26

An executive pension plan is an occupational money purchase pension scheme arrangement with an insurance company.

Most company directors and senior executives of small and medium sized enterprises are members of executive pension plans (EPPs) or their rival small self-administered schemes (SASSs), which are essentially part or non-insured EPPs and were developed from EPPs in the late 1970s and later. Many controlling directors have preferred SSASs, but EPPs still have a place. EPPs and SASSs share most of the same advantages and disadvantages compared with, say, personal pensions.

EPPs first became available to controlling directors in 1973. Before that date controlling directors were not allowed to participate in any form of occupational scheme, and any pension provision had to be made by way of retirement annuity contributions.

EPPs were affected relatively little by the *Pensions Act 1995* requirements. Some of these requirements did encourage a few employers to consider EPPs instead of retaining influential directors in other forms of occupational scheme, such as final salary arrangements.

The introduction of the new defined contribution regime with effect from 6 April 2001 now makes it possible for EPPs to be established on that basis. However, in the build up to the changes brought in by the *Welfare Reform and Pensions Act 1999*, there was little indication that EPP providers would intend establishing EPPs on a defined contribution basis.

EPP funds are managed by insurance companies and earmarked for the individual director or employee.

Over the last few years, changes have been made to the maximum EPP funding rules. These rules, laid down by the Inland Revenue, govern the maximum contributions which may be applied to EPP. These have had the effect of:

• reducing the level of contributions that can be made into EPPs, with the greatest impact on younger employees; and

• bringing contribution limits for EPPs into line with the maximum contributions that can be made to SSASs.

These rule changes might have lessened their appeal relative to other pension schemes, but EPPs remain an important pension and tax-planning tool.

EPPs are designed to provide pension and other benefits for controlling directors as well as other senior employees and executives. However, any employee may be a member of an EPP Benefits can be accumulated in earmarked funds for particular members, and these individuals can exercise significant control over the type and amount of their own personal and survivor benefits.

EPPs play a particularly important role in directors' pension and tax planning for small companies.

An EPP may be established as a selected individual's sole pension arrangement or to top up benefits available from an occupational scheme available to employees generally; an EPP therefore often used to be known as a 'top hat' scheme.

A group of selected individuals may all be members of one EPP or a separate EPP may be established for each participant.

EPPs generally provide a wide variety of investment options.

Controlling directors   6.27

A controlling director, for practical purposes, is a member who, at any time after 16 March 1987 and within ten years of retirement or leaving service or leaving pensionable service, has been a director and, either on his or her own or with one or more associates, has beneficially owned or been able to control, directly or indirectly or through other companies, 20% or more of the ordinary share capital of the company.

Controlling directors have specified rules which affect them and do not apply to other employees. The Inland Revenue says that these rules are needed because controlling directors can generally determine the employer's affairs, as well as their personal position.

Controlling directors generally want to ensure that the right balance is struck between their own remuneration package and the continuing viability of their companies. For the entrepreneur who established a successful company, an EPP can be an important component of both personal financial planning and the company's taxation and growth strategies.

SSAS v EPP choice   6.28

Many controlling directors prefer the flexibility and additional facilities offered by a SSAS (see **6.31** below) to the relatively straightforward structure of an EPP. The EPP may be a suitable investment vehicle for controlling directors who do not want or need the sophistication of an SSAS because:

- they wish to invest less than is really economical for a SSAS;

- they may not want the relative complexity and additional administration involved in a SSAS;

- they may prefer the investment of funds to be undertaken by an institution;

- they are not concerned with purchase of property, loans or shares in the company within the fund.

- the insurance company offers conventional loan facilities on the basis of the EPP investment;

- EPPs have drawdown facilities. Although occupational scheme drawdown is less flexible than personal pension drawdown, EPPs also have the option to transfer to a personal pension with its full drawdown facility. The drawdown rules (see **6.14** above) can similarly apply to SSAS which may also be transferred to personal pensions. Changes have been made to the transfer regulations which introduced further restrictions from 6 April 2001.

Appeal of EPPs for other directors and employees   **6.29**

EPPs offer flexibility and choice to non-controlling directors, senior executives and key managers and personnel who may want more emphasis on pension benefits than cash remuneration within the overall remuneration package. Indeed, EPPs are now probably more widely used for directors and other executives who do not control their own companies than for entrepreneurs, whose choice is more typically a SSAS.

For executives, the EPP has a number of attractions:

- An EPP can be used as the sole means of pension provision. This may be necessary if the employer does not operate an occupational scheme; or it may be desirable if the executive does not want to join the group scheme operated by the employer.

- An EPP allows the executive to choose, for example as part of a flexible benefit scheme, the exact proportion of pension contributions in relation to total remuneration (within Inland Revenue limits). In contrast, it is much harder to quantify the amount invested for an individual employee into a final salary scheme.

- Substantial sums can be invested by an employer in relative confidentiality – and so avoid creating public precedents for other employees. It is important that no sex discrimination occurs.

- Executives who move jobs frequently may prefer to have a money purchase scheme than join a succession of final salary arrangements.

- With the abolition of carry forward for personal pensions from April 2001, the ability of an EPP to fund for past service may well be more attractive when an executive has not started making pension contributions until the business has been established for several years.

- An employee can choose, again, within a flexible benefit scheme, to sacrifice bonuses/salary, subject to the special rules surrounding salary sacrifice (see **6.53** below). The employer saves NICs and substantial amounts can be invested, generally on a sporadic basis. Although this may be achieved in a personal pension the maximum contribution limits may restrict the amount sacrificed.

- As a flexible benefit option, the EPP can be used to top up final salary or group occupational money purchase schemes. This is very suitable for executives who are approaching retirement, but whose occupational pension is providing too low a level of benefits. FSAVCs are not available to controlling directors.

- Up to tax year 2000/01 it was not possible for executives who were already members of an occupational scheme to take out a personal stakeholder pension in respect of the same source of earnings. From 6 April 2001, the concurrency arrangements of the new defined contributions scheme allow such executives (other than controlling directors) to contribute to a personal or stakeholder pension, up to £3,600 (gross) a year so long as they generally earn less than £30,000 pa (executives normally earn more than this). However, executives would typically be interested in the ability to have a higher contribution, as well as the other benefits of an EPP set up as an occupational scheme.

Each employer can establish only one SSAS. So EPPs, personal pensions or FURBS (see **6.32** below) are therefore the only other available possibilities.

EPP pension benefits   **6.30**

The benefits from an executive pension plan are governed by the same rules and restrictions as apply to occupational pensions generally. In principle, benefits at retirement are available as a pension for the member and his or her spouse and/or dependants. Part of the member's pension can be commuted and drawn as a tax-free cash sum.

The maximum pension benefits are subject to the tax regime that applies to the member, based mainly on his or her entry date into the scheme – pre 1987, 1987/89, post-1989 (see **6.13** above). If a potential EPP member who does not already have a pension scheme does not want their benefits to be subject to benefit restrictions, then an EPP set up under the defined contributions regime, or a personal pension, should be considered.

Small self administered schemes (SSAS)

6.31

A SSAS is officially defined as 'a scheme with less than twelve members where at least one of those members is connected' with another member, or 'with a trustee or an employer in relation to the scheme'. Also that 'a scheme is defined as self-administered if some or all of the income or other assets are invested otherwise than in insurance policies'.

A SSAS is essentially an occupational pension scheme, generally for controlling directors, with a number of important differences relating to:

- investment powers;

- PSO approval and supervision;

- charges.

In the past, this was an important difference as compared to EPPs relating to funding requirements. Now, however, EPPs and SSASs have been broadly brought into line and are still able to accept higher contributions than those applicable to personal pensions.

The attractions of a SSAS are access and control. The trustees who are also members have access to the assets of the fund to self-invest in ways that will benefit the sponsoring company. They can keep control of their fund, within the limits laid down by the Pension Schemes Office (PSO) regulations and with the assistance of their professional advisers. Control becomes an increasingly important factor as the size of the fund grows.

Normally, only controlling directors becomes members of a SSAS, because even senior employees should not generally be exposed to the additional risks associated with the typical SSAS investments. Exceptionally, senior executives may be included, but normally only after they have given a disclaimer which both acknowledges and accepts the additional risks involved.

A SSAS is not usually allowed more than eleven members. In practice, most SSASs have between one and three members as controlling directors of a private company.

The Inland Revenue reserves the right to treat schemes with twelve or more members as a SSAS, if it believes that the numbers have been artificially inflated with a view to avoiding the SSAS regulations.

Conversely, a small scheme with eleven or less members who are unconnected with each other may not necessarily be treated as a SSAS, eg if it comprises the directors of a public company, because with a SSAS, one or more or the members have to be connected.

A company is not permitted to have more than one full SSAS. The regulations prohibit the Inland Revenue from granting approval to a SSAS for a company that already has a current SSAS in force. A single SSAS can be established for a number of companies, providing they meet the normal Inland Revenue rules governing associated companies.

Where an individual draws remuneration from more than one company in a group, and all the companies are included in a single SSAS, benefits in respect of each employment must be paid for by contributions from the respective companies.

The Inland Revenue does not permit contributions to be paid by one company for benefits which are based on remuneration or service from another. Alternatively, each company in a group can set up its own separate SSAS. Then, any individual who works for two or more companies can be a member of several SSASs.

There is considerable potential for conflicts of interest in a SSAS, because the members fulfil different roles. A member will generally be simultaneously:

● a director of the sponsoring company which makes contributions to the SSAS for the benefit of the members and their beneficiaries;

● a member and therefore one of the beneficiaries of the SSAS benefits;

● one of the trustees aiming to run the SSAS for the benefit of all the members and beneficiaries.

There is scope for these roles to come into conflict at some future date, if relationships were to break down, eg as a result of a boardroom split or simply divorce.

A SSAS is a pooled fund and investments are not earmarked for individual members. There is, therefore, scope for members to take different views about investment strategy. For example, members nearing retirement might prefer a lower risk approach than younger members. With EPPs or personal pensions, the policy proceeds are allocated to each specific member and cannot be paid to any other member of the scheme.

There is a principle that all occupational pension schemes must be established for the sole purpose of providing relevant benefits on retirement or death. This principle applies to SSASs in the same way as other schemes, despite the emphasis placed on the investment freedom which they offer. Therefore, the Inland Revenue is concerned to ensure that SSASs do not give non-relevant benefits to the members or persons connected to them.

Regulations provide that the Inland Revenue only approves investments which do not confer direct or indirect benefits on members, eg a SSAS cannot buy a holiday home for use by a member or his or her family.

Unapproved pension schemes   6.32

Unapproved schemes have always been an option open to employers, but until 1989 were rarely seen for tax reasons. However, by virtue of the *Finance Act 1989* (*FA 1989*) the use of unapproved schemes became a practical and, in certain circumstances, an attractive proposition. All the benefit is available in cash form

FA 1989 introduced the Earnings Cap. The level of the cap was originally set at £60,000, and has risen to £97,200 for the 2002/03 tax year (see further **6.54** below).

It also abolished the rule that employees could not enjoy the tax benefits of an approved scheme if they were also members of an unapproved arrangement.

Unapproved schemes fall into two categories:

- *Unfunded Unapproved Retirement Benefits Scheme (UURBS)* – The employer promises a benefit to the employee but does not establish a fund to provide for this benefit. The employer establishes a 'book reserve' to cover the potential liability. The employee is taxed on benefit payable under the scheme at point of receipt.

- *Funded Unapproved Retirement Benefits Scheme (FURBS)* – The employer makes specific provision through an external fund. This is normally set up as a discretionary trust fund in similar fashion to that used for an exempt approved scheme. The employee is taxed on any contributions made to the scheme as a benefit in kind. At retirement he is allowed to uplift the entire fund tax free. However, if he chooses to draw a pension, this will be taxed and effectively the employee would be taxed twice.

Thus far, the unfunded route has been the more popular for the provision of pension benefits, because it is appropriate for large companies who have to recruit high earning employees and also because it has no immediate adverse cash flow implications for either employers or employees. But there is the call on funds later and if not documented properly the employee can have no guarantee to any benefits on leaving. They may not be happy with unfunded promise unless the company is wealthy.

Bear in mind that an unapproved scheme is an occupational scheme. Individual circumstances will determine whether it is better to join a personal pension or an exempt approved occupational scheme.

Within the constraints of Inland Revenue rules and regulations, these can be used as flexible benefit options for topping up pensions, particularly to those vehicles above. They are also useful where the Inland Revenue has set limits (see **6.13** below) particularly imposed by the Earnings Cap.

Contracting out of SERPS   6.33

Contracting out means that if an occupational pension scheme meets a certain benefit standard both employer and employees are excused from paying the full rate of NICs, no further State earnings related pension scheme (SERPS) pension accrues. Whenever the Government has proposed to build an additional State pension on top of the basic flat rate pension, it has also proposed an option. (PPs can contract-out for rebate only).

Defined contribution schemes may be contracted out of SERPS by satisfying the following:

- Whenever the NIC rebates have been received the principle remains that protected rights (minimum contributions paid in) are accumulated separately from any other employer and employee contributions.

- When received the NIC rebate (standard and age related) becomes a minimum contribution due to the scheme trustees for prompt investment.

- A contracted out money purchase scheme may also have a contracted-in section for members who do not wish to be contracted-out.

- If a scheme ceased to be contracted out before 6 April 1997 the members could be bought back in to SERPS. The SERPS benefits purchased would then reflect the value of the protected rights assets. Schemes that have continued to be contracted-out since 6 April 1997 were not able to buy back the protected rights back into SERPS.

The NIC rebate system applying to a contracted-out money purchase scheme is as follows:

- For 1997/98 and 1998/99 a flat rate of 3.1% of banded earnings and an age-related additional percentage (earnings between the lower and upper limits for NIC).

- From April 1999 at flat rebate of 2.2% of band earnings and age related percentages.

- Different rules apply to the way in which invested rebates (protected rights) delivered before and after April 1997 are applied when the scheme members retire.

Defined benefit schemes may be contracted-out of SERPS by satisfying the 'reference scheme test'. In a flexible benefit scheme either a 'core' benefit would need to be maintained at the level required to meet the reference scheme test, or the scheme itself would cease to be contracted-out. Members could then only contract-out at an individual level, (eg if the flex pension is operated through an appropriate vehicle such as a personal pension scheme).

Death-in-service benefits 6.34

Some scheme benefits, such as incapacity pensions and spouses death-in-service pensions, are based on a member's potential future service up to normal retirement age, as well as his or her completed pensionable service.

Lump sum death-in-service benefits 6.35

In a flexible benefits scheme, employees are often given a choice over the level of lump sum life assurance benefit to be provided in the event of their death in service. Typically, an employee can choose between two, three or four times their 'base' salary (ie their salary before any 'flexing adjustments'), depending on their needs. A core level of benefit is recommended, but some employees may not need four times salary life cover because, for instance, they do not have any dependants.

The maximum lump sum on death-in-service is:

- four years' final salary (capped for a post-89 member); or

- £5,000 if greater;

- plus a refund of the member's own contributions, with interest, which could be their actual investment growth on the contributions.

Retained lump sum death benefits must be taken into account where the lump sum payment on death from the current employer's scheme exceeds two years' final remuneration (excluding any refund of members' contributions).

Final remuneration can include items excluded for maximum pension purposes such as share option gains. It can also be taken as the actual rate of basic salary at death (though fluctuating pay must be averaged, in the same way as for pension purposes); or it can be taken as the total earnings received in a particular 12-month period ending in the three years preceding death.

The restrictions which apply to the calculation of final remuneration for controlling directors' pensions do not apply to death-in-service benefits.

Where the member is able to flex accrual rate by, for instance, choosing 1/60ths instead of 1/80ths, there is scope for adverse selection against the scheme/employer. In these circumstances, it may be necessary to use a fixed accrual rate for benefits based on prospective service.

Death-in-service pension benefits 6.36

The basic maximum payment for the survivor's life is:

- two-thirds of the maximum member's pension which would have been payable at normal retirement age, assuming no change in the member's current salary;

- for the surviving spouse/dependant of a member who would have been able to complete 20 or more years by normal retirement age, the maximum is 4/9ths of the final remuneration;

- this is limited by the Earnings Cap in the case of post-1989 members;

- In calculating maximum death-in-service survivor pension, retained benefits are ignored.

For members who would have been unable to complete 20 years by retirement age, the maximum survivor's pension for each regime grouping is as follows:

- Pre-1987 members – the maximum survivor's pension is a fraction of final salary according to total years of actual-plus-prospective employment to normal retirement age. As all current pre-1987 members have more than ten years' service, the maximum widow's benefit in all cases is 4/9ths of final remuneration.

- 1987/89 members and post-1989 members – the maximum survivor's pension is 1/45th of final salary (as defined above for death-in-service and restricted by the Earnings Cap in the case of post-1989 members) for each year of total actual-plus-prospective service to normal retirement age, up to a maximum of 20 years.

Dependants' additions   6.37

Whatever a member's approval regime, one or more surviving dependants can be given pensions. The total must not exceed the maximum pension that the member could have received at normal retirement age on the basis of current salary.

No one dependant can draw more than two-thirds of that pension. If the dependant is a child, the survivor pension must stop at age 18 or when full-time education ends, if later. A wife, husband and under-age child are automatically regarded as dependants even though they may not be strictly dependent financially.

An unmarried partner (a common law husband/wife or same sex partner) can be treated as dependent, even though the relationship is one of interdependence, where, for example, the member's death would deprive the partner of his or her customary standard of living.

Death during deferred retirement   6.38

If the employee defers retirement and dies before actually retiring, the maximum survivor benefits can be either those appropriate to:

- death-in-service; or
- death after retirement.

The death after retirement treatment automatically applies if the employee took any benefits at normal retirement age.

Death-after-retirement survivor benefit   6.39

Regardless of the retired member's approval regime:

- the maximum survivor's pension on death after retirement is two-thirds of the maximum pension which the member could have received at retirement, increased in line with the RPI between retirement and death;

- other dependants, including children and persons treated as dependent, can be given survivor pensions on the same terms as for death-in-service pensions;

- retained benefits are ignored in calculating maximum death-after-retirement survivor pension.

Some schemes also allow dependant's pensions on death in service to be flexed.

Where death benefits are increased, medical evidence may be required. This is not, however, always the case.

Additional Voluntary Contributions   6.40

Employees may be able to use part of their flexible benefit allowance or credits for Additional Voluntary Contributions (AVCs). If the employer is willing to 'match' these contributions, up to a certain level, it can make the AVC option particularly valuable. AVCs are also very tax efficient (see **6.41** below).

From April 2001, some members of occupational pension schemes have been allowed concurrent membership with stakeholder pensions (and traditional personal pensions). For these individuals, it might be more beneficial if they paid their AVCs into a stakeholder pension (as opposed to the company AVC arrangement). However, before doing so, they must ensure that they will not lose out on any employer matching contributions.

All occupational schemes have been required to offer in-house arrangements since 6 April 1988. The benefits can accrue on a money-purchase basis, a flat additional-amount basis, or on an added-year basis.

FSAVCs have been available since 26 October 1987 and are accumulated (or invested) separately from the employer's scheme. This allows members greater flexibility and control over their pension arrangements.

An FSAVC is set up by an outside pension provider such as a bank, building society, unit trust or insurance company. The scheme must have the sole purpose of providing relevant benefits and be established under irrevocable trusts. Apart from death benefits, FSAVC benefits must accrue on a money-purchase basis.

There are three main eligibility conditions for either type of arrangement:

- the employee has to be an active member of a UK occupational scheme;

- controlling directors are not allowed to contribute to an FSAVC, but may pay in-house AVCs;

- members of simplified defined benefit schemes are not allowed to contribute to an FSAVC.

From 6 April 2001, members of occupational schemes may contribution to a personal pension in any tax year, as well as, or instead of, AVC arrangements if they have earned no more than the 'remuneration limit' (£30,000 for tax year 2001/02) for that year in any of the five preceding tax years (ignoring years before 2000/01). However, this does not apply to members who are currently controlling directors or have been controlling directors in any of the five preceding tax years (ignoring tax years before 2000/01).

Tax treatment of AVCs 6.41

AVC arrangements have the main tax advantages of other pension schemes. Investment growth is generally free from income and capital gains tax and contributions receive full income tax relief but the tax credit on UK dividends may not be reclaimed.

Income tax relief on in-house AVCs is granted as follows:

- Monthly or annual contributions receive income tax relief through the net pay system by being deducted from pre-tax earnings. This ensures immediate tax relief, at the member's marginal rate.

- Special contributions (single payments) can sometimes be made under the net pay system. If this is not possible, the member should pay the contribution gross, but before they pay any contributions, members should ask their local Inspector of Taxes to confirm how and when relief will be granted.

The rules for tax relief on FSAVCs are more straightforward.

- FSAVC contributions are paid net of basic rate income tax regardless of whether they are monthly, annually or special.

- If the member is a higher-rate taxpayer, further relief can be claimed through the Tax Office, so that full income tax relief is received on the contributions. Normally this is achieved by adjusting the member's tax coding.

AVC benefits   6.42

The purpose of an AVC is to secure extra pension or life cover. Cash cannot normally be taken directly from an AVC. However, there are four exceptions which allow AVC benefits to be commuted for cash:

- In-house AVC arrangements entered into before 8 April 1987.

- If the member retires because of serious ill-health. Commutation is permitted only if the member is similarly commuting the entire main scheme benefits. There is a tax liability on any part of the AVC cash sum which would not have otherwise been available as cash under a pre-8 April 1987 AVC arrangement.

- If the total pension benefit, including the main scheme pension does not exceed £260 a year. The same potential tax charge applies as for commutation on the grounds of serious ill-health – unlikely, of course, in practice.

- If a member buys added years under, for example, a statutory pension scheme, these can be used to provide some tax-free cash benefit.

AVCs can also help boost the overall level of cash available from the main occupational scheme for members subject to the *Finance Act 1989* regime and interim regime.

Tax-free cash can be calculated as 2.25 times the member's pension before commutation. The pension deriving from AVCs can be included within this pension figure with the trustees agreement.

Contributions   6.43

The maximum employee contribution allowed to all occupational schemes, including voluntary contributions, is normally 15% of total annual remuneration. This must, therefore, include any contractual employee contributions made to the main scheme.

If the main scheme is a contracted-out money purchase scheme, the maximum also includes the employee's redirected NICs. He or she could, in addition, where eligible, pay up to £3,600 gross into a personal pension scheme.

An employee is free to make both in-house AVCs and FSAVCs, provided total contributions are within the 15% limit, when added to any main scheme contributions. He or she could, in addition, where eligible, pay up to £3,600 gross into a personal pension scheme.

Within any one tax year, the Inland Revenue permits an employee to contribute to only one FSAVC in respect of the same employment.

Annual remuneration for AVCs and FSAVCS is not restricted to the main scheme definition of pensionable salary and can include all benefits assessable to tax under Schedule E Case I or II (eg bonuses, commissions, P11D benefits).

If the Earnings Cap (£97,200 for the 2002/03 tax year) applies to the member's main scheme benefits, it will similarly apply to any in-house AVC or FSAVC arrangements. For FSAVCs, the maximum contribution is calculated based on the employee's remuneration during the tax year.

For contributions to the main scheme or to in-house arrangements, the limit is usually calculated on remuneration for the scheme year, but tax relief is limited to 15% of remuneration for the tax year, subject to the maximum benefits which may be provided in accordance with Inland Revenue limits.

AVC death benefits   6.44

Pensions provide one of the most cost-effective and flexible ways to arrange life assurance. In many cases it makes sense to maximise the use of pension-based life assurance before arranging cover that is not so tax-privileged. Tax relief is available on the contributions and the benefits may be paid wholly or largely free of tax.

In-house AVCs are assets of the trust of the main occupational scheme and FSAVCs are written under a separate master trust. Any death benefits from in-house AVCs and FSAVCs are, therefore, paid to beneficiaries chosen by the trustees under a discretionary trust and are free from inheritance tax.

The recipients of the AVC benefit can be different from the recipients of the main occupational scheme benefits. AVCs can also purchase additional life cover, by re-directing contributions to fund individual term assurances.

The terms of each policy can be chosen by the member, but it cannot be later than the normal retirement age of the main occupational scheme. The additional life cover cannot be assigned, because it is an asset of the trust.

The total lump sum benefit payable must not exceed four times final remuneration plus a refund of member's contributions with interest, when aggregated with any other benefits in respect of this and previous employment. Within these limits, there is no restrictions on the level of death-in-service benefits that can be provided and the entire contributions can be used to secure it.

A widow(er)'s/dependant's pension can also be provided. This can be up to two-thirds of the member's maximum pension entitlement, assuming he or she remained in service until normal retirement.

There is an exception if the main occupational scheme is a simplified money purchase scheme. The maximum contribution to secure death-in-service benefits is restricted to 5% of remuneration; but there is no restrictions on the level of benefits this can secure, ie no maximum lump sum of four times final remuneration.

Once the member has purchased a pension, payments stop on death, unless there is a balance of any guaranteed minimum period; or provision for a spouse's or dependants pension.

The total payout could be less than the fund value at retirement if the pensioner dies soon after retiring or after the end of a guaranteed period.

Purchasing added years with AVCs

6.45

Within a final salary scheme, it may also be possible to purchase 'added years'. Not all employers are happy to do this due to risk but wealthier companies still do.

The purchase of added years secures extra years' service in the scheme, on which benefits are calculated and paid. For example, a member who has 15 years' service and has bought five added years will receive a pension based on 20 years' service.

Salary inflation has to be taken into account because the added years' method secures benefits which are linked to an unknown salary at retirement. The employer may be prepared to take on this commitment or, alternatively, the rates offered to members may reflect very high assumptions for future salary inflation.

Contributions are normally expressed as a percentage of pay and, therefore, the benefits provided and the amount paid increase every time the member receives a pay rise.

The cost of buying added years depends on the member's age at the outset and the selected payment terms. The overall cost of buying added years can be relatively expensive for the benefits obtained, although these are guaranteed under the scheme. In effect, the scheme/employer bears the risk (as for all defined benefit schemes) of added years. Where salary growth is expected to be slow, money purchase benefits may be a better option.

Contracting out

6.46

An in-house AVC cannot be used for contracting out of SERPS. An FSAVC can be a vehicle for contracting out of SERPS.

If AVCs were used for contracting out, it would do so as a personal pension. However, the benefits would be included in an Inland Revenue benefit limit test, whereas protected rights from other appropriate personal pensions are not.

Minimum contributions to FSAVCs in respect of contracting out do not get tax relief added to members' shares. Whereas tax relief is added for personal pensions. In practice, it is, therefore, unlikely that any provider would operate an FSAVC contracting out.

Topping up pensions via flexible benefit   6.47

Employees can be offered a range of possibilities for making additional contributions to their pension provision via a flexible benefit scheme. To some extent, the number of options will depend on the employer and individual circumstances.

Added years   6.48

Employees in a final salary scheme can sometimes buy added years. This may be worth considering if, they intend to stay with the employer until retirement age. Equally, it will be attractive if their earnings are likely to rise at least as fast as earnings generally, or faster. If they rise faster than assumed in the added years offer, the employer would be subsidising the purchase.

The AVC purchase terms are generally attractive because of their charging structure.

Executive pension plans   6.49

The employer could set up an executive pension plan (EPP) for the individual. This may be advantageous if the proposed contributions are sufficiently large to make the extra administration worthwhile.

The employee's remuneration could be structured (eg by bonus or salary sacrifice) so that contributions paid by the employer are higher than the maximum 15% of earnings applicable to employee contributions.

The EPP can generate a tax-free sum. This could be particularly valuable where the main scheme does not provide maximum tax-free cash under the Inland Revenue rules.

It may also be advantageous where the employee has the choice between taking tax-free cash from the main scheme, but only at the expense of losing an index-linked pension. The member could take the full index-linked pension from the main scheme and draw the tax-free cash from the EPP.

Care is required with any salary or bonus sacrifice arrangement, because it reduces an employee's final remuneration. EPPs also have the advantage of saving employer's and possibly employees' NICs.

Money purchase AVCs   6.50

Employees can contribute to a money purchase AVC scheme either in-house or on a free-standing basis.

The FSAVC basis may be more attractive for some employees because the benefits can be taken at a different time from the main scheme benefits, if the employee leaves service before retirement. Taking AVCs can now be deferred

It may provide investment diversification outside the main scheme, and it usually gives greater choice.

The in-house scheme may be preferable where the costs are lower, or the range of funds compared to the FSAVC is at least as good. It may also be preferable where the range of funds suits the client's attitude to risk.

An in-house scheme will almost always be preferable where the employer makes some form of matching contribution, eg 1% for each 2% AVC.

Personal pensions   6.51

From 6 April 2001 a member accruing benefits under an occupational pension scheme can contribute to a personal pension (including a stakeholder pension) in respect of the same earnings if they meet eligibly criteria.

Contributions are limited to £3,600 gross a year and contributions under this 'concurrency rule' cannot be made if the member has another source of earnings.

Benefits provided by these contributions do not count towards occupational pension scheme benefit limits. Up to 25% of the fund (excluding protected rights) can be taken as a tax-free cash sum.

For those eligible the pension/stakeholder option could be more flexible and is a better option than an FSAVC and an in-house AVC.

Non-pension investment   6.52

A pension scheme has the advantages of tax relief on the contributions and tax-effective roll-up of the funds. This should allow for a better rate of return than most investments. Increasingly, Individual Savings Accounts (ISAs) are being considered as a viable alternative to FSAVCs or in-house money purchase AVCs.

ISAs which replaced PEPs from 6 April 1999, offer tax benefits which for many people are similar in value but with lower contribution limits.

The ISA fund is free from UK tax on investment income and capital gains – like a pension fund. However, tax credit repayment for UK dividends on ISAs (and PEPs) has been 10% from 6 April 1999 and will cease on 6 April 2004. No tax credit repayment in respect of UK dividends has been payable to pension funds since 2 July 1997.

The contributions into an FSAVC are wholly tax allowable, but the benefits which have been drawn as a pension annuity are fully taxable.

In contrast, the ISA qualifies for no tax relief on the contributions, but the proceeds are tax-free and can be taken in any way and at any time the client wishes.

Clients who are 22% taxpayers when they make pension contributions and when they draw the benefits gain no advantage from tax relief, relative to investing in ISAs. Indeed the tax credit repayment on UK dividends until 2004 favours ISAs over AVCs. But if they are 40% taxpayers in their contributing years and 22% taxpayers in retirement they will see a tax benefit in AVCs over ISAs. An ISA, like most other investments, can be drawn on at any time and in any form. There is no need to purchase an annuity.

If the employee can afford to invest in both AVCs and ISAs simultaneously, they can both be useful components in the overall retirement planning package.

Salary sacrifice

6.53

A popular method of increasing the combined employee and employer contributions to a pension scheme is salary sacrifice. This is an arrangement whereby the employee agrees to take a reduction in their contractual salary and the employer pays a corresponding amount into their pension scheme as a contribution.

This effectively reduces employer NIC on this proportion of salary, the employee also saves NIC and PAYE and benefits from the tax advantages associated with the occupational scheme.

This arrangement has to be approved by the Inland Revenue. Care must be taken as reducing contractual pay may affect Earnings Caps, maximum contribution rates, and benefits such as life cover.

In a flexible benefit scheme these salary sacrifice contributions can be classed as 'employer' contributions and, therefore, not deemed as party of salary or earnings.

Figure 2: Example of employee NIC savings using flex

	No flex	*Using flex*
	£	£
Contractual Salary	20,000	20,000
Employee contributions (5%)	1,000	0
Flex contributions (5%)	0	1,000
Income Tax	2,957	2,957
Employee NIC	1,547	1,447
Net pay	14,496	14,596
Employee saving		100
Employer saving NI?		119

Note: The example in Figure 2 is a very simplistic example of NIC savings via Flexible Benefits.

Earnings Cap   6.54

The tax advantages that apply to exempt approved occupational pension schemes are substantial. In the late 1980s, the Treasury became increasingly concerned about their cost and this led to the introduction of the Earnings Cap.

The Earnings Cap imposes limits on the benefits which may be provided by an exempt approved scheme – and also on the contributions which can be paid to a personal or stakeholder pension. Additional, ordinary and additional voluntary contributions by employees to occupational pension schemes are limited to 15% of the Earnings Cap.

The Earnings Caps applies to those who joined exempt approved schemes, that were set up before 14 March 1989, on or after 1 June 1989 and to members of schemes established on or after 14 March 1989.

There are provisions safeguarding the interests of employees who might otherwise be affected by the cap. Scheme members can be moved between different schemes with the same employer without becoming capped, and existing pension commitments can be safeguarded in the event of a take-over, merger, or company reconstruction.

With the introduction of the Earnings Cap, higher earners who changed jobs found that the whole of their income could no longer be pensioned under approved arrangements. Alternative provision was required to take account of their earnings over the cap.

The Earnings Cap was originally fixed at £60,000 for the tax year 1989/90. The level of the cap each year is normally increased in line with the retail prices index (RPI), and rounded up to the next higher multiple of £600, although the level of the cap was frozen between 1992/93 and 1993/94.

Over the long term, average earnings tend to rise faster than retail prices, and the value of the cap will thus reduce as a proportion of most employees' earnings.

Before considering an unapproved scheme, it is normally important to ensure that the employee is funding for the maximum benefits from exempt approved arrangements that the Inland Revenue permit on earnings up to the level of the cap. In some circumstances, other forms of remuneration, for example, additional salary, may be more appropriate for particular individual, than unapproved pension benefits.

The two main legal requirements that affect including pensions in a flexible benefits are the Earnings Cap and the Inland Revenue.

Sometimes it is better to provide a pension via a PP, particularly where individual has substantial previous company benefits which diminish the value of his company pension. This is particularly relevant when the pension is flexed paying for a benefit he may not get

Where pension is included as a flex option, the only tax consequences – apart from not taking advantage of the privileges available on pensions – are that other alternatives, eg cash – may actually increase taxation (increased income tax liability for the employee and increased employer's NIC).

Legal issues   6.55

There is not, nor is there likely to be, one single piece of comprehensive legislation covering occupational schemes. Those responsible for operating pension schemes have to bear in mind seven distinct areas of law:

- Trust law, relating to the rights of the scheme members and the duties or trustees and employers;

- Contract law, relating to employment contracts between employers and employees;

- Employment law, which can override scheme rules with special rights and protections arising from UK and European Union law;

- Social Security law, greatly expanded by the *Pensions Act 1995*, the *Welfare Reform and Pensions Act 1999* and the *Child Support, Pensions and Social Security Act 2000*;

- Tax law, governing tax relief and maximum permissible benefits as prescribed by the Treasury and the Inland Revenue;

- Financial Services law, regulating the management of scheme investments;

- European Union law and decisions handed down by the European Court of Justice.

This chapter refers briefly to each of these areas of law in turn, although most of the detail is set out in other relevant chapters.

Issues for employers and trustees 6.56

Some of the legal issues for employers and pension scheme trustees are as follows:

- Approved pension schemes are subject to Inland Revenue limits, both in terms of contributions paid-in and benefits paid-out. If these limits are breached, the pension scheme may lose its approval status and tax privileges. The administration of a flexible benefits arrangement needs to include benefit testing.

- Most Inland Revenue limits are based on salary. Where an employee reduces his or her salary under a flexible benefits scheme, this can affect the maximum contributions that can be paid into any pension arrangement and the maximum benefits that can be paid out. This point should not be overlooked.

- Where an employee is given an option over the level of benefits to be paid in the event of death in service (eg life assurance benefit and spouse's death in service pension), some scheme trustees may decide that it is appropriate to obtain the spouse's consent before giving effect to any reduction in benefits. In the author's view this is not strictly necessary, but not everyone agrees.

Employees may seek advice from employers and/or trustees as regards the best options for them. There is no general duty in law to give such advice and it is recommended that they do not do so. The giving of advice is strictly regulated and penalties can be levied against the unauthorised. The employee handbook (see **CHAPTER 9**) should provide employees with most of the information they need to make informed choices. Individual advice should be obtained from authorised financial advisers.

An employee's pension promise may be set out specifically in his or her contract of employment as well as the pension scheme documentation. The incorporation of the pension scheme into a flexible benefits arrangement with a change in 'core' pension may have a knock-on effect on the contract – which cannot be changed unilaterally.

Under the *Transfer of Undertakings (Protection of Employment) Regulations 1981 (SI 1981 No 1794)* (TUPE), new employers are not, currently, required to provide any protection to pension arrangements for staff transferred as a result of a business transfer, however, a recent ruling means that early retirement and redundancy pensions are. So, at present, from a pensions perspective, there is no need to make any special arrangements following the transfer of an undertaking; new employees will just be offered the same flexible pension arrangement as existing employees.

However, the TUPE position with regard to pension is set to change and, may embrace pensions in future. This may prevent transferred employees from being included within a flexible benefits arrangement.

Finally, before the pension scheme can be flexed, scheme amendments will invariably be required, as well as a new scheme booklet. Amendments to a pension scheme's trust deed and rules must comply with its amendment provisions and with all legislative requirements. Also, the consent of the scheme trustees will invariably be required before a pension scheme can be effectively modified.

7 — Tax Implications

This chapter includes the following:

- Introduction
- Employee's position
- Employer's position
- Tax definitions
- Eligible for tax relief benefits
- Non-taxable benefits
- Benefits in kind
- Voluntary benefits
- Holidays
- Company cars
- Share schemes
- Rates and contributions 2002/03

Introduction   7.1

The correct management of tax in a flexible benefits scheme is not only a legislative requirement but also an important part of maximising the benefits the scheme delivers and minimising the costs. The tax treatment of individual products is similar to those benefits found in a normal benefits scheme. However, when mixed together, particularly with the use of trading salary, they can change employee's resultant net pay in a different way to that expected.

In looking at the tax and National Insurance contributions (NICs) implications of introducing the flexible benefits scheme there are two main issues that need to be considered:

- the employees potential tax liability on the receipt of the benefit; and

- the entitlement of the employer to claim a tax deduction for the cost of the benefit.

The tax position of employee benefits ranges considerably. For instance, employer contributions to most approved pension schemes, as covered in **CHAPTER 6**, are not taxed as 'benefit in kind' and do not attract employer or employee NICs.

On the other hand, some benefits are treated by the Inland Revenue as benefits in kind and also attract NICs. It is, therefore, essential that the tax situation is clarified before the scheme is launched and this is communicated very clearly to employees.

Tax due is collected by amending an employee's tax coding which is commonly changed once the benefits have been reported to the Inland Revenue at the end of year reporting via Form P11D.

Employee's position   7.2

It is important that both the employer and the employee understand their tax treatment so they can make an informed choice.

A typical flexible benefits scheme, as we have seen, consists of a salary element; an element comprising benefits taxed under specific benefit-in-kind rules and voluntary benefits, which are benefits that are selected from a menu to be purchased by the employee.

It is important for employees to be conscious of any potential benefit-in-kind liability arising on other benefits as this will affect an employee's take-home pay. Additionally if they are members of a final salary scheme and they choose to trade their taxable benefit for a non-taxable benefit, it could affect the way their final salary is calculated.

Employer's position   7.3

The main issue for the employer is to ensure that any costs payable by the employer are allowable as a deductible expense in determining its taxable profits. Expenses are deducible if they have been incurred in earning the profits of the business and cost incurred to reward employees falling into this category.

Tax definitions   7.4

The following is a summary of definitions of the terms used in this chapter together with a description and outline of their tax treatment and effect on net salary as a stand-alone benefit (as opposed to inclusion of the flexible benefits scheme).

Salary   7.5

The following salary definitions are:

● Contractual (shadow) gross pay – this is the employee's contractual salary before any deductions, including 'trading salary'. It is used to calculate pension contributions, bonus calculations, maternity pay, redundancy, etc.

● Payroll gross pay – this is the employee's actual pay after deduction of 'salary traded'. Also referred to as notional pay.

● Net pay – this is the resultant pay due to an employee, after all deductions including PAYE and NICs.

Eligible for tax relief   7.6

These include Pensions, Additional Voluntary Contributions (AVCs) and other such benefits. Net salary given up will be far less than the amount of any benefit paid. Payroll gross pay has remained unchanged and NICs are not affected.

Non-taxable benefits   7.7

This includes benefits such as medical screening and is not liable to income tax. Electing for a non-taxable benefit may have implications on final salary calculations and AVCs. Employee NICs are based on payroll gross pay.

Benefits in kind   7.8

These include benefits such as private medical insurance where the employer pays for the benefits and the cost is not recovered out of net pay. Tax due is collected by adjustment of PAYE tax codes. Employee NICs are based on payroll gross pay. These will be higher for selling holidays and lower for buying.

Voluntary benefits   7.9

These include benefits such as dental care, critical illness, etc. Because these benefits are deducted from net salary after tax, they are not taxable. Employees have already paid tax and National Insurance via salary and will not have to pay again for voluntary benefits chosen.

Holidays   7.10

This includes trading up or trading down holidays. Taxable pay (PAYE) has been reduced/increased, which may have final salary calculation and AVC implications. Employees' NIcs are based on payroll gross pay. These will be higher for selling holidays and lower for buying.

Special provisions   7.11

This includes benefits such as employee share schemes and company cars, for which the Inland Revenue has developed special formulas. This is covered in more detail in sections **7.17** and **7.22**.

Eligible for tax relief benefits   7.12

The tax implications on pensions and AVCs that are eligible for tax relief have been covered in the main in **CHAPTER 6**. However, there are two further important implications for employees and employers in terms of flexible benefits. These concern the net effect on pay of including AVCs in the flexible benefits scheme.

Figure 1: Eligible for tax relief (AVCs)

	22% Taxpayer		40% Taxpayer	
	AVCs	*No AVCs*	*AVCs*	*No AVCs*
	£	£	£	£
Contractual (shadow/payroll gross pay):	20,000	20,000	40,000	40,000
Purchase of AVCs (5%):	1,000	—	2,000	—
Tax payable on:	19,000	20,000	38,000	40,000
Tax payable:	4,180	4,400	15,200	16,000
Net pay:	14,820	15,600	22,800	24,000
Final result – paid AVCs of:	1,000		2,000	
At a cost of:	780		1,200	
Note: Payroll gross pay has remained unchanged. NICs are not affected.				

The Table in Figure 1 shows the effect on both a 22% taxpayer and a 40% taxpayer before and after choosing to pay AVCs.

No adjustment is made to shadow salary. Therefore, this is the same as payroll gross pay and there is no effect upon the amount of NICs paid.

Tax relief is given on any AVCs paid and therefore the amount of employee's salary subject to tax is reduced.

The effect of this is shown on the bottom of the Table. You can see that more has been paid into their pension fund by way of AVCs than their net salary has been reduced by. The 40% taxpayer also makes a bigger saving than the 22% taxpayer.

Non-taxable benefit   7.13

The Table in Figure 2 illustrates the effect of choosing a non-taxable benefit on both a 22% and 40% taxpayer.

Figure 2: Non-taxable benefit

	22% Taxpayer		40% Taxpayer	
	AVCs	*No AVCs*	*AVCs*	*No AVCs*
	£	£	£	£
Contractual (shadow) gross pay:	20,000	20,000	40,000	40,000
Purchase of medical screening:	500	—	500	—
Payroll gross pay/tax payable on:	19,500	20,000	39,500	40,000
Tax payable:	4,290	4,400	15,800	16,000
Net pay:	15,210	15,600	23,700	24,000
Final result:				
Purchase medical screening worth:	500		500	
At a cost of:	390		300	
Note: Pay on gross pay has remained unchanged. NICs are not affected.				

In the example illustrated in Figure 2, the value of employee's shadow salary is reduced by the benefit in order to arrive at their payroll gross pay.

The amount on which both tax and NICs is calculated is reduced. This illustration only takes account of the reduction in tax paid; it would be too complicated to illustrate any National Insurance effect.

The effect of this is that a benefit has been purchased that is worth more than the amount by which their net salary has been reduced. Again the higher rate taxpayer saves more than the basic rate taxpayer.

This choice reduces the amount of employee's reward subject to tax and may, therefore, have implications for pension payments as well as AVC contributions.

Benefits in kind   7.14

As explained in the introduction at **7.1** above, benefits in kind include benefits such as private medical insurance, where the benefits are paid for by the employer and the cost is not recovered out of net pay. Tax is collected by adjustments to the PAYE tax code and employee NICs are based on payroll gross pay. Benefits in kind also include cars, which are covered at **7.17** below.

Since April 2000 all taxable benefits in kind that were not currently liable for NICs became liable for Class 1A payments. There was also some relaxation of tax reporting rules in relation to benefit in kind provided for work purposes where there were some insignificant private use. There were also changes to NIC liability on non-cash vouchers when a third party provided them.

Essential taxation of benefits in kind is charged on the amount equalled to the cash equivalent of the benefit. This is the cost of the benefit less any contributions made by the employee. This tax charge includes premiums paid by the employer for members of the employee's family in respect of health insurance. Tax on this type of benefit is paid at the personal taxation income tax rate set by the Inland Revenue.

For the tax year 2002/03 the Inland Revenue have made the following additional concessions:

- Group transport will attract no benefit in kind on works buses or a subsidy to public bus service, loan of cycle and cycle safety equipment.

- A loan of computer equipment to employees will be tax free, however, this is not available if it is restricted to directors and senior staff or the value of the computer equipment exceeds £2,500.

The preferential tax treatment on computers makes it ideal for inclusion in the flexible benefits scheme, particularly if the organisation is trying to encourage wider use by its employees of web-based technology at home.

Another popular flexible benefit, driven by tax advantages, is season ticket loans. Where the total of all loans outstanding do not exceed £5,000 there is no benefit in kind tax liability. If the company offers interest free or cheap loans, which exceed £5,000, then there will be a benefit in kind charge. The benefit in kind charge is the difference between the official rate of interest and the amount actually paid.

There are some statutory exemptions to taxation on benefits in kind including work place nurseries, canteens and accommodation which is necessary for the employment and mobile phones. Also expenses payments intended to reimburse employees for the cost of travelling and entertainment.

See **5.33** above as an example of using childcare vouchers to utilise the NIC savings to offer a more attractive benefit.

The Table in Figure 3 includes an illustration for both a 22% and a 40% taxpayer.

Figure 3: Benefits in kind

	22% Taxpayer		40% Taxpayer	
	AVCs	*No AVCs*	*AVCs*	*No AVCs*
	£	£	£	£
Contractual (shadow) payroll gross pay:	20,000	20,000	40,000	40,000
Purchase of benefits in kind:	(500)		(500)	
Payroll gross pay:	19,500	20,000	39,500	40,000
Tax code personal allowance:	(4,385)	(4,385)	(4,385)	(4,385)
Benefits in kind:	500		500	
Tax payable on:	16,615	15,615	35,615	35,615
Tax payable:	3,435	3,435	14,246	14,246
Net pay (payroll gross pay – tax payable):	16,065	16,565	25,254	25,754
Final result:				
Benefits purchased:	500			
At a cost of:	500			
Note: Taxable pay has remained unchanged. Employee NICs are based on payroll gross pay.				

Should employees wish to purchase a benefit in kind they are not already entitled to, the cost will be adjusted against their shadow salary to arrive at their payroll gross pay.

As already explained, the tax will be collected by reducing their PAYE tax code. This code sets out the amount they can be paid through the payroll before they start paying tax.

Although their payroll gross pay has been reduced, the amount of remuneration of which tax is paid has remained the same. The amount of tax payable also remains the same and their net pay (the difference between payroll gross and tax payable) is reduced by the same amount as has been deducted from their shadow salary ie the cost of the benefit.

Employees' NICs are based on payroll gross pay. Therefore, if their salary is below the threshold for paying maximum NI contributions, they will make a small saving.

Voluntary benefits   7.15

Because the benefits are deducted from net salary after tax they are not taxable. Employees have already paid tax and NI via salary and, therefore, do not have to pay it again for the benefits they have chosen. There is no effect on payroll gross pay tax or NICs.

In essence, the employer is acting as a paying agent for the provider so care must be taken to ensure that an adequate contract between them and the provider clearly shows payment due out of net pay. The tax advantage for the employer is that there are no NICs due, as apposed to benefits in kind.

Holidays   7.16

One of the most popular elements of the flexible benefits scheme is trading holidays. Essentially, employees are swapping salary for time. As PAYE and NI is charged on salary the simplistic view is that if they buy more holiday they reduce their tax and NI burden and vice versa.

Figure 4 illustrates a 22% taxpayer. The principles are the same for a 40% taxpayer.

Figure 4: Holidays

	22% Taxpayer		
	No change	Trade down	Trade up
	£	£	£
Contractual (shadow) gross pay:	20,000	20,000	20,000
Trade down/up 5 days holiday:	—	385	(385)
Payroll gross pay/tax payable on:	20,000	20,385	19,615
Tax payable:	4,400	4,485	4,315
Net pay:	15,000	15,900	15,300
Final result;			
Holiday traded down/up:		385	(385)
At gain/(cost) of:		300	(300)
Note: Taxable pay has been reduced/increased by £385 (Pension/AVC implications). Employee's NICs based on payroll gross pay.			

The value of any holidays traded down or up will be adjusted against the employees shadow salary to arrive at their salary paid through the payroll.

Both tax and NICs are calculated on payroll gross pay. The Table in Figure 4 only shows the effect of the change upon taxation, if they are below the maximum earnings threshold for paying NICs the effect will be a little greater.

As you can see from the Table, if they choose to increase the amount of annual holiday they would like to take, their net salary reduces by less than the value of the shadow salary. Conversely, if they choose to reduce the amount of holiday they would like to take, their net pay increases by less than any notional additional gross salary paid to them.

The Inland Revenue, therefore, taxes employees for working harder, but eases the burden for them if they want to take life a little easier!

Company cars   7.17

After 5 April 2002 the Government has changed the way it taxes company cars. Their intention is to place a green levy on car users to persuade them to drive less and use more fuel-efficient vehicles. Running in parallel with this issue has been an increasing trend in the UK for organisations to move away from running large company car fleets.

These two factors combined has seen an increase in employers offering cash as an option for the company car. (See **CHAPTER 5.34** for an example of a personal lease plan.)

The existing rules applying before 6 April 2002 are based on a percentage of the list price of the car. If a company car is used for private purposes, then the benefit will be 35% of the car's list price when new, if the annual business mileage is below 2,500 miles.

The tax charges for the benefit will be 35% of the list price for a business mileage of between 2,500 and 17,999 miles and 15% for business mileage of 18,000 miles or more.

The list price is the price published by the manufacture/importer/ distributor for retail in the UK. The price paid for the car is irrelevant.

After 5 April 2002, the tax charge on the benefits of a company car will be based on the levels of carbon dioxide (CO_2) emissions. There will be no reduction for business mileage or for older cars (cars over 4 years old).

Cars with an approved CO_2 figure   7.18

The charge will be increased from 15% of the list price if the CO_2 is emitted above the qualifying level. The increase will be by 1% for every extra 5 grams per kilometre (g/km) over that level.

The maximum charge in any event will be 30% of the car's list price. The initial qualifying level will be reduced as cars become more fuel-efficient.

Cars with no approved CO_2 emissions figure   7.19

In this case the charge will be according to the engine size, but will still operate as a percentage of the list price of the car.

Engine Size	Percentage of car's price on which tax will be charged
0–1,400 cc	15%
1,401–2,000 cc	25%
2,101 cc plus	35%

3% will be added for diesel cars, but the maximum charge will still be 35%.

Older cars, ie those registered before 1 January 1998 will have slightly different percentage rates.

Engine Size	Percentage of car's price on which tax will be charged
0 – 1,400 cc	15%
1,401 – 2,000 cc	22%
2,001 cc plus	32%

If a car has no approved CO_2 emission figure and no cylinder capacity, then the fixed charge will be 35% of the list (32% if the car is older). If the car is solely electric, the charge will be 15% of the list price.

The new rules   7.20

These new rules are still subject to consultation. There may be a supplement waiver for diesel cars with very low CO_2 emissions and possible discounts for other 'environmentally-friendly' cars (ie those running on gas, petrol and gas combinations).

The scales of charges are illustrated in Figure 5.

Figure 5: Car scale charges

G/km of CO$_2$			
2002/03	*2003/04*	*2004/05*	% of list price
165	155	145	15★
170	160	150	16★
175	165	155	17★
180	170	160	18★
185	175	165	19★
190	180	170	20★
195	185	175	21★
200	190	180	22★
205	195	185	23★
210	200	190	24★
215	205	195	25★
220	210	200	26★
225	215	205	27★
230	220	210	28★
235	225	215	29★
240	230	220	30★
245	235	225	31★
250	240	230	32★
255	245	235	33★★
260	250	240	34★★★
265	255	245	35★★★★

Diesel supplements:

  ★ add 3% if car runs solely on diesel

  ★★ add 2% if car runs solely on diesel

  ★★★ add 1% if car runs solely on diesel

  ★★★★ maximum charge so no diesel supplement

Example 7.21

Figure 6 below illustrates how this works in practice and illustrates how this will impact drivers.

Figure 6: Example

Omega Est 2.2I CDX Auto – Petrol £24,010 CO_2 248 Combined OMG 27.4	
Current tax @ 18,000 business miles (40% tax payer)	= **£1,400** (15%)
2002/03 tax irrespective of business miles (40% tax payer)	= **£2,977** (31%)
Rover 75 Tourer 2.0 CDT SE Connoisseur Auto – Diesel £23,340 CO_2 190 combined MPG 40.9	
Current tax @ 18,000 business miles (40% tax payer)	= **£1,400** (15%)
2002/03 tax irrespective of business miles (40% tax payer)	= **£2,147** (23%)
Rover 75 Tourer 2.0 CDT SE Connolsseur Man – Diesel £22,165 CO_2 160 combined mpg 48.8	
Current tax @ 18,000 business miles (40%) tax payer	= **£1,300** (15%)
2002/03 tax irrespective of business miles (40%) tax payer	= **£1,595** (18%)

Share schemes 7.22

Using share schemes with flexible benefit packages is complex because the interaction between the tax treatment of share options, the 'value' of those options and performance criteria that are attached to them make it difficult to incorporate them into a flexible benefits scheme. However, the provision of a share scheme package is becoming more and more common. Indeed, there is an increasing expectation amongst employees that such a scheme be put in place.

The changes in tax and NI treatment brought about by the 2002 Budget have been a major boost for employee share schemes. Their inclusion in a flexible benefit scheme is an additional way for employees to save for retirement, especially those who have exceeded their Inland Revenue limits and have no capping. They also offer substantial savings by allowing the organisation to remix how employees can trade salary and benefits for share options.

This area of employee benefits and tax planning is very complicated and readers are recommended to seek specialist advice. However, for sake of illustration, the following example shows some of the tax advantages of a Save-As-You-Earn (SAYE) Scheme.

Save-As-You-Earn (SAYE)

- Employees save money with authorised bank/building society.

- Monthly savings up to £250 for three or five years.

- End of contract – tax-free bonus.

- If funds left for further two years – additional bonus.

- Option granted over shares the fund is expected to but in three/five/seven years.

- Discount up to 20% permitted on market value on grant.

- All employees must be invited to join.

Tax consequences:

- No income tax on grant or exercise of option (even if discount on market value on grant up to 20%).

- No tax on bonus at end of contract (even if option not exercised).

- CGT chargeable on sale (sale proceeds less exercise price).

  ☐ Taper Relief

  ☐ Annual exemption

Rates and contributions 2002/03   7.23

The following rates and contributions are current at the time of writing. They are for illustration only to help readers analyse their own unique situations.

Income tax rates   7.24

Tax year	Taxable income	Band	Rate	Tax Band
2001/02	£0–£1,880	£1,880	10%	£188.00
	£1,881–£29,400	£27,520	22%	£6,054.40
2002/03	£0–£1,920	£1,920	10%	£192.00
	£1,921–£29,900	£27,980	22%	£6,155.60

National Insurance contributions   7.25

Note that as of April 2002, SERPS has been replaced by the State second pension (SP2).

Contracted into S2P			
Employees' Class 1 (rates calculated on total earnings).			
2001/02		*2002/03*	
Earnings per week	Employee	Earnings per week	Employee
Below £87	Nil	Below £89	Nil
£87–£575	10% on earnings above £87 pw	£89–£585	10% on earnings above £89 pw
Over £575	£48.80 pw	Over £585	£49.60 pw

Employers' Class 1			
Earnings per week	Employer	Earnings per week	Employer
Below £87	Nil	Below £89 p.w.	Nil
£87 and over	11.9% on earnings above £87	£89 and over	11.8% on earnings above £89

Contracted out of S2P		
	2001/02	*2002/03*
Rate reduction on employee band earnings	£72–£575	£75–£585
Employee	1.6%	1.6%
Employer band earnings		
Employer – salary related schemes	3%	3.5%
Employer – money purchase schemes	0.6%	1.0%

Earnings limit						
	2001/02			*2002/03*		
	Weekly	*Monthly*	*Annu-ally*	*Weekly*	*Monthly*	*Annu-ally*
Lower	£72	£312	£3,744	£75	£325	£3,900
Upper	£575	£2,491	£29,900	£585	£2,535	£30,420

Class 1A: 2001/03
Employer rate on value of car and fuel benefits: 12.2%

Self-Employed			
		2001/02	*2002/03*
Class 2	Flat rate = if earning over £3,955 p.a.	£2.00 pw £104.00 pa £3,955 pa	£2.00 pw £104.00 pa
Class 3	Rate = On profits	7% (max £1,755.55) £4,535– £29,900 pa	7% (max £1,806.35) £4,615– £30,420

Voluntary			
		2001/02	*2002/03*
Class 3	Flat rate =	£6.75 pw	£6.85 pw
	On profits	£351.00 pa	£356.20 pa

8 — Employment Law Issues

This chapter includes the following:

- Introduction
- Terms and conditions of employment
- Changing a contract
- Breaches of terms and conditions
- Discrimination
- The Employment Act
- Equal opportunities
- Business transfers

Introduction   8.1

The subject of employment law is very complex and the consequences of not meeting legal and strategy requirement can be severe. It is strongly recommended that when setting up the project team an employment lawyer is included to ensure compliance and good practice.

The five main employment law issues that affect and are affected by flexible benefits are:

- terms and conditions of employment;
- discrimination;
- *Employment Act 2002*;
- equal opportunities;
- business transfers.

Each and all of these in one way or another will impact on the design and implementation of the new scheme.

Terms and conditions of employment   8.2

The contract that links the employer with the employee is the Contract of Employment. Both reward and benefits are usually written into this contract in such a manner that any subsequent changes to them represent a change in agreement.

A contract is a promise, or a set of promises, that the law will enforce. In an employment contract, the employee promises to perform certain tasks for the employer, who in turn promises to reward the employee. These promises are enforceable because they are legally binding: if one party breaks a promise then the other party will be entitled to seek damages for breach of contract (and possibly constructive dismissal).

Contracts of employment are made up of a variety of terms and conditions that establish the rights and obligations of both the employer and the employee. There are four main types of terms:

- express;
- implied;
- incorporated; and
- statutory.

Express terms   8.3

These terms expressly (specifically), record the agreement reached between the employer and the employee. The terms can be spelt out either in writing, eg 'You are entitled to 20 days holiday per year', or agreed verbally, eg 'Your starting and finishing times will be 9 am to 5 pm'.

Using the example above it is easy to see that if employees are offered the option to trade up or trade down that this could be a direct change in the express terms and condition of their employment. In this instance their contract would have to be changed or modified.

Implied terms 8.4

These are terms which the law implies can be legally read into a contract of employment, where the contract is silent on a specific issue. So, even though the terms are not written down or agreed verbally they are nevertheless part of the contract. Implied terms can be split into two categories.

- Terms automatically implied by common law because they are regarded as part of every contract, eg the duty of mutual trust and confidence between employer and employee, the duty of care, eg for the employer to provide a safe place of work.

- A term that can be implied because it represents the true intention of the employer and the employee at the time the contract was originally made, ie although nothing was formally agreed, both parties would have included it in the contract if they had really thought about it at the time. For instance, where a term is universally adopted in the company and is so clear-cut, reasonable and well known by both parties that it is included in the employment contract.

This is one of the most contentious parts of the Contract of Employment as very often the implied intention of the employer has arisen out of traditional practice rather than design. For instance, free use of the company pool car when employee's vehicles have broken down.

Incorporated terms 8.5

These are terms which are incorporated into contracts from other sources such as collective agreements, working rules, disciplinary codes, staff handbooks, etc. These terms are either:

- express — the contract states that that some of its terms are regulated by a collective agreement;

- implied — the terms of a collective agreement are incorporated into individual contracts because this is what the parties agreed to when the contract was formed and have been consistently applied.

The law requires the statement of written particulars of employment to include a section which says whether or not a collective agreement forms part of the terms and conditions of employment.

Statutory terms   8.6

These are terms which are either imposed or implied by statute concerning the rights of employers and employees. For flexible benefits the main ones to consider are:

- The *Equal Pay Act 1970*, which imports an equality clause into every contract.

- The *Sex Discrimination Act 1975*, the *Race Relations Act 1976* and the *Disability Discrimination Act 1995* provide the right to equal treatment and not to be discriminated against.

- The *Employment Rights Act 1996* provides many rights, including time off for public duties, the right not to have unlawful deductions made from wages, the right to a minimum statutory period of notice, maternity leave, parental leave, emergency family leave rights, the right not to be unfairly dismissed, etc.

- The *Working Time Regulations 1998* (*SI 1998 No 1833*) limit working time and provide for a minimum period of paid annual leave.

- The *Part-time Employees (Prevention of Less Favourable Treatment) Regulations 2000 (SI 2000 No 1551)* which prohibit discrimination against part-time workers unless the treatment is justified on objective grounds.

Changing a contract   8.7

A contract of employment is a legally binding agreement. Once the contract is made, the employer and the employee are bound by its terms and neither party can alter the contract without the agreement of the other. If the basic design and framework of the flexible benefits scheme is going to radically change the Contract of Employment or the mechanism for choosing benefits affects the above terms, then the organisation can only affect this in the following ways:

- the employer and employee agree to the change – this is variation by mutual consent;

- the terms of the existing contract may allow for changes to be made by the employer – this is variation by contractual authority;

- individual contracts may be varied by the terms in a union agreement or those subsequently negotiated and incorporated into an agreement – this is also a form of variation by contractual authority.

Where mutual agreement cannot be reached, or there is no contractual authority to make a change, an employer can attempt two other options, both of which have considerable risks:

- the employer simply imposes the change with or without advance warning – this is a unilateral variation; or

- the employer terminates the existing contract with notice and substitutes a new one – this is also a unilateral variation.

Change by mutual consent 8.8

If the Flexible benefit scheme requires a change to the terms and conditions of employment, the simplest method, both from a practical and legal point of view, is to persuade the other party to agree to the change.

The basic legal position is that the terms of an employment contract are determined at its formation and clear evidence of mutual agreement will be needed to establish that terms have been varied.

Any change that is imposed by the employer in the absence of agreement will be a breach of contract entitling the employee to seek damages for breach of contract, or possibly, where there is a fundamental breach, to leave employment and claim constructive dismissal.

An employee must have agreed to any changes in terms and conditions voluntarily. If it can be shown that he or she was under threat of dismissal or some other form of duress then it is not possible to call this change by mutual consent. This is often achieved by including a section on the preference form where the employee agrees and accepts these changes.

Mutual agreement to change will only be effective where it has been properly brought about in accordance with the principles of contract law, ie offer, consideration, acceptance and an intention to be legally binding.

A difficulty with this principle in change by consent is the concept of consideration, ie there must be some benefit passing from each of the parties to the other. However, courts tend to look at cases in a common sense way. For example, an agreement to change in benefit entitlement is accompanied by an improvement in flexibility and choice.

Handy hints for change by mutual consent

- Establish what changes are needed and why.

- Identify the employees who will be affected and the likely consequences.

- Develop a strategy for negotiation, eg the change might cause some inconvenience so maybe you can offer improvement(s) to other terms.

- Consult with the employees affected and consider negotiation or some form of compromise to achieve the desired result.

- Ensure details of the final agreement reached are unambiguous, with the timing and changes clearly spelt out.

- Confirm the changes in writing and obtain signed acceptance.

Change by contractual authority 8.9

In order to impose a variation without being in breach of contract, the employer must act within the terms of the contract. Contracts of employment sometimes include express flexibility clauses which give the employer the right to vary the terms of employment. These may be specific, such as a term dealing with an employee's reward purchase or benefit entitlement. Clauses need to be clearly drafted in express written terms, highlighting the scope of the new scheme.

However, an employer cannot make any changes it wants to the contract simply by inserting a global contractual term to that effect. At best, this type of clause will only give the right to make changes of a minor and non-fundamental nature.

An express term in a contract, giving the employer the right to vary contractual terms, can be limited by implying into the contract a term which affects the exercise of that right. For example, say an employee was instructed, in accordance with a clause in his contract referring to flexible benefits, to transfer from one type of pension to another with little notice. This could amount to a fundamental breach of the implied term that the employer would not act in such a way as to undermine the mutual trust and confidence of the employment relationship.

It is a well-established rule of construction in contract law that any ambiguity will be resolved against the party who seeks to rely on it to avoid obligations under the contract.

Handy hits for change by contractual authority

• Establish what changes are needed and why.

• Identify the employees who will be affected.

• Establish the contractual authority allowing the right to vary terms.

• Consult the employees, highlighting the contractual right to vary terms.

• Consider the affect on individuals and any reasonable adjustments that could be made.

• Ensure that final changes will be within the terms of the contract.

• Issue written notice of change as appropriate.

• Obtain signed acceptance from the employees.

Variation through the terms of a collective agreement   8.10

Where a change in terms and conditions is negotiated with a trade union, the issue arises as to whether the agreement reached with the union has the effect of varying the terms of the individual contracts of union members, or indeed others in the workforce.

Incorporation of a collective agreement into the employment contract is the normal way in which a change agreed by a union on behalf of an employee becomes legally effective. If a contract of employment expressly or impliedly incorporates such agreements made between the employer and the relevant trade union from time to time, then the making of a new agreement will vary the terms under which the employee is employed. In such circumstances, whether or not the employee is a member of the union is irrelevant.

The normal way in which collective agreements are incorporated into an individual contract is by express reference in the contract itself. There should be little doubt now as to express incorporation as the right to written particulars under the *Employment Rights Act 2002* requires that an employee is aware as to whether the terms in a collective agreement apply to the contract or not. These considerations also apply to the concept of workforce agreements under the *Working Time Regulations 1998 (SI 1998 No 1833)* and the *Maternity and Parental Leave Regulations 1999 (SI 1999 No 3312)*.

Imposed unilateral variation   8.11

This is where an employer simply imposes a unilateral change to the contract. This is a breach of contract. Whether it is a fundamental breach will depend on the circumstances of the change introduced and the impact on the employee and the employment relationship. Employers are strongly advised not to use this approach. Sometimes employees choose to work under the new terms without putting up any resistance. However, there can be a number of costly consequences for an employer who imposes change – the employee could:

- claim to have been unfairly constructively dismissed, although the employer could plead in the alternative that, while there may have been a breach, it was fair and reasonable in the circumstances;

- stay at work under protest and bring a complaint on the basis that the changes are radically different compared to the previous contract and in effect the previous contract has been terminated;

- bring a claim for breach of contract in the Employment Tribunal;

- work under protest and bring an action for damages for breach of contract in a civil court;

- bring a claim concerning illegal deductions from wages if a pay reduction was involved; or

- simply refuse to accept the breach and refuse to work under the new terms, which presents the employer with a further problem, ie either dismiss the employee or back down.

While claims may be able to be defended on the basis that any change was objectively justified, if it was fair, such a defence will have no effect in a breach of contract claim.

Effecting change by termination with notice and the offer of a new contract   8.12

This is an extremely rare way of effecting changes in a Contract of Employment for flexible benefits. If the organisation has reached the stage where this is the only alternative then it is probably due to other reasons such as contractual harmonisation or organisational restructure. It is, however, of use to understand how this works as, although it may not be as a direct result of introducing the flexible benefit scheme, it may affect its design and implementation.

An employer faced with an employee who refuses to agree to a change may choose to terminate the old contract with full contractual notice and offer the employee new terms and conditions. There will be no breach of contract in these circumstances, so the employer is not laying himself open to any civil action or constructive dismissal claim. But the termination will be a dismissal which can give rise to an unfair dismissal claim even if the employee has accepted the new job.

In an unfair dismissal case the employer must show a potentially fair reason for dismissal within the categories set out in the *Employment Rights Act 1996 s 98(1), (2)*. In the context of business reorganisations and changes in terms and conditions, the usual statutory reason pleaded is 'some other substantial reason'. The employer has to show a reasonable belief that a sound, good business reason existed, and a tribunal would need to reach the view from the evidence that the employer had acted reasonably in all the circumstances of the case, which will include full consultation with the affected employees.

It should be borne in mind that the concept of a redundancy for the purpose of collective consultation is a wide one which covers, for example, a dismissal effected to implement a change in employment terms and, in these types of situation, the employer is still required to consult as if it were a redundancy situation where 20 or more employees are involved.

There are still real, but unavoidable risks for employers by dismissing and offering a new contract. While there can be no breach of contract there is the risk of an unfair dismissal claim. An employee does not necessarily have to leave his employment to bring an unfair dismissal claim in such circumstances. He or she could stay on and work under the new contract and still present a claim to an Employment Tribunal concerning the old contract. To defend such a claim, an employer would have to show a sound business reason for the change which could be objectively justified. This means:

- there must be a real need for change within the business, ie a genuine commercial objective;

- the change must be an appropriate means of achieving the commercial objective;

- the advantages to the business must outweigh any disadvantages to the employees affected.

Void terms 8.13

Any agreement or attempt to insert a provision into a contract which excludes or limits statutory rights under the various Employment Acts will be void and unenforceable, eg a term which does not allow for the minimum statutory paternity pay be taken under the *Employment Act 2002*.

Breaches of contracts of employment 8.14

To fully understand the ramifications of flexible benefits in Contracts of Employment, organisations need to understand what their position is in terms of breaches of contract.

Types of breach 8.15

Where a part of the contract is not adhered to then the party who has suffered damage can make a claim for breach of contract in respect of any losses incurred because of that breach. One party to the contract will be entitled to terminate the contract where the party in default has:

- repudiated the contract, ie has indicated by words or conduct that he or she does not intend to honour obligations under the contract; or,

- actually committed a fundamental breach of contract.

Effect of the breach 8.16

Where one party commits a breach the innocent party can either:

- refuse to accept the breach and therefore treat the contract as continuing; or

- accept the breach and treat the contract as at an end.

Generally, a repudiation or fundamental breach by one party has to be accepted by the other party before the contract ends. If an employer accepts an employee's breach and the contract comes to an end, then the employer dismisses the employee, subject of course to the employee's right to complain of unfair dismissal.

Remedies for breach of contract claims 8.17

The damages payable to an employee following a breach of contract have one basic purpose – to put the employee into the position he or she would have been in had both parties performed their obligations under the contract. In the context of flexible benefits and employment contracts, damages could entail compensating an employee who may have been worse off by the introduction of the new scheme by the equivalent amount that he or she would have been entitled to had the contract not been breached. Therefore, damages are limited to the period between the time of the claim and the point at which the contract could have been lawfully terminated, subject to right to complain re: unfair dismissal.

Claims in Employment Tribunals 8.18

A breach of contract claim can be brought before an Employment Tribunal if the claim arises or is outstanding on the date of claim. Where such a claim is brought by an employee, the employer can make a counter-claim in respect of any breaches of contact by the employees. Other than claims for damages or for sums due in respect of personal injury, a claim can be lodged for:

- damages for breach of a contract of employment or any other contract connected with employment;

- a sum due under such a contract;

- the recovery of a sum in pursuance of any enactment relating to the terms or performance of such a contract.

Any contract claim to an Employment Tribunal must be presented within three months of the date of breach. There is no service qualification required to be eligible to make a contract claim.

Where a tribunal finds that the whole or part of a sum claimed in proceedings is due, it will order the respondent to pay such subject to an upper limit of £25,000 per claim.

Claims in civil court 8.19

Prior to the extension of jurisdiction to tribunals employees had to sue in the normal civil courts for such contractual sums. The extension does not diminish that right but clearly it is expected that an employee, who considers that his employer owes him or her money or its equivalent in benefits, will want to have a claim for these decided at the same time.

Nevertheless, if the amount claimed under the contract (other than redundancy payments, basic awards and unfair dismissal compensation) exceeds £25,000, the employee will have to sue in a civil court because the amount of the claim will put it beyond the tribunal's jurisdiction. Claims can be heard in County courts (up to £50,000), or the High Court (over £50,000) and must be brought within six years of the cause of action arising.

Discrimination 8.20

If not assessed properly during the design stage, introducing a new flexible benefits scheme may possibly give rise to direct and indirect discrimination claims, for example:

- The structuring of premiums for certain benefits could indirectly discriminate against women who form the majority of part-time workers who, in turn, have been excluded from all or part of the scheme.

- Benefit entitlement is structured in such a way that it refers to either male or female gender and as such may discriminate against employees undergoing gender re-assignment, particularly where it can be shown that he or she is being treated less favourably.

- The buying and selling of holidays could indirectly discriminate against certain racial groups by forcing them to take their holidays at different parts of the year not suitable to their religion, because of cover required for those who have traded up their holiday allowance.

- The product portfolio included in the flexible benefit scheme could discriminate against disabled people if it is strongly biased towards able people.

Changes should, therefore, be examined carefully to ensure there are no discriminatory implications, remembering that in indirect sex and race discrimination claims it is a defence for the employer to argue that the requirement is objectively justified because of a genuine business need.

In direct discrimination claims concerning disability, it is open to the employer to justify going ahead with a change which impacts adversely on a disabled employee if it can be shown that it was not reasonable or practicable to make adjustments to accommodate the disabled person or that making adjustments would make no difference to the situation.

Employment Act 2002   8.21

The *Employment Act 2002* received Royal assent on 8 July 2002 and relates to work and parents. It contains a number of provisions, covering several subject areas. In many cases the Act amends current legislation. However, clauses in the Act relating to pay and administration of statutory paternity and adoption pay and fixed-term work, are free standing and do not amend existing legislation.

The main areas that affect flexible benefits are summarised below.

Statutory Paternity Pay (SPP)   8.22

- Statutory right to SPP for fathers following the birth of a child or the placement of a child for adoption.

- SPP will be paid in respect of a single block of up to two weeks and regulations will provide for the father to choose to be paid for a single period of one week or two weeks.

- SPP is only payable for paternity leave taken within 56 days of the date on which the child is born or placed for adoption.

- The rate of SPP will be set in regulations and in 2003 it will be the lesser of £100 or 90% of the employee's average weekly earnings.

- SPP will be available to an employee who has:

  ☐ met the service and relationship qualification Statutory Paternity Leave (SPL);

  ☐ given appropriate notification;

  ☐ average weekly earnings which are equal to or above the lower earnings limit applying to National Insurance Contributions (NICs).

- SPP will be administered by employers in the same way as Statutory Maternity Pay (SMP), ie large employers will be able to recover 92% of SPP paid out; small employers (in 2002/3, those with NICs due in a year of £40,000 or less) will be able to claim 100% plus an added payment (in 2001/2 of 5% for Statutory Maternity Pay) to compensate for employers' share of NICs payable in respect of SPP. Regulations will provide for employers to apply for advance payments of SMP if necessary where the amount they have to pay out in SMP exceeds NICs due.

- Where an employer fails to pay SPP, the Inland Revenue will become responsible for the payment. Liability will also fall on the Inland Revenue from the first week in which an employer becomes insolvent.

- To ensure compliance, employers must:

  ☐ keep appropriate records and make periodic returns to the Inland Revenue;

  ☐ produce those records for inspection by the Inland Revenue;

  ☐ provide information about entitlement to SPP to their employees.

- To further ensure compliance, the Inland Revenue will be able to:

  ☐ obtain information from both employers and applicants for SPP;

  ☐ impose penalties where there is refusal or repeated failure to comply;

  ☐ make decisions on entitlement in the event of dispute.

Statutory Adoption Pay (SAP) 8.23

- There is a statutory right to SAP for adoptive parents around the placement of a child for adoption. However, it will not apply to step-family adoptions or adoptions by a child's existing foster carers – whether the child is being adopted within the UK or from overseas.

- SAP will be available for a period of up to 26 weeks.

- The rate of SAP will be set in regulations, however, in 2003 it will be the lesser of £100 or 90% of the employee's average weekly earnings.

- SAP will be available to an employee who has:

  ☐ at least 26 weeks continuous service with the same employer by the week in which an approved match with the child is made;

  ☐ given appropriate notification;

  ☐ average weekly earnings which are equal to or above the lower earnings limit applying to NICs.

- The administration and enforcement of SAP will be exactly the same at that for SPP above.

Maternity leave and maternity pay 8.24

- Changes will be made to the two maternity benefits for pregnant working women: Statutory Maternity Pay (SMP), which is administered and paid by employers; Maternity Allowance (MA), which is paid by the Department for Work and Pensions (DWP). Both are currently paid for a maximum of 18 weeks. All the changes are to take effect in 2003.

- The payment period of MA and SMP will be extended from 18 to 26 weeks.

- There will be an increase in the standard rate of MA and SMP to £100 a week, or 90% of weekly earnings if this is less than £100.

- In the case of SMP a woman will receive 90% of her average weekly earnings for the first six weeks for which SMP is payable (as now). For the remaining 20 weeks, the woman will receive a prescribed standard rate of a £100 a week, unless this exceeds her earnings-related rate (90% of her average weekly earnings), in which case, she will receive the earnings-related rate for the entire pay period.

- There will be an increase in the minimum period of notice that must be given to an employer/by an employee for SMP from 21 days to 28 days.

- An employee's entitlement to SMP will be safeguarded from the 15th week before the EWC on her satisfying the employment and earnings tests and giving notice where appropriate. As now she must have ceased to work for the employer but the requirement that she ceases work 'wholly or partly because of pregnancy or confinement' will be omitted. This safeguards a woman's entitlement to SMP should her employment end for whatever reason after the beginning of the 15th week.

- An employer will be allowed to offset his SMP payments against any payments due to be made to the Inland Revenue as may be prescribed in regulations.

- Regulations may also provide for employers to apply for advance funding if the amount they are due to pay in SMP will exceed the tax, National Insurance and other allowable payments due to be made to the Inland Revenue.

- Employers will be able to recover SMP from tax and other payments due to the Inland Revenue and not just from NICs as now.

- Regulations will provide for employers to apply for advance payments of SMP if necessary where the amount they have to pay out in SMP exceeds allowable payments due to the Inland Revenue.

Fixed-term work   8.25

- The European *Directive 1999/70/EC* concerning the framework agreement on fixed-term work was agreed on 28 June 1999 and was due to be implemented in the UK by 10 July 2002.

- The purpose of the framework agreement is to apply the principle of non-discrimination to those in fixed-term employment and to establish a framework to prevent abuse arising from the use of successive fixed-term employment contracts or relationships.

- Following a consultation exercise, the Government intends to prevent pay and pensions discrimination against fixed-term employees, even though on account of its legal base, this directive does not apply to pay and pensions.

- The Act (*Employment Act 2002*) enables the Secretary of State to make regulations preventing less favourable treatment of fixed term employees as compared to permanent employees and preventing abuse arising from the use of successive periods of fixed term employment.

- These regulations will, in particular, specify:

  ☐ circumstances in which fixed-term employment is to have effect as permanent employment;

  ☐ circumstances in which fixed-term contracts are to be taken to be successive;

☐ classes of person taken to be fixed-term and permanent employees;

☐ circumstances in which fixed term employees are taken to be, or not to be, treated less favourably than permanent employees and amend provisions in current primary legislation that allow for some or all fixed term employees to be treated less favourably than permanent employees.

Equal opportunities   8.26

As with discrimination, flexible benefit schemes need to be structured in such a way as to offer equal access and opportunities to all. The governing legislation is summarised below.

Sex and race discrimination   8.27

The *Sex Discrimination Act 1975* and the *Race Relations Act 1976* both render certain kinds of discrimination unlawful and have similar, and often corresponding provisions. It makes discrimination on the grounds of gender, ie male or female, marital status or/and gender reassignment, unlawful.

The *Race Relations Act 1976* deals with discrimination on the grounds of race, colour, nationality, or ethnic or national origin. It makes it unlawful to discriminate against job applicants, employees, the self-employed and contract workers.

Three types of discrimination are unlawful:

● Direct discrimination – treating a person less favourably than another person purely on the grounds of sex, marital status, gender reassignment or race in like for like circumstances.

● Indirect discrimination – offering a flexible benefit which appears to apply equally to everyone, but which in reality disadvantages people of a particular sex or race and where the employer cannot objectively justify the requirement.

● Victimisation – where a person is treated less favourably because he or she has alleged that discrimination has taken place or has acted as a witness in a discrimination case.

Less favourable treatment on the grounds of pregnancy or a pregnancy related reason, (such as an illness arising from pregnancy), is deemed to be automatic sex discrimination.

Employers can lawfully discriminate in jobs where being a specific sex or race is a genuine occupational qualification (GOQ); lists of jobs set out in the Acts are exhaustive.

Positive discrimination, other than in a GOQ situation is not permitted, but employers can encourage employees of one sex or race to apply for jobs where that sex or race is drastically under-represented. However, final selection must be based on merit, irrespective of sex or race.

It is unlawful to publish or cause to be published any document or advertisement which indicates or which might be reasonably understood to indicate an intention to discriminate.

It is unlawful for an employer to instruct any other person to discriminate or to induce another person to discriminate by bribery, threat or placing that person at a disadvantage.

Disability Discrimination Act 1995   8.28

The purpose of the *Disability Discrimination Act 1995* is to end discrimination against disabled people in employment and in the access to goods, facilities and services.

A disabled person is someone with a physical or mental impairment who has a substantial and long-term (ie 12 months or more) adverse effect on his or her ability to carry out normal day-to-day activities.

Normal day-to-day activities include mobility, manual dexterity, physical co-ordination, continence, ability to lift, carry or move everyday objects; speech, hearing or eyesight; ability to concentrate, remember, ability to learn or understand or perception of the risk of physical danger.

People who suffer from progressive conditions, eg multiple sclerosis, muscular dystrophy, HIV, AIDS, automatically come within the definition of a disabled person. This needs to be carefully assessed in terms of underwritten benefits.

Discrimination for a reason relating to disability is unlawful in respect of:

- job applicants;

- employees;

- apprentices;

- contract/agency workers; and

- the self-employed.

There are two types of unlawful discrimination:

- Direct discrimination occurs where a disabled person is treated less favourably for a reason relating to disability, compared with a person to whom that reason does not apply and the less favourable treatment cannot be justified. An employer also discriminates if the duty to make reasonable adjustments to working arrangements or the physical features of a premises applies, to remove any barrier to employment, but is not met (see below): and, the failure cannot be justified.

- Victimisation occurs where a person is treated less favourably because he or she has alleged that discrimination has taken place or has acted as a witness in a discrimination case.

The Act places a duty on employers to make reasonable adjustments to accommodate disabled people to help overcome the practical effects of their disability.

The duty applies where any arrangements made by the employer, or any physical feature or the premises, place a disabled employee or a disabled job applicant at a substantial disadvantage.

Making adjustments to premises – this could include structural or physical changes such as widening a doorway for a wheelchair or providing appropriate contrast in décor to help the safe mobility of a visually impaired person.

Examples of adjustment to working arrangements could be the allocation of some of the disabled person's duties to another person or transferring the disabled person to fill an existing vacancy.

Where the duty applies, employers may be able to justify not making the adjustment on the basis that it was not reasonable or practicable, eg cost, disruption, etc.

If a disabled person unsuccessfully applies for a job, a tribunal must assume that disability was the reason, if the wording of the advert shows an intention to discriminate.

Part-time workers   8.29

The *Part-time Workers (Prevention of Less Favourable Treatment) Regulations 2000 (SI 2000 No 1551)* were introduced on 1 July 2000. They apply to England, Scotland and Wales. There are similar laws in Northern Ireland.

The regulations give part-time workers the right not to be treated less favourably in their terms and conditions than comparable full-time workers, unless the organisation can justify the different treatment. This means that, for instance, they cannot be excluded from a flexible benefit scheme unless the organisation can justify it.

You can only justify treating part-time workers less favourably if you can prove that it is necessary and appropriate to achieve a real business aim.

A full-time worker is a worker who works the normal full-time hours for your business. A part-time worker is a worker who works less than the normal full-time hours for your business.

The regulations cover: part-time employees working under a contract of employment; and workers who are not genuinely self-employed, working part-time for your business. This could include agency workers or workers on a fixed term contract.

A part-time worker can compare their terms and conditions with a comparable full-time worker. The comparable full-time worker must work for the same employer and be doing similar work under the same type of contract.

A worker who changes from full-time to part-time hours can compare their terms and conditions with their previous full-time contract. This also applies to someone returning part-time after a period of absence, such as an employee returning from maternity leave, as long as she is not away from work for longer than 12 months.

A part-time worker can write to his or her employer asking for a written statement of the reasons for treating them less favourably. A statement must be provided within 21 days.

Fixed-term workers 8.30

On 9 March 2001 the Department of Trade and Industry launched a consultation period outlining the Government's proposals for the introduction of the Fixed-Term Work Directive. This period ended on 31 May 2001.

The DTI have revealed that although the Fixed-Term Work Directive was to come into effect on 10 July, the Government will not be introducing Regulations on time. The Government states that it will be taking advantage of the provision within the Directive which allows Member States with particular difficulties a further year to implement the changes and insists that appropriate time will be given before any Regulations are brought into effect.

The draft Fixed-term (Prevention of Less Favourable Treatment) Regulations 2001 apply only to employees. The definition of a fixed-term contract has been broadened to comply with the Directive. The draft Regulations will apply to contracts of employment which:

- are made for a specific term which is fixed in advance; or

- terminate automatically on the completion of a task or the occurrence or non-occurrence of a specified event. (Note: a qualifying specified event does not include the individual attaining the normal retirement age, nor does it include a breach of contract entitling the employer to summarily dismiss the employee.)

The draft Regulations will provide fixed-term employees with a number of new rights.

Less favourable treatment 8.31

A fixed-term employee may not be treated less favourably than other comparable permanent employees, either in respect of the terms of their contract of employment or by being subjected to any other detriment by any act or deliberate failure to act of his employer.

However, arrangements both in respect of pay and membership of, or rights under, an occupational pension scheme are expressly excluded.

To determine whether a fixed-term employee has been less favourably treated, they must identify an appropriate comparator who is:

- employed by the same employer; and

- engaged in the same or broadly similar work, having regard to whether they have a similar level of qualification, skills and experience; and

- who works at, or is based at, the same establishment as the fixed-term worker (or where there is no comparator at the same establishment, who meets the first two requirements above).

An employer may only avoid a claim of less favourable treatment if she/he is able to demonstrate that the treatment complained of is justified on objective grounds.

Written statement   8.32

If a fixed-term employee believes that her/his rights under the regulations may have been infringed, she/he is entitled to request a written statement from her/his employer giving particulars of the reasons for the treatment. Employers are required to provide a written statement within 21 days of the employee's request. Should tribunal proceedings follow, the written statement is admissible as evidence and the tribunal may draw any inference which it considers is just and equitable if an employer refuses to provide a statement, or the produced statement is evasive or equivocal.

Right to receive information of alternative vacancies   8.33

Fixed-term employees are entitled to be informed by their employer if any suitable available vacancy arises at the establishment during their period of employment. Employers are able to satisfy this positive duty if they can demonstrate that the vacancy has been communicated to the fixed-term worker within an advertisement which the fixed-term employee has a reasonable opportunity of reading in the course of her/his employment or where the employee has been reasonably notified of the available vacancy in some other way.

Unfair dismissal   8.34

A new right of automatic unfair dismissal is provided where, if the principal reason for dismissal (including a dismissal where the fixed-term contract terminates automatically on the completion of a particular task or upon the occurrence or non-occurrence or a specified event without being renewed) is that the fixed-term employee has:

- brought proceedings under the Regulations;

- requested a written statement under the Regulations;

- given evidence or information in connection with such proceedings brought by any employee;

- done anything under the Regulations in relation to the employer or any other person;

- alleged that the employer has infringed the Regulations;

- refused to forego a right conferred on him by the Regulations.

Remedies   8.35

An employee may complain to a tribunal that a right under the Regulations has been infringed. Claims must be brought within three months commencing with the date that either the less favourable treatment/detriment occurred or, where an act or failure to act forms part of a series of similar acts, the date of the last of these acts. The employee is under the burden of proof to identify the grounds for the less favourable treatment or detriment.

The tribunal can make the following orders/awards:

- a declaration as to the right of the complainant and the employer;

- an award of compensation;

- a recommendation that the employer take, within a specified period, reasonable action to obviate or reduce the less favourable treatment.

Limitation on successive fixed-term contracts   8.36

If an employer engages an employee on a fixed-term contract, and the employee has been previously employed on a fixed-term contract or succession of fixed-term contracts and in continuous employment for a period of four or more years without a break in continuity of employment, then the contract is deemed to become a contract of indefinite duration unless the employer can show that engagement on a fixed-term contract can be justified for objective reasons. This new right commences from the date the Regulations come into effect and time engaged on fixed-term contracts prior to the Regulations being in force may not count towards the qualifying period of four years' continuous employment.

Business transfers   8.37

Because one of the main reasons for implementing a flexible benefits scheme is to harmonise different sets of benefits during business transfers, it is important to understand the employment law considerations are the same.

Employees are prevented by the *Transfer of Undertakings (Protection of Employment) Regulations 1981 (SI 1981 No 1794)* (TUPE) from contracting out of their rights under the Regulations and in particular, to mutually agreeing to any contractual changes directly related to a business transfer which put them in a worse position even if other changes they agree to are to their benefit.

This places the following key obligations on the new employer:

● The new employer effectively 'steps into the shoes' of the old employer and takes over all the rights and obligations arising from the transferring employees' contracts of employment, including those contained in collective agreements with a union.

● The new employer becomes responsible for all employment liabilities, eg outstanding tribunal cases, but this does not include liabilities for criminal offences. Amendments to the Acquired Rights Directive will give the option to provide that the old employer's outstanding debts in relation to employees do not pass to the new employer in order to save jobs when the undertaking of the transferor is insolvent.

Restrictions imposed on new employer   8.38

The new employer is prevented from:

● imposing changes to fundamental contractual terms, including pay and benefits as the Regulations allow employees to resign and claim constructive dismissal if any imposed changes directly related to the transfer put them in a worse position;

● dismissing employees for a reason directly related to the transfer, as this will be automatically unfair.

However, dismissals may be fair if they are for a genuine economic, technical or organisational reason.

Even a consensual variation in the terms of an employee's contract is prohibited if the transfer of the undertaking is the reason for the variation and the change puts the employee in a worse position, even if these are offset by advantages so that overall he or she is not put in a worse position.

TUPE, states that any provision of any agreement, whether part of a contract of employment or not, will be void if it tries to exclude or limit the employee's rights under the Regulations. These include, the right to have all of the terms and conditions enjoyed under the previous contract with the old employer fully protected. This is a major reason for using flexible benefits to harmonise different sets of benefits.

The case, therefore, still remains that employees cannot agree to accept a variation to their terms and conditions, even if they want to, when they transfer to a new employer, if the reasons for the variations are due to the transfer and the changes put the employee in a worse position. This must be considered carefully in respect of flexible benefits.

Employee protection 8.39

Automatic unfair dismissal occurs when an employee is dismissed or made redundant, either before or after the transfer, purely because of the transfer itself and for no other reason. There is a one-year service qualification needed to bring a claim for unfair dismissal.

Dismissal can be fair only if it can be proved that it was not because of the transfer itself, or was because of the transfer, but either the old employer or the new employer can show that there was an economic, technical or organisational reason 'entailing changes to the workforce'.

Examples are:

- Economic – turnover has dropped, so to remain profitable some employees have to be made redundant.

- Technical – employees do not have the technical know how or experience to do their jobs because of the introduction of new equipment/machinery.

- Organisational – the merging of transferring staff into existing structures shows a surplus or overlapping of responsibilities.

'Entailing changes to the workforce' means that in looking at the whole workforce there is a sound economic, technical or organisational reason for making changes to the *number* of people employed or the *functions* they perform, ie redundancies. It does not mean that employers can change or harmonise terms and conditions of employment, including pay and benefits.

Time lapse between transfer and dismissal   8.40

One of the areas of ambiguity with TUPE (*SI 1981 No 1794*) is how much time must elapse after a transfer before any dismissals will cease to be connected with it, by virtue of TUPE. Although a dismissal may be years after the transfer, if it was connected with the transfer: the chain of causation has not been broken. It is likely to be taken as unfair dismissal under TUPE.

Constructive dismissal   8.41

Within the context of dismissal, TUPE (*SI 1981 No 1794*) incorporates the concept of a constructive dismissal as added protection for employees. For a claim to be successful purely within the context of TUPE, the employee has to show that there was a *substantial* change to his or her *detriment*. This includes pay and benefits.

In the context of a transfer of an undertaking it is not necessary for the employee to point to a repudiatory breach of contract by the employer (as the employee would have to do under the law of unfair dismissal in the *Employment Rights Act 1996*); rather the employee need only show that he or she suffered a substantial detrimental change to his or her working conditions. This relates purely to a claim with TUPE – there may be instances where the normal unfair/constructive dismissal principles apply in transfer situations as set out below.

As outlined above, in these circumstances, the employer would not be able to offer an economic, technical or organisational defence for changes to terms and conditions. As has already been seen, employers will fall foul of the Regulations if they attempt to impose changes directly related to a transfer. The fairness of the change, even if related to business efficiency, will be no defence.

Contracting out will be void 8.42

Any provision in a contract which seeks to exclude or limit an employee's rights under the Regulations or prevents an employee from presenting a claim to an employment tribunal concerning a failure to maintain terms and conditions, a failure to consult or unfair dismissal, will be automatically void and unenforceable.

9 — Documentation

This chapter includes the following:

- Introduction
- Announcements
- Employee handbook
- Preference forms
- Benefit statement
- Scheme manual
- Pensions documentation
- Legal requirements
- E-Communication/documents
- Total reward statements

Introduction   9.1

To a large degree, the success or failure of a flexible benefit scheme can hinge on the quality of the company's communications. Scheme documentation is an integral part of these communications and, by getting the documentation right, a company will go a long way towards successfully promoting the scheme and ensuring its effective installation.

The most important issue, though, is that employees clearly understand what options are available, the consequences of the choices they make and accept responsibility for them. This means that education is more important than promotion and the role of documentation, in delivering this objective, is key.

The organisation needs to look in detail at the documentation that is required in advance of the new scheme's installation, the documentation that is required at the time of establishment, and the documentation that is required post-installation.

In this instance, documentation means all written communication – be it paper based or electronic.

When the scheme 'goes live', employees will need full details of its operation, a statement of their current benefits, and a medium for selecting their preferred benefits (or preferred level of benefits, where a core element is compulsory). The documents used to meet these needs are as follows:

- surveys;

- announcements;

- employee handbook;

- preference form;

- benefit statement;

- scheme manual;

- company newspapers/bulletins.

Surveys   9.2

As we have seen in **CHAPTER 4**, there is little point in going ahead with a flexible benefit scheme if evidence reveals that there is no demand for it. By gauging interest in a proposed scheme, well in advance of its suggested launch date, a company can save itself a lot of time and money, as well as work.

There is a need to ascertain how employees perceive their current remuneration and benefits package, and to gain an insight into any new benefits that they might want. Also how they wish to be communicated to.

A popular way of achieving this is to issue an employee survey. This could cover support for the existing reward package, demand for new benefits and any desire for greater flexibility over benefits. The survey could also be supplemented or followed-up by 'face-to-face' communications (eg focus groups), allowing employees, or at least a cross-section of them, to publicly air their views.

Assuming that there is a positive employee reaction to suggestions of greater flexibility in benefit provision and that the scheme is given the 'go-ahead', this information can then be used to successfully sell the whole flexible benefits concept to employees.

More information on how this process is managed and an example of an employee survey is in **APPENDIX 1**.

Announcements   9.3

The new scheme strategy needs to involve some form of announcement covering the decision to introduce a new flexible benefits scheme, an outline of how the scheme will work, and details of opportunities for employees to obtain further information, for example workplace presentations.

At this stage, the scheme should also be given a name. 'Branding' a scheme will help people identify with it and facilitate the promotion of the scheme. This is covered in more detail in **CHAPTER 10**.

To ensure that interest is maintained in the period between the issue of the initial announcement and the formal launch of the scheme, the company could use publicity materials, for example, posters and issue regular 'update' bulletins.

Figure 1 illustrates an example of a scheme announcement bulletin.

Employee handbook   9.4

The scheme guide or handbook is one of the most important documents for employees. It has to provide full details of a potentially quite complex arrangement in a manner that will enable employees to fully understand and appreciate the flexible benefits scheme.

Some handbooks are quite short whilst others can run to over 30 pages. Regardless of length there are three important points to note. The handbook should:

- be divided into appropriate sections, covering items such as the mechanics of the scheme; core benefits, flexible benefits; and the implications of different options such as tax and National Insurance (NI). Consideration should be given to having the handbook professionally produced using, for example, pictures to break up the text;

Figure 1: Example of a scheme announcement bulletin

YOUR CHOICE

This is your personal invitation to attend a Road show to let you know all about the new flexible benefits scheme, 'Choice Benefits'. This will take place...............................

As part of our new strategy of offering a more personal response to an individual's specific needs, we are introducing 'Choice Benefits' which is a flexible benefits scheme. This is a forward thinking, modern innovation in which you are able to take control over your own employee benefits package.

THE BENEFITS OF CHOICE

We will be able to offer each individual a mix of certain employee benefits to suit their individual personal circumstances. This means exactly what it says. Some of the benefits are 'flexible'. Other benefits are what are called 'core' benefits, this means that the company has a duty of care to provide these, at a certain level, to everybody.

Each employee's remuneration package has a total value, made up of salary and benefits. Each benefit within the total package has its own value. The flexible benefits can be arranged in a way to suit your personal circumstances. Everybody's circumstances are different and you will be able to re-arrange your flexible benefits to suit your altered needs. (Full scheme details are available in 'Choice Benefits – The Facts' which is available from Communications).

Of course, you need not change anything at all. You may be completely happy with the mix that you already have – that's fine. However, we want to cater for everyone's needs and adapt to your changing lifestyles, streamlining and improving the total employee benefits package, and offering a new adaptability and excellence of service to suit your lifestyle.

Please do try to make time to attend the Road show, but if this is not possible and to find out about individual consultations, please telephone ....

on Tel...

YOUR CHOICE – YOU BENEFIT

- cover concisely most of the questions that employees are likely to ask. A balance needs to be struck between comprehensiveness and conciseness. In any event, the handbook should include details of where employees can obtain further information;

- be issued to all relevant employees, giving them plenty of time to make informed decisions. There should be ample opportunity for having questions answered before employees have to commit themselves to choosing particular benefits or levels of benefit.

It is likely that at least part of the handbook will need changed every year (eg tax and NI information). Therefore, it may be more practical and cost-effective for the handbook to be issued in the form of a ring binder or looseleaf, avoiding the need to re-issue complete handbooks every time a page becomes obsolete. It should also be accompanied by the other essential installation documents, such as the benefits statement and the preference form, forming a flexible benefits 'pack'.

Employee handbooks will require regular updating. Staff will be using the handbook to decide the make-up of the their benefit package, and it is imperative that their decisions are based only on current data and information (eg up-to-date tax information).

An example of an employee handbook is in **APPENDIX 1**.

Preference form 9.5

The preference form is one of the most important documents within a flexible benefits scheme. It summarises the various fixed and flexible benefit that are available, their options and costs. Most preference forms are produced in a format that allows the employee to calculate the mix of their various choices to ensure that they have not exceeded their flexible benefit allowance (as offered in the scheme), Inland Revenue and legal limits. These calculations can be paper based, on a PC or within a web-enabled format.

This document acts as an enrolment form and enables employees to clearly set out the benefits that are to be altered. Some employees may not want to 'flex' any of their benefits and this is fine. For these employees, there is still a need for them to complete the preference form but only to select an option of 'no change in benefits'. A decision not to change existing benefits is still a choice.

The preference form is also an important legal document. Not only is it a formal record of the employee's choice, it also confirms that the employee has accepted the consequences of their choice (this does not affect their statutory rights). Finally, it may also contain a clause whereby the employee agrees that their choice constitutes a change to their terms and conditions of employment.

Although a paper copy of the preference form can be provided with the employee handbook, it is usually in a form that is completed 'on-line'. A web or PC-based preference form cuts down on paper-work and can be used with appropriate software to model various 'what if' scenarios (whereby staff enter their options and the system shows the implications of those options, such as the impact on their benefit allowances).

For both manual and computer records, it is important that steps are taken to ensure the security of personal data such as compliance with the *Data Protection Act 1998*.

Normally, benefit options can only be changed annually and are effective from the scheme review date. However, more frequent changes are possible upon the occurrence of a 'lifestyle' change (eg birth, death or marriage – see **5.39** above). In either event, a new preference form should be completed and sent to the scheme admin-istrator.

The preference form itself may also have to be updated, at least annually, to ensure that the information contained on it remains current.

An example of a preference form can be found in **APPENDIX 1**.

Benefit statement 9.6

Each employee will receive their own personal benefit statement, specifying the benefits they receive at present and the value of those benefits. It imperative that the employee checks his or her statement and that any errors are corrected.

After reading the employee handbook and ensuring that they under-stand how the flexible benefit scheme works, employees should check their benefit statement and, if applicable, complete the preference form.

Personal benefit statements are an important part of the flexible benefit scheme as they confirm the final choice of the employee and act as an official record. Pre-installation of the new scheme, the personal benefit statement should clearly show exactly what the employee is receiving. This is broken down into core elements and those elements that can be flexed.

Figure 2 shows a simple illustration of the three basic constituents of the employee's reward package; annual salary, cash benefits and benefits in kind.

Figure 2: Personal benefit statement

Personal Benefit Statement		
1 January 2002		
Personal Details		
Title:	Date of joining:	
Surname:	Normal retirement date:	
Forename(s):	Current contractual hours:	
Marital status:	Grade:	
Annual salary	**Core**	**Flex**
Current basic salary:		
Additional pay:		
Cash benefits	**Core**	**Flex**
Mortgage subsidy:		
OTE incentive bonus:		
Pension:		
Company car:		
Fuel card:		
Healthcare:		
Education subsidy:		

Personal Benefit Statement		
1 January 2002		
TOTAL CASH BENEFITS		
Benefits in Kind	**Core**	**Flex**
Annual holiday entitlement		
Outstanding balance of loans		
Life assurance		
Eye examination voucher		
Corrective spectacles voucher		
Staff introductory bonus		
Long service awards		
Sick pay		
PHI		
Hospital fund		
Mobile phone for business use		
SAYE		
Shares		
Allocated parking space		

Personal Benefit Statement Notes	
Cash Benefits	
Current basic salary	This is your current basic salary.
OTE commission	This is your On Target Earnings Commission.
Territorial allowance	This is your location allowance.
Mortgage subsidy	This payment is subsidy on your mortgage
OTE incentive bonus	This is your on-target incentive bonus.

Personal Benefit Statement Notes	
Pension scheme	This is the company's contribution to your pension.
Company car	This is your car allowance that you are entitled to on your current grade.
Fuel card	This is based on the annual national average mileage.
Healthcare	This is the company's contribution to your private medical insurance for both you and your family, if applicable.
Education subsidy	This is the tuition fees paid by the company for your chosen course of study.
Benefits in kind	
Annual holiday entitlement	This is your annual holiday entitlement converted into cash.
Outstanding balance of loan	This is the balance of your company loan.
Life assurance	This is the tax-free lump sum that your beneficiaries receive should you die during your employment with the company.
Eye examination voucher	This voucher can be obtained from the HR department and entitles you to a free annual eye examination.
Corrective spectacles voucher	This voucher can be obtained from the HR department and contributes £50.00 towards the cost of a pair of VDU spectacles.
Staff introductory bonus	If you introduce a friend to the company and they begin employment with us, you will receive a bonus of £1,000: £500 on their joining and £500 when they have been here for more than 6 months.
Long service awards	On your anniversary dates of 10 years, 20 years and 25 years and 30 years you will receive a bottle of champagne, a certificate of achievement and vouchers to the value of £100, £200 and £250 and £300 respectively.

Personal Benefit Statement Notes	
PHI	This is a long-term sickness or disability plan which provides financial assistance for employees working 16 hours per week or more, who become permanently disabled through injury or sickness.
SAYE	The company's first Save As You Earn Scheme was launched in April 1998. There may be a further issue of shares next year.
Sick pay	Sick pay entitlement is calculated by length of service, as follows:

Length of Service	Full pay	Half pay
0–6 months	No pay	
6 months to one year	4 weeks	Nil
1–5 years	8 weeks	8 weeks
5–10 years	13 weeks	13 weeks
over 10 years	26 weeks	Nil

Hospital fund	This is a health plan that offers cash benefits if you have healthcare treatment. It is an optional staff benefit and application forms can be obtained from the HR department.
Mobile phone	You are provided with a mobile phone for business use only where the company meets all costs.
Share	This is the number of company shares that you have been awarded to date.
Allocated parking space	You have an allocated space at the company's office.

On the form illustrated in Figure 2 there are two columns to allow the employer to state which benefits are core and which are flex. For those benefits with a mix of core and flex, for instance private medical insurance, the respective columns will reflect what percentages are applicable. The notes that accompany the benefit statement may also contain references to the new flexible scheme.

Post installation the benefit statement should now show what products have been selected as core and those which are flexible. Once checked and agreed by both employer and employee this becomes the official record for the remainder of the scheme year (unless there is a lifestyle change – see **5.39** above) and becomes the 'post installation' benefit statement for the next scheme year.

Scheme manual   9.7

The 'scheme operations manual' is a guide for administrators and is concerned with process, quality control and service standards. Rather than draw up a new manual from scratch, employers may prefer to revise their existing process manuals.

Pension documentation   9.8

Both personal pension schemes and stakeholder pension schemes are classified as 'investments' under the *Financial Services and Markets Act 2000*. Employers may provide factual information on such arrangements but cannot, unless authorised to do so, give advice. Promotional material relating to stakeholder and personal pensions, which an employer proposes to issue to employees, should be approved by an authorised person.

Occupational pension schemes are not classed as investments under financial services legislation but, in any event, employers and trustees should, as a general rule, avoid giving advice to individual members. There is no duty to provide such advice and not doing so avoids any assumption of responsibility for its accuracy.

Disclosure of information regulations   9.9

Both occupational pension schemes and personal pensions are subject to minimum disclosure requirements under separate sets of disclosure of information regulations (*Personal Pension Schemes (Disclosure of Information Regulations 1987 (SI 1987 No 1110)* and *Occupational Pension Schemes (Disclosure of Information) Regulations 1986 (SI 1986 No 1046)*. When communicating pensions, it is, of course, imperative that the regulatory requirements are complied with. Essentially, the disclosure of information regulations provides that 'basic information' must be given automatically to pension scheme members; while 'individual information' only has to be given on request.

The individual items that have to be disclosed is beyond the scope of this book, but it should be noted that:

- the disclosure regulations do not confer on any member an entitlement to obtain information which is not relevant to their own rights;

- when basic or individual information is provided, it should invariably be accompanied by an address that the recipient can use to obtain further details. This requirement is often over-looked.

In the case of occupational pension schemes, the trustees are responsible for compliance with the disclosure of information regulations. For personal pensions, compliance rests with the provider.

Stakeholder pension schemes 9.10

Since 8 October 2001, most employers have had to nominate a stakeholder pension scheme for their 'relevant employees' (essentially, employees who are not already covered by an existing pension arrangement and who have been employed for more than three months with earnings in excess of the lower earning limit for National Insurance purposes – see **7.25** above).

Before nominating a scheme, employers must consult with relevant employees over their choice of arrangement. After nominating a scheme, employers must provide relevant employees with sufficient information 'to get in touch with it' (ie the name and address of the scheme provider).

Also, representatives of the stakeholder provider must be given 'reasonable access to relevant employees for the purpose of supplying them with information about the scheme'.

Even where an employer is not obliged to nominate a stakeholder pension scheme, it may choose to do so voluntary as, for example, an alternative AVC vehicle for occupational pension scheme members who are eligible for concurrent membership with personal/stakeholder pensions. Communicating such an arrangement can be quite complex and comments above, on financial services legislation (see **9.8** above), should be borne in mind.

Combined pension statements 9.11

The *Child Support, Pensions and Social Security Act 2000* and regulations made under the Act contain provisions relating to 'combined pension statements' (covering sSate and private pension rights). The regulations allow an individual's State pension information to be provided to pension scheme trustees and managers, unless the individual concerned objects. Previously, the individual had to actively consent to his/her information being disclosed. The premise behind the change is to increase the take-up of combined pension statements and ensure that individuals are properly informed as regards their need to save. There is, however, no obligation for schemes to provide combined pension statements.

Money purchase illustrations 9.12

The *Child Support, Pensions and Social Security Act 2000* also provides for regulations to be made which will require annual benefit statements to include an illustration of the future benefits that might become payable. The basis for calculating illustrations is to be determined by reference to guidance notes produced by the Faculty and Institute of Actuaries.

The regulations will apply to members of occupational and personal pension schemes (including stakeholder schemes, but excluding retirement annuity contracts) which provide money purchase benefits (including money purchase AVCs).

Unlike combined pension statements, money purchase illustrations will be compulsory (probably, from 2003).

Legal requirements 9.13

When considering reward documentation from the point of view of a new employee, the first consideration is *Part I* of the *Employment Relations Act 1996*. This provides that a new employee must be provided with a written statement of his/her particulars of employment. The statement must be given within two months and must include:

● details relating to the employee's remuneration;

● terms and conditions relating to holiday entitlement;

● terms and conditions relating to pensions and pension schemes (normal practice is just to refer to a separate scheme booklet).

If there is a change in any of the items in the statement, details of the change must be given at the earliest opportunity and, in any event, within one month.

Data Protection Act 1998 9.14

Another consideration, affecting new and existing employees, is the *Data Protection Act 1998* (*DPA 1998*), which replaces the 1984 legislation (*DPA 1984*). Communicating reward clearly involves the processing of personal information and those controlling that information (in DPA parlance, 'data controllers') must, broadly speaking, ensure that:

- they have 'notified' with the Information Commissioner (processing personal information without notifying is a strict liability offence, but data controllers that have already registered under the 1984 Act do not need to notify under *DPA 1998* until their existing registration expires).

- each employee (or 'data subject') consents to the processing of his/her personal information (in certain circumstance, consent might be inferred);

- certain information (eg details of the data controller) must be given automatically to data subjects, and such subjects have the right to prescribed information on request; and

- they enter into contracts with those processing personal information on their behalf (such persons are know as 'data processors').

Above all else, data controllers must comply with the eight data protection principles, which underpin the whole *DPA 1998*. These principles can be summarised as follows:

- processing of data must be fair, lawful and specific;

- data must be accurate, adequate and relevant, but never excessive nor retained for longer than necessary;

- data must also be processed in accordance with the rights of data subjects and not transferred to countries without adequate protection.

N.B. The above summary does not take into account the transitional provisions or limited exemptions under *DPA 1998*.

A more detailed section on the *Data Protection Act 1998* can be found in CHAPTER 13.

E-communication/documentation 9.15

This is covered in more detail in **CHAPTER 10**. Where documentation may be provided in electronic, rather than paper, form. The following additional areas need to be analysed as they could be relevant:

● information provided over an intranet or internet will be of little use if the intended recipients do not have access to a PC;

● it is important to get the design of the website right;

● in some instances, it will not be possible to comply with the disclosure of information regulations (see **9.9** above) by electronic means (eg information that has to be provided by post). This issue may also apply to other statutory requirements.

There could be *Data Protection Act 1998* issues.

In relation to e-communication, it is important to ensure, again, that disclosure regulations, and other statutory requirements, are not being breached.

Total reward statements 9.16

More and more organisations today are moving towards the concept of total reward statements. The technology required to design and install a flexible benefit makes the step towards this relatively easy and indeed enhances both the promotion of the scheme and the education of its members. As the benefit statement illustrated at **9.6** above, such statements cover all or most of the items that make up a person's remuneration and benefit package.

The total reward statement consists of personalised data, output and information along with all details relating to an employees reward package. In summary it contains anything and everything that an employee receives for contributing to the organisation.

It is a snap shot view of the main employment cost and obligations and communicates how and various components of reward fit together. Its main advantage is improving the overall perceived value of what an individual receives from an organisation.

Some reward statements go further, quoting the cost of or comparison to the high street replacement value of the benefit. These can be added to other employment costs to give the total perceived value of reward that the employee enjoys.

As with benefit statements the total reward statement can be used to confirm flexible benefit choices.

The main components and their sources of data required for a total reward statement are:

- basic pay, variable pay and other cash entitlements from payroll;
- pensions;
- shares/incentives;
- benefits (including flexible benefits);
- Form P11D (to illustrate tax implications of flexible benefit choice);
- other reward such as statutory entitlements, holidays, training etc. The design, development, implementation and administration of total reward statements are very similar to flexible benefits and the main points covered in this book would apply. There is an example in Figure 3 at **9.18** below.

Legal requirements   9.17

In terms of legal requirements, if a total reward statement is being issued to a new employee, compliance with the *Employment Rights Act 1996* may apply. If so, the prescribed information must be supplied within the set timescales.

In any event, personal information is being processed and the data protection principles must be observed. It might be useful to include a note on the statement, asking the recipient to ensure his/her details are correct. This could help ensure compliance with the fourth data protection principle, which requires personal data to be accurate and up to date.

Advice should be avoided because of financial services legislation and the possibility of assuming a responsibility for its veracity.

Minimum requirements under the disclosure of information regulations (see **9.9** above) must be observed. For instance, it is generally advisable to include an address that recipients of information can use for further information.

Total reward statement notes 9.18

The notes accompanying total reward statements are important and can serve a number of purposes:

- first, they should make it clear that the statement is provided for information only and that the items on it are not guaranteed. A caveat along these lines should make it less likely that individuals will rely on the statement without first checking their entitlements';

- second, they should make it clear, where applicable, that the some benefits may need to be changed without warning and/or may be payable only if certain conditions are met';

- third, they can be used as a reminder to, for example, keep pension scheme death benefit nomination forms up to date; and

- finally, they can refer the reader to other documents (such as the pension scheme booklet) for further information on particular benefits.

The above covers documentation requirements for the flexible scheme itself. It is important to remember, however, about 'consequential documentation matters'; ie changes to existing legal and explanatory documents.

Changes to pension scheme rules and booklets have already been mentioned. Revised documents may also be required for ancillary benefits, such as private medical/dental insurance and permanent health insurance arrangements.

New service contracts may also be required – see further **8.7** above.

Figure 3 illustrates an example of a Total Reward Statement.

Figure 3: Total Reward Statement

TOTAL COMPENSATION STATEMENT
YOUR PAY
Your base pay and additional earnings at the end of the year were:

TOTAL COMPENSATION STATEMENT	
Total pay (before tax) Overtime Annual bonus Other earnings.	
Your taxable earnings were therefore:	
INCENTIVES As a result of your own, your team's and the business' objectives having been exceeded last year, you received the following incentive related rewards:	
Performance Bonus	
You were allocated . . . . share options that may be redeemed in 2004. As the issue price of . . . . their value was	
In total you received incentives of:	
INSURANCE **Death Benefits**	
If you die while employed your dependants will receive a death benefit equivalent to three times your annual pensionable pay which, based on your pay is	
The cost of this insurance is borne by your employer at a cost of:	
Disability Benefit	
Should you be disabled while employed, you will receive a benefit equal to . . .% of your pay. This is currently equal to	
The cost of this insurance is borne by your employer at a cost of:	
Medical Aid	
You are a member of . . . . Health. The cost of this benefit is shared between you and your employer. You paid . . . . which is deduced pre-tax from your pay.	
Your employer pays . . . . . .% of this benefit	
The total cost to the company of providing these insurance benefits is:	

TOTAL COMPENSATION STATEMENT	
RETIREMENT ACCUMULATION	
Your employer helps you prepare financially for your retirement via The . . . . company retirement Fund. The contributions you and your employer make, and the investment income earned by these funds, accumulate to your account within the Fund.	
Your contribute 6% of your pensionable pay that was deducted prior to paying tax from your pensionable pay.	
The company contributed . . .% of your pay, equivalent to:	
The company also paid the administration and management costs of the fund (being . . .% of pay) which amounted to:	
The total cost to the company to provide these retirement benefits is:	
LEAVE	
Annual Leave	
Last year you were entitled to . . . . . . days annual leave. The value of this, based on you pay was:	
Sick Leave	
You took . . . . . . day sick leave valued at:	
The total cost to the company of your leave entitlements is:	
OTHER BENEFITS	
Your company provided you with the following further benefits:	
Parking	
You received a company subsidy towards your parking amounting to:	
Staff Discount	
The company provided you with a discount on your financial planning. Last year the average subsidy was:	
The total cost to the company of providing these benefits was:	

TOTAL COMPENSATION STATEMENT	
TOTAL COMPENSATION	
Adding together all these amounts, your total compensation is:	
SUMMARY OF YOUR TOTAL COMPENSATION	
Pay	
Non-pay benefits (refer to below)	
Incentives	
Insurance	
Retirement accumulation	
Leave	
Other benefits	

Notes:

- While every care has been taken in preparing this statement it is for information only and does not confer any right of entitlement to any of the benefits shown

- Company policy, current legislation, individual scheme rules and/or insurance policy limitations govern all benefits payable. These may be changed at any time.

- The section on retirement and death benefits should be read in conjunction with your retirement scheme booklet and annual benefits statement you receive in connection with the scheme.

- The values shown for each of the non-pay benefits represent your share of the approximate aggregate costs to the company of providing those benefits.

- When you retire, or if you suffer long-term incapacity of disablement, you may also be entitled to receive benefits from the State.

- If you believe that any of the details in this statement are incorrect, or if you need any further information, please contact the Human Resources Department.

10 — Scheme Launch and Communication

This chapter includes the following:

- Introduction
- Definition of communication
- Communicate stakeholders
- Managing perception
- Proactive communication
- Communicating at different levels
- Developing an integrated communication strategy
- The use of technology
- Financial counselling
- Communication checklist

Introduction   10.1

While many aspects of a company's management have an impact on the 'bottom line', communication is a fundamental skill without which survival and success would be impossible.

Today, verbal communication is more about managing expectations and perceptions. There is discussed in more detail at **10.9** and **10.12** below.

A flexible benefits scheme should be uniquely branded based on internal marketing. The vision and mission set must be meaningful and based on the desired outcome relevant to the organisation.

Information gathered from the feasibility study can be used to develop a communication strategy that will ensure employees have a clear understanding of the new strategy; how it affects them individually and their part in making it work for both them and the organisation.

Education is the vital component of communicating a flexible benefit scheme. Employees should understand the options available to them and the consequences of their discussions as they will, ultimately, be responsible for them.

The design and launch of the benefits scheme should concentrate on effective communication to all staff and others involved. To achieve this there are four basic steps:

- obtain top team endorsements for the scheme;

- identify current communication strategy and develop an appropriate strategy for benefits;

- ensure that all personnel involved in the communication process have received comprehensive training in communication skills and possesses adequate knowledge; and

- agree a format for communication.

Definition of communication   10.2

The most basic definition of communication is the means of passing intelligence and/or information from one place to another. True communication is a two-way flow of information based on listening, recording, looking and responding.

As we have seen in **CHAPTER 1** there are many forces of change in our modern world that are affecting communication. These range for societal changes to rapid globalisation. We are living in a virtual society based on perception rather than reality. This is against a background of continuous change and ambiguity.

There are four basic types of communication:

- Verbal – The most common. Spoken, video, telephone, media, recording, interviewing. The base of all human interaction.

- Visual – The most impact. Body language, gestures, video, media, posters, and presentations. The basis of perception.

- Written – The formal bit of communicating. Letters, memos, faxes, instructions, contracts. The basis of business communication.

- Electronic Communication – e-mail, web-enabled, intranet, internet, mobile phone, WAP. The basis of modern communication.

The most powerful is the combination of them all.

Measuring communication 10.3

As communication has a fundamental impact on the performance of an organisation it is important to measure the value that it adds. For example:

- internal performance measurement and external;

- improved bottom line;

- improved environment;

- happier workforce;

- improved productivity;

- never ending improvements;

- greater speed, flexibility and cost-effectiveness.

Communication stakeholders 10.4

As a flexible benefit scheme is dependent on partnership with all their stakeholders, the ability to communicate effectively takes on a greater importance

The main stakeholders in a flexible benefits scheme are:

- *Employees* – to be motivated employees must be properly led, informed and involved in the business. There will be no buy into flexible benefits if products and services are not marketed properly. Employees will not maintain interest if they are not 'cared for' (eg pre-and post-launch support).

- *System and product suppliers* – suppliers will fail to deliver consistently and at the right time, place and price if they are not engaged in a mutually beneficial partnership built on regular, honest contact.

- *Senior management* – they will only provide funds if presented with a sound proposition to them. The scheme needs to retain their confidence on an ongoing basis.

- *Company community* – goodwill and support depends on the perception created and influencing skills.

All of these groups effect and are affected by the communication process.

The challenge with communication is that it is affected by even the smallest comment made, very often out of context. It is, therefore, vital to understand how the various communication stakeholders will influence the strategy the company is developing.

Different people react in different ways to communication. It is important to understand that each individual and group reacts in his or her own unique way. Again, it is vital to understand this basic chemistry in the organisations unique situation.

Managing perception   10.5

As explained in the introduction above, communication these days is more about managing expectations and perceptions. Very often the reality of the situation is clouded by judgements based on the perception of those involved. To really understand communication you must first of all understand perception.

Perception is the active psychological process in which stimuli are selected and organised into meaningful patterns.

Normally this process is carried out instantaneously and without consciousness. It is a mental activity of processing information received through stimuli, selecting the important elements and applying the individual's perceptual framework to it.

Perceptual selectivity   10.6

The first two most important elements that determine our perceptual selectivity is a stimulus and the context in which it occurs. If employees are presented with a complex flexible benefit scheme during a period of great uncertainty then this may compound their concerns rather than alleviate them than if a different time was chosen. Other factors that affect perceptual selectivity are expectations (learning, motivation and personality) and past experience.

Past experience is an important issue when considering the communication of a flexible benefit scheme particularly if previous initiatives have not worked out or have stalled.

Influencing factors 10.7

Once an individual has selected the information they are going to consider they then will apply a series of other influencing factors before deciding on their reaction. These include:

- physical environment;
- psychological characters;
- needs;
- motives;
- goals;
- past experience; and
- social and cultural environment.

Needs, motives and goals are the main drivers behind the success of the flexible benefit scheme but if incorrectly managed can also work against it.

Stereotyping and the halo affect 10.8

The two most common consequences of this in terms of how people perceive others in the situation that they are in are:

- The halo affect – this is where, based on our perceptual world we attribute the benefit of the doubt to the information presented based on previous experience.
- Stereotyping – this is where, to save time, we assume that the information presented is similar to circumstances before.

The best way to explain how these two work together is to consider an individual crossing the road. To begin with all stimuli (sight, sound, smell, touch) are assessed but only those that are moving continue to remain in the conscious. For instance, if the car on the right hand side is not moving it quickly moves from our sub-conscious to our conscious.

As they try to cross the road in order to manage the multitude of information being gathered in, they will only respond to those stimuli that change. For instance, if the car does not move it will not register. If during the course of their journey, stimuli that are not moving change, then this will register (eg a car starts to move off).

This is the only way that we can safely cross the road and the same principle applies to the way we perceive any large amounts of information presented. If a communication is delivered in the same fashion and style, it becomes part of the background and is quickly ignored. To maintain employee interest in a flexible benefit scheme the organisation must continuously change the way information is presented.

This is used to a great effect by advertisers who use branding to influence individual choice. Colours, sounds and smell help to establish a background which is easily recognisable and immediately shifts the perspective set to that associated with it. For instance, the colour orange suggests a mobile phone or a low cost airline.

In a flexible benefits scheme this needs to be used to its maximum effect choosing the name of the scheme, the colours associated with the documentation etc, to create a brand that influences the perceptive set of the individual. Continually changing the format in which information is delivered helps to maintain the interest of the audience.

Proactive communication   10.9

Two-way dialogue is vital to ensure that employees clearly understand the decisions that they are making and accept responsibility for the consequences. Proactive communication, as the name suggests, is a two-way interactive dialogue between employer and employee.

It is based on being positive and mutually beneficial messages and ensures that situations are handled effectively because it empowers and enables individuals within the communication process. In a flexible benefit scheme, communication needs to be responsive to the company needs as well as employee demands, as communication is a powerful catalyst.

Effective communication skills   10.10

Effective communication skills are based on:

- clarity, consistency and openness;
- understanding the cycle of change;
- identifying where individuals, groups, departments, divisions and the organisation is on the cycle
- using communication to move people around the cycle;
- managing as a listener;
- supportive communication;
- using proactive communication to lead.

Using proactive communication   10.11

The key steps to using proactive communication to develop a flexible benefits scheme are:

- use communications to explore and decide where you want to be (feasibility study);
- use communication to find out where you are (feasibility study);
- use communication to manage the required actions to effectively install the new scheme;
- monitoring and feedback;
- clarity and simplicity;
- no use of complex words or phrases;
- plain English indicates clear thinking.

The main objective of effective communication is to manage expectations and perceptions. It would be ideal if the organisation could deliver a flexible benefit scheme that was beyond and above that what was expected. This entails establishing exactly what is expected from all stakeholders and what is required to exceed those expectations.

The key to this is to design a communication strategy (see **10.18** below) that is straight forward and not over complicated and does not involve any communication propaganda. It should be simple, interesting and solicit the response that the organisation has set out to generate.

Communicating at different levels 10.12

Each group of individuals interacts with and reacts to communication in a different way. Its behaviour is influenced by its own unique perception of the situation and the role that they will play within the flexible benefits scheme. Because of the nature of communication it is difficult to be precise in terms of the key points to consider when it comes to communicating at different levels, however, the following is a guide.

Senior management 10.13

The senior management team is interested in how the flexible benefits scheme will allow the organisation to achieve its main objectives and prosper. However, they are also potential members of the scheme.

They will need information to make their decision to invest in the new scheme as well as ongoing statistics to monitor progress. They need to be satisfied that all is proceeding well and that employees perceive the new scheme as a positive improvement in the recognition and reward that the organisation gives them.

Senior management will also be playing a pivotal role in terms of launching and facilitating this part of the scheme so they need to be communicated to in such a way that allows them to do this comfortably. Senior management may also have obligations to ensure that legislation is being adhered to and financial reporting is correct.

Employees 10.14

The majority of this chapter concentrates on formal communication with employees. However, it is important to ensure that the strategy allows the organisation to 'walk the talk' to ensure proper education and buy in. The messages delivered must be consistent to ensure no ambiguity and misinterpretation of information.

The scheme managers must learn to listen, be brave and trust the communicators and react to constructive criticism. In a sense they need to dress the part to reinforce the brand that is beginning to develop.

System and benefit suppliers   10.15

These suppliers will be key to the successful administration of the new scheme. Communication processes should help to build and reinforce the relationships with them and, in the sense, treat them like customers. Very often a good relationship built on good communication can yield advantages, such as free additional services and marketing.

Financial   10.16

As with most projects in an organisation, the flexible benefits scheme needs to generate reports that allow the monitoring of progress against the original plan. This reporting should be structured and proactive as well as accurate and clear.

For those organisations that have put a flexible benefits scheme in to reinforce shareholder value, it is even more important to feed back the progress of the flexible benefit scheme as a value added exercise and one that will improve market value.

Regular financial monitoring of costs are important because they will encourage the senior management to continue to endorse and support the scheme over many years to come. It may be that in the second or third year extra funds will be required to introduce a novel product area or upgrade the systems and infrastructure to cater with more members.

Community   10.17

Every organisation is a community in itself and also belongs to a wider one. Modern managements strive to improve the image of the organisation in both the local and wider business community and, indirectly, encourage a perception of best employer.

The community may even contribute to the flexible benefit scheme. For instance, the local leisure centre may provide some of the services. This in turn gives an opportunity, through good communication, to promote the image of the organisation on a wider basis.

Developing an integrated communications strategy   10.18

When developing a communications strategy it is important, first of all, to recognise the difference between informal and formal communication. The grapevine in any organisation is the most powerful form of delivering messages, however, it is the most uncontrollable. It can work for or against but either way it cannot be ignored.

A good communication strategy should acknowledge this powerful catalyst rather than trying to exploit it. For instance, if the flexible benefits scheme is being launched in several sites, then emphasis should be placed on the first presentation going well to ensure that the message spreads in advance of the next one held at another site.

The most powerful form of formal communication is a one-to-one meeting. In an ideal world this would be the best way to educate individuals and promote the flexible benefits scheme. However, in reality there is not enough time to do this and the process would be costly.

The closer you can mimic this 'one-to-one' philosophy the better the communication strategy will be. For instance, one of the advantages of having an interactive web based scheme is that individuals can interrogate the system, ask their own individual questions and work out their own options in their own way.

Announcement   10.19

The usual strategy adopted with a flexible benefits scheme is to begin the process by sending out a letter to individuals, informing them that the company is considering a new initiative in terms of employee benefits. As with advertising this notice does not contain any answers but merely states the intent of the organisation to do something.

Over the course of the next few weeks, publishing regular articles in the in-house magazine supplement this, or memos sent out to employees, setting the scene for the launch of the new scheme. These tend to start off fairly simplistic and gradually build up more detail. This is a process adopted by advertisers and helps individuals adjust to a new way of thinking, allowing them to take on board an increasing amount of information.

Next, a letter or memo is sent inviting them to the launch of the new scheme. This should be the only time that the organisation tries to sell the concept to their employees. Beyond this, the process should be one of making an informed decision.

Launch 10.20

The launch itself should be tailored to the unique culture of the organisation. If the company has a fairly cynical workforce then a glitzy road show (presentations etc) would be more of an opportunity to make fun of the process than to learn from it. However, if the workforce is fairly easy going, such an event may be the best way forward.

Whichever the situation the organisation must make sure that the road show encourages people to attend and also to listen. It is more important for employees to clearly understand what their options are and the consequences then it is to choose a benefit without any thought.

The prime objective of a road show is:

● to introduce individuals to the scheme; and

● make them aware of how it will work;

● the process involved in making choices;

● the products available and their costs;

● the tax treatment on the scheme; and

● how this will affect their individual rights and contracts.

The length of the presentation should be no longer than an hour. Product providers should be encouraged to set up stalls around the edge of the presentation so that individuals can find out more information about their products. This ensures that the presentation does not become boring or tedious with individual products and detail.

The whole of the above strategy needs to be endorsed by the senior management. It is their responsibility to ensure that the product is tried and tested and the organisation has their buy in before the first road show/presentation. If the company sets up a communication working party at the beginning of the project including several members of the senior management team, this process will be easier.

Surgeries and helplines 10.21

Usually as a result of the presentation, the majority of employees will have a clear understanding of what is on offer, the process and how to go about making their choices. However, there may be a small amount of people that still need further help. Running a series of surgeries and/or helplines can provide this help. The amount of time available and resources usually dictates the level of this support.

Communication catalyst 10.22

The success of the above process is very much dependent on the company's choice of individuals to run it. When choosing the communication catalysts, the first thing is to consider is who the most respective communicators are in the organisation. These are usually people who are quite willing to voice their concerns about a project as well as their endorsement. Employees will feel that their opinion is unbiased.

Although it may seem a good idea to have the most positive people as the communicators, it will not help if they have the reputation of agreeing with everything. They need to be able to back up what they are saying with intellectual debate and the company must ensure a contingency plan is in place to cater with any comments they may have.

At the end of the day it is the mix of people that will be the success of the strategy.

Key tasks, action points and target dates 10.23

Just like the discussion on project management in **5.1** above, the communication strategy needs to have a plan of action (time scales, key tasks and responsibilities). Because it is the most unpredictable element of the scheme it must be closely managed and monitored.

Communications as a whole should already be on the management agenda. If it is not then the introduction of the flexible benefits scheme may act as a catalyst for this to happen.

Sometimes the introduction of a flexible benefits scheme has to be delayed to allow the management to develop on overall communication strategy and implement it and sometimes the flexible benefits scheme provides the vehicle for this to happen.

Culture   10.24

Good communication should be instinctive and the flexible benefits scheme should support this and underpin the key corporate messages that have already been delivered in the organisation. The style, language and branding of the scheme should closely reflect those of the organisation.

For instance, if one of the key themes flowing through the organisation at the time of the launch is quality control then the flexible benefit scheme must also major on quality control. The worst thing that could happen is if the flexible benefits scheme was perceived to be lacking in terms of quality control at the same time as the organisation is insisting on it as a core competency.

As well as the organisation's communications strategy there should be individual strategies that help to drive all the above through. For instance, the relationship with a supplier should ensure that their levels of communication are at least equal to those of the organisation. If the company is issuing a fairly in depth employee handbook the provider should also supply the same quality and level of information.

Feedback and modification   10.25

The last part of developing an integrated communication strategy is to develop systems and procedures that allow the close monitoring of the current situation. The organisation should not be afraid to correct its communication strategy and modify it as a reaction to the information obtained. For instance, if the initial feedback from the scheme launch is that the bulk of employees do not understand the scheme, then clearly the organisation needs to address this. This could be through a relaunch of the scheme or placing greater emphasis on promoting the follow up surgeries. This will ensure that employees will have a second chance to find out about the products and services.

The use of technology   10.26

Technology is there to assist and enhance the flexible benefit scheme, not to dictate it. Technology is topical and grabs the headlines but is no good without a focused and considered strategy supporting it.

The gains cannot always be quantified in money terms. Organisations should take into account intangible gains, for example positive staff motivation and brand image.

Before deciding how to use technology to communicate, it is necessary to consider and decide 'who, what, where and when'? Answers to these will steer the organisation towards the correct 'how'?'

Target audience 10.27

When deciding who their target audience is going to be, organisations must consider the following points.

- Who would their information be relevant to?

  ☐ Pensions information would be of more interest to older staff rather than new graduates.

  ☐ Younger staff would probably like to see links to non-work based sites, whilst those with family might like to be steered towards seeing their financial information from all sources to give the wider picture.

- What is the employee's technical profile?

  ☐ Are they likely to be comfortable using technology to reference information?

  ☐ Do they have the required technology readily available?

- What are the overall flexible benefit aims?

  ☐ To attract people to the company?

  ☐ To retain and focus on current staff?

  ☐ To maintain contact with past employees and provide a long-term contact point?

What is going to be communicated? 10.28

Information is the primary content, but there are different ways to offer it:

- Produce electronic versions of current hard-copy information (but do not just duplicate it exactly without thinking of the usability factors).

- Collate or link to different sources for topics that might be of interest.

- Pre-empt up and coming issues (be proactive not reactive).

- Offer electronic contact via email for queries and questions (this will ease the pressure on the helpline).

- Present the company as the organisation would like to be perceived.

- If focusing on current staff, introduce a complete package including an overall financial and/or lifestyle monitoring.

Where and when to introduce technology   10.29

This is very much dependant on the company ethos:

- Is time spent not working on company issues seen as wasted?

- Getting employees to actively use technology by introducing non-work related items, can improve the core skills of your staff. Address 'moderation' and 'monitoring' to ensure it does not get out of hand.

- Everyone has a life that cannot always be managed out of office hours. Acknowledging this and offering a solution that meets employees half way can be a positive HR exercise, for instance, considering standalone PCs in a segregated environment.

- Employees will initially need some support but this will reduce quickly.

Home use of PCs and the intranet is expanding, but not as quickly throughout all age groups. Consider your target audience:

- PCs in the home are more actively used than links via the television scenario.

- Families with children will invariably be introducing technology at home because it is an increasing requirement for education.

- Companies need to consider what then happens when employees leave.

How to introduce technology   10.30

An Intranet is an excellent way to test the idea(s). It is within the companies control and they have a 'captive audience' to trail various scenarios and get feedback. The main points to bear in mind are:

- Companies should not just keep to work-related information; they should introduce some topical but carefully considered general items.

- They should make sure there is a dynamic mechanism to encourage two-way dialogue.

- They should promote it and get buy in across the employees and management.

- Cost can be contained (small and simple is often best anyway), introduction should be at a steady pace and not an 'all or nothing' solution.

- Technology is always changing so organisations should not get caught up in constant upgrading or waiting for the right moment.

- If they are out of their normal field of expertise, companies should seek expert advice. It is a complex area and can be costly if not thought through.

Security   10.31

There are plenty of people who spend all their time trying to break into websites. It is a fact of life and companies should ensure that:

- security is a main consideration and depends on content;

- there is adequate cost provisions dependant on hosting in-house or externally;

- content should be kept up to date and timescales for upgrades should be kept as short as possible; and

- any password security used to access the system is effective and robust.

A popular password nowadays is to let employees choose, say, three text strings (eg pet's name, father's date of birth, mother's maiden name) and put these together into a single string. Then every time they log on, they will be asked for differently numbered characters from this string (eg 3rd, 10th and 15th characters).

Key issues to consider   10.32

Companies should concentrate on producing a site that is focused and speedy, that has a simple quick mechanism in place for updating

214

current and adding new content. Time spent at the planning stage is worth it in the long term. Technology should have its own strategy.

Companies should not underestimate the ongoing overhead for password entry. Various options exist for password entry; they should consider their target audience. They should match the security to the actual risk, taking care not overdo it, but make a conscious decision on what is necessary.

Disclaimers are crucial. Companies must ensure employees are given a clear picture of the accuracy of (or the reliance to place on) the information provided.

Companies should state clearly that it is the hard copy of documentation that is legally binding, if they offer an electronic version, it must be made obvious that the employee should refer to the hard copy before making decisions, etc.

Although electronic signatures are now technically 'legal' in some situations, it has not been sufficiently challenged in court yet to know what issues this will give rise to. So companies should tread carefully still.

Employees assimilate information in different ways and so it is good to present information on the site in more than one way. Some web-based sites allow employees to tailor their access screens. For example, include all documentation in full via menus and catalogue pages. Then also think about the questions the employee would ask and present the answers by pulling together the various segments distributed around the site.

Employee financial counselling 10.33

Employees' benefit packages are complex and often involve choices to be made at different stages of an employee's career. Traditionally, employees have taken 'core' benefits for granted because, to all intents and purposes, they were out of their control and their perceived benefits long term.

By introducing a flexible benefits scheme, the company will be moving the emphasis of ownership for control and management of benefits from the employer to the employee. Because of this and to ensure that the perceived advantages of a flexible benefit scheme are reinforced, education through employee financial counselling, on a structured basis, will be vital.

The key stages of setting up these processes are:

- Agree format of financial counselling surgeries.

- Set up individual consultations to allow employees to enter the scheme in the most appropriate manner, eg make an informed decision about the initial mix of benefit they require.

- Agree and set up a regular review process for employees, eg agree frequency and level of support.

- Agree parameters for extraordinary consultation eg changes in lifestyle, such as bereavement.

- Agree format and frequency for annual surgeries to update staff on scheme changes, changes in legislation etc.

Communication checklist 10.34

The communication stage of designing and implementing a flexible benefits scheme is complex, to say the least. Most companies work to a pre-determined checklist. The following is an example:

- **Design unique brand and style:**
    - ☐ research and employee profiling;
    - ☐ product – to suit the organisations needs;
    - ☐ name – the foundation stone;
    - ☐ format for literature.

- **Proactive communication:**
    - ☐ based on internal marketing, not just issuing information;
    - ☐ top team endorsements;
    - ☐ identify and use current communication strategy;
    - ☐ employee communication;
    - ☐ two way communication;
    - ☐ education is top priority;
    - ☐ responsive plan.

- **What needs communicating?**

  - ☐ benefit options;

  - ☐ implications of personal choice, eg tax;

  - ☐ branding;

  - ☐ the values of your organisation, reinforcing employer brand;

  - ☐ mergers and acquisitions;

  - ☐ honesty;

  - ☐ employees must clearly understand their options and take responsibility for their decisions.

- **Who is being communicating to?**

  - ☐ top team;

  - ☐ executive committee;

  - ☐ management structure;

  - ☐ team talks;

  - ☐ employees;

  - ☐ potential employees;

  - ☐ shareholders;

  - ☐ marketplace (including product suppliers).

- **What media can be used?**

  - ☐ internal marketing literature;

  - ☐ announcement letters;

  - ☐ scheme handbook;

  - ☐ in-house magazine;

  - ☐ launch meetings;

  - ☐ management meetings;

  - ☐ theme and branding as product;

  - ☐ electronic;

  - ☐ presentations.

- **Who will be the communicator?**

  - ☐ Who are the most respected communicators?

217

- ☐ Who are the most positive?
- ☐ Who are the most negative?
- ☐ What is the right mix?
- ☐ Avoid Chinese whispers.

- **Timing:**
  - ☐ company strategy;
  - ☐ must be integrated elements of business plan;
  - ☐ pre-launch meetings and adaptations;
  - ☐ management and employee input;
  - ☐ launch;
  - ☐ taking into account annual pay rises, holiday periods, etc;
  - ☐ monitoring, feedback and adaptation.

- **Overcoming communication difficulties:**
  - ☐ suspicion;
  - ☐ 'the best way to upset someone is to mess with their money';
  - ☐ perception;
  - ☐ involvement;
  - ☐ knowing your audience is knowing they aren't you;
  - ☐ people at different life stages need different methods of communication;
  - ☐ decide what to say, and say it three times;
  - ☐ don't oversell;
  - ☐ be honest;
  - ☐ if there is an overall reduction in the companies benefits budget, say so, at least employees now have choice;
  - ☐ the message is more important than the medium;
  - ☐ overused e-mail? Try paper.

- **After the launch:**
  - ☐ monitoring;
  - ☐ questionnaires;

- [ ] one to one meetings;
- [ ] communicate successes back to members;
- [ ] adapt and add to system once running smoothly.

Help is at hand with

www.pensionsPro.com

See how much time and money you could save.
Visit www.pensionsPro.com for your *no obligation 7-day trial*.
Alternatively call our online sales team on **020 8686 9141 ext. 5233**.
Please quote reference W27.

pensionsPro is an online site dedicated to providing comprehensive, authoritative, accurate and up-to-date information for pensions professionals.

The site provides a unique range of online business tools, giving an unsurpassed wealth of information and official materials, together with guidance and interpretation written and updated by experts in the industry. This means that you have all the information you need in one place – saving you time and money, whilst being assured of accuracy and quality.

To give you ultimate flexibility, there are several subscription modules available. For more information and/or to take-up our no obligation trial, please complete and return the form below.

☐ **I would like to take up your no obligation 7-day trial**
☐ **I would like more information**

Title _____ Name _____

Surname _____

Email _____

Job Title_____

Company _____

Town _____

Country _____ Postcode _____

Telephone_____ Facsimile _____

One site, all the answers

2

Caroline Berry
Butterworths Tolley
2 Addiscombe Road
Croydon
Surrey
CR9 5ZX

See how much time and money you could save.
Visit www.pensionsPro.com for your *no obligation 7-day trial*.

www.pensionspro.com

One site, all the answers

11 — Management and Administration

This chapter includes:

- Introduction
- Basic administration process
- Organisational requirements
- Integration with other systems
- Setting up the management and administration system
- System options
- Web-based administration systems
- Administration audit

Introduction   11.1

The administration of flexible benefits can be complex, time consuming and expensive and is often cited as the major barrier to choosing such a scheme. However, the effective use of technology now offers the opportunity to alleviate historical and administrative problems. It is important that a realistic appraisal of a company's capabilities is carried out during the feasibility study in order that the best solution can be implemented.

One of the key objectives of the new scheme may be rationalisation and/or harmonisation of existing benefits administration. If this is an area where cost savings have been identified, then this must be the overriding factor in any design or implementation.

There are basically two options for the organisation to administer a flexible benefits scheme – in-house administration and outsourcing administration.

In-house administration 11.2

The advantage of keeping administration in-house is the flexibility and control that the company derives. The starting point for the successful management of administration is a database of personnel records that is accurate and contains sufficient information about employees.

Companies that run administration in-house often use specialist software to help them perform the day-to-day functions. Accuracy of records on the personnel database is essential, as it will be used to pre-populate enrolment forms and other documents.

Outsourcing administration 11.3

The nature of a flexible benefits scheme is such that there are inevitable 'bottle necks' at inception and each renewal, when the amount of paperwork and administration is substantially greater than at any other time of year.

Outsourcing administration to a third party avoids the problem of having to deal with the disruption that this causes to the business. One of the major factors that will drive a company's decision will be the experience of their staff in handling benefits administration.

Those with relatively little experience may find comfort in relying on the resources of a third-party administration centre, whilst those used to administration may find the loss of control inhibiting.

See further CHAPTER 12.

Basic administration functions 11.4

Before choosing which option, the employer needs to consider the administration functions that need to be performed. These include.

- producing personalised enrolment forms;

- processing employees' choices;

- producing statements confirming benefit choices;

- providing member details to benefit providers;

- providing details of leavers to benefit providers;

- liaising with payroll department/external payroll bureau;

- providing P11D details;

- liaising with product providers.

Basic administration process 11.5

The diagram in Figure 1 below is a typical process chart for a flexible benefits scheme. Because each scheme is unique there is no definitive process but this illustration contains most of the elements required. Although, in this illustration the scheme booklet and preference form are shown outside the administration system, for most modern schemes they are part and parcel of the technology.

In essence the administration system consists of inputs, process and outputs. It needs to be accessed by two main groups of people, administrators and employees. It also needs to send information to other parts of the organisation such as payroll and HR, as well as product providers.

Administrators need access to the system to be able to correspond with employees and generate reports. They also need to be able to add joiners and delete leavers as well as making mid-term adjustments for lifestyle changes.

They will be responsible for authorising and changing requests, and generating the monthly payroll file as well as ensuring premiums payable to providers are actioned.

Employees need access to the system to be able to look at the products available and understand their entitlements. The administration system needs to be able to cope with both core benefits and flexible benefits as they are usually part of the same scheme.

Most flexible benefit schemes now have an intuitive interface that allows individuals to customise their access to the scheme to make it user-friendly.

As well as product information and purchase options, employees will also need to understand their salary sacrifice limit, running totals and Inland Revenue limits, (eg pension contributions).

The administration system needs to have a fairly robust audit trail for troubleshooting and quality control.

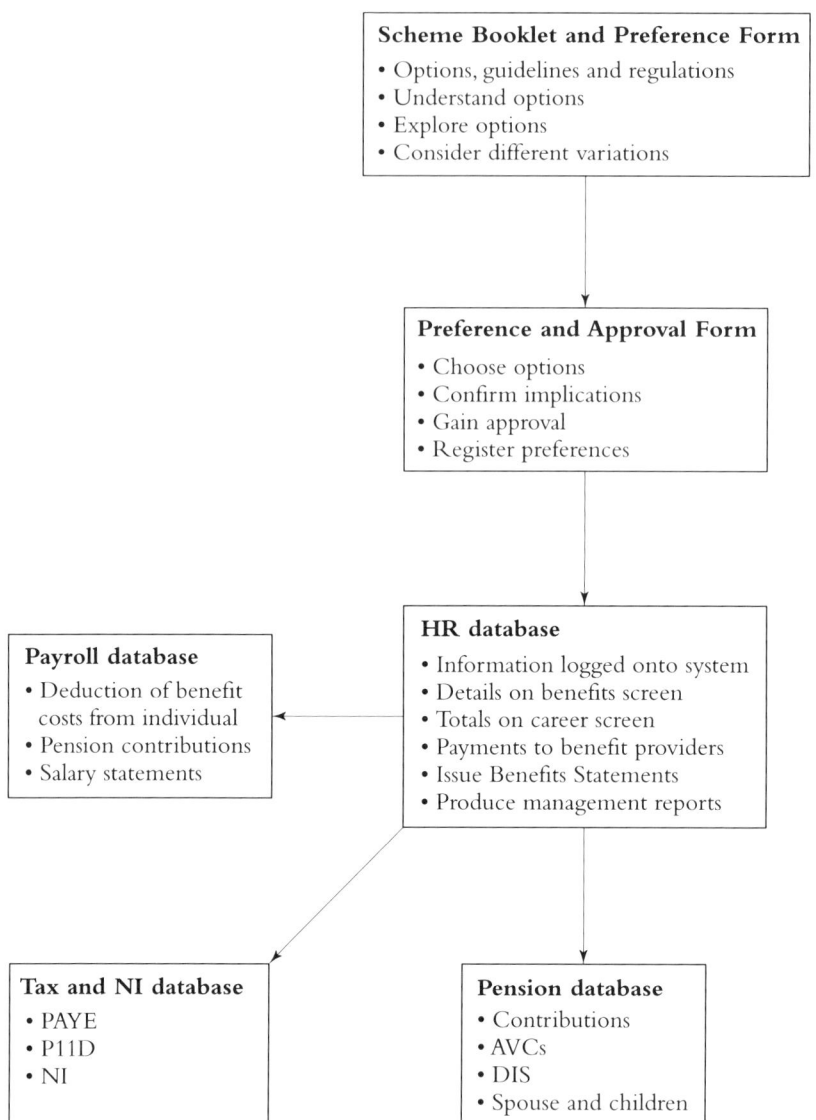

Figure 1: Flexible benefits – Typical process flowchart

Other systems in the company will also need modifying to cope with the new flexible benefits scheme. For instance, the payroll system will have to be modified to cater for a shadow salary as well as the existing contractual salary calculations.

Note: This chart details the basic process of individual selection, calculation, approval and processing of flexible benefit options. It assumes that a scheme booklet and professional preference form has been produced which contains costings for each option along with limits on selection.

Inputs 11.6

The main inputs in to the processing part of the administration system for a flexible benefit scheme are product and employee data.

Product inputs include elements such as options, entitlement and pricing. They are processed in such a way that employees can model their choices and the administrator can process them easily and effectively.

Employee input includes elements such as personnel data, job details and benefit entitlement. Reporting filters are often included to make it easier to monitor and control groups of individuals. For instance, this could be an analytical evaluation of employees by department.

Calculation and processing 11.7

The system takes the above input and applies the rules, regulations and guidelines (outlined in previous chapters)**CHAPTER 3**) to produce a set of outputs that can then generate the necessary action. For instance, the employee may choose to trade some of his or her salary to increase holiday leave; the system calculates what this means in monetary terms and produces a set of outputs that allows money to be deducted from payroll and added to holiday entitlement. At the same time, outputs are sent to the tax and National Insurance (NI) database to enable Inland Revenue calculations to be processed.

Outputs 11.8

The main two outputs from the system are employee and administration access. This enables effective two-way communication. Because most systems are now based on employee self service, an output is required to enable them to enroll on the benefit plan. Outputs are also required when changes are made by individual employees because of a life event change (see **5.39** above) or leaving or joining the organisation. The interface with payroll is important not only to ensure deduction of benefit costs from individuals but also to facilitate calculations based on both contractual gross pay and payroll gross pay.

As with any such complex initiative an important output from the system will be reporting and managing information. This is required as part of the management audit of the system and to ensure the flexible benefits scheme is reaching its desired objectives.

As explained in **9.6** above, benefit statements are required post and pre-enrolment. Obviously the system needs to generate these in a consistent and accurate manner.

Product providers will require outputs that tell them which employees have chosen which combination of benefits. These outputs also will allow the organisation to calculate premiums payable and manage any adjustments required at the end of the year due to leavers, joiners, life event changes etc.

The final part of the system output is an employee directory and audit trail that will allow the administrator to manage the overall set up and quality of the scheme.

Organisational requirements   11.9

Over and above that detailed previously the administration system will need to cater for inputs and outputs from five other areas within the organisation:

- payroll – deductions, pension contributions and salary statements;

- tax and NI – PAYE, P11D, and NICs;

- pensions – contributions, AVCs, DIS and dependants;

- HR – personal data, job details, reporting filters, benefits, reward details and career details;

- management audit.

Integration with other systems   11.10

Depending on which system the organisation chooses, the interface with other databases will either be electronically or via normal forms of communication. Whatever the choice, they will require the same data and information to be able to process the employees' choice.

These will include employee data, enrollment data, payment data and entitlement as well as information on leavers, joiners and those opting for a life event change. The timing and accuracy of this information will affect the overall administration of the flexible benefit scheme.

The best form of interface between separate databases is electronic. This means a seamless flow of information that is instantaneous and does not require any intervention.

In a totally integrated system, were HR, payroll, flexible benefits, P11D and management accounts are all part of one system, the administration process is automated. This requires fewer personnel to administer and support the process.

At the other end of the scale, the database may be totally separate and unable to communicate at all, even via common spreadsheets such as Excel. Here information has to be printed out from one database and manually inputted into another. This is time consuming, open to inaccuracy and requires extra personnel.

Although the first example is clearly the best alternative, it is also the more expensive. However, the introduction of a flexible benefit scheme may be a catalyst for the organisation to review the whole of its HR system and infrastructure.

A more common form of interface is to link the separate databases with a common spreadsheet manager. This downloads output from one database into, say, Excel and then uploads it back into the other, having converted it into the appropriate language.

Which ever combination is chosen, the interface between the flexible benefit administration system with the other database is vital and should be dealt with early on in the project design and strategy.

Setting up the management and administration system   11.11

The management and administration of a flexible benefits scheme is more of a co-ordination of resources rather than a process. This is due in the main to the assumption that each individual benefit provider will administer each of its own individual databases including registration, ongoing support etc.

As the organisation will probably have existing IT systems covering payroll, P11D, HR etc, the first objective is to determine how best to fit in the new scheme's systems. This will have been covered in the feasibility study (see **4.1** above) at the beginning of the project. Planning at this stage will also be affected by the choices of the organisation to either run the scheme in-house or to outsource it to a third party provide (see **12.24** below).

Whichever route is chosen there are several actions that need to be taken. The first of these is to define and set the service standard for all parts of the flexible benefits scheme. For instance, the turn–around time from enrollment to the generation of a new benefit statement.

At the commencement of the project, the organisation needs to put together an administration manual covering working practices, methods of transmission of data etc. Not only will this save time in the long run but will also act as a double check for the processes being developed.

A management accounting system needs to be set up to ensure relevant and accurate information is provided to the senior management team and accounting department. This information will be used, for instance, to determine the cash flow required to fund the scheme.

Employees' benefit records may have been set up on an existing database but will now have to be modified to reflect the new entitlement for each individual. It may be that the current HR system, where traditionally benefits have been managed, requires a new separate screen to show the flexible benefit choices.

As mentioned above, there is a requirement to ensure processing of payments to the benefit providers from the organisation. But thereThere isalso a need to ensure that whatever payments are due direct from employees,employees (ie not from payroll deduction have at leastdeduction) have also been flagged up. If this part of the system is automated it will save time later and reduce the onus on the organisation to chase up individual payments.

The final part of setting up the management and administration process is to define the parameters by which this scheme is going to be measured and monitored.

Administration staff will require training well in advance of the system going live from the systems providers to enable them to 'troubleshoot' as well as manage the process.

System options   11.12

There are a number of ways that a flexible benefits scheme can be set up:

- paper based;
- voice response system;
- computer based;
- web based.

Paper-based enrolment   11.13

This has been the traditional method used. The process of producing an enrolment form for each employee can be simplified by using software to interface with the company's personnel record system.

The result is, typically, a form which is pre-populated with an employee's personal details, their flex fund and the cost of each option. One of the benefits of using a paper-based enrolment system is that it is the cheapest and easiest way of reaching all employees as it is not reliant on access to PCs.

Whilst the mass production of enrolment forms can be achieved relatively easily, the administration of completed forms can involve a vast amount of data input, which is both time consuming and expensive.

Voice response system   11.14

To avoid the need to key in the choices of employees, some companies have introduced telephone systems, which allow staff to register using a touch-tone telephone. These choices are then linked in with the flexible benefits administration system.

Computer-based enrolment   11.15

With the use of PCs becoming widespread both in the workplace and at home, access to technology allows employees to model their benefits 'online'.

The availability of an Intranet is important in making online choices widely available within a company, however, the use of 'PC booths' is an alternative for employees who do not have exclusive use of a PC. There are also developments in software that allows employees to access their benefits over the Intranet; this gives the added benefit of enabling choices to be made at home. This is covered in more detail **11.16** below.

Employees access their benefits file by entering their personal ID and password, which gives confidentiality over personal information. They are then able to look at various scenarios by choosing different levels of benefits.

When they are happy with their choices they are submitted electronically, avoiding the need for production of a significant amount of paper. Their saved choices are stored and can be accessed by employees throughout the year, thus forming an electronic benefits 'handbook'.

Employing such technology will clearly add to the overall cost of the project but longer-term cost savings need to be taken into account. Providing information about the scheme and each of the benefits in an electronic format may replace the need for a scheme guide and there will certainly be substantial ongoing savings in administration time and costs as a result of the functionality of such systems. Obviously compatibility with existing company systems and networks is essential and the use of technology needs to be built into the initial stages of any project.

Web-based administration systems 11.16

There is a growing interest and demand for web-based administration systems. This is an illustration of a typical flexible administration system.

The principle of the Internet (and Intranet) is a web of communication lines connecting together servers at multiple locations. In order to make information, applications, etc available on the Internet, the minimum requirements are a server to host the data and the necessary connection in to the Internet via an Internet Service Provider (ISP). The cost of this is minimal as is the reliability and security it provides. Therefore, all a hosting service provides is a server and Internet link. This can be done by the company providing the servers, security and the Internet links to an ISP to 'host' their applications and data internally or by the use of a third-party provider to supply some, or all, of these services. There are a number of issues, however, to consider when looking at hosting services which have considerable impact on the service provided and on the resultant cost.

The Process Chart illustrated in Figure 2 below is based on an administration system set up for a web-based flexible benefits scheme. The system itself has a series of inputs based on product and employee data which is then processed to generate a series of outputs which are interfaced with other parts of the organisations system and product providers.

There are two levels of access: employee and administrator. These allow both to access the system from a remote location via the Internet or Intranet (if a stand-alone in-house system).

Outputs are fed to product providers, payroll, tax and NI, pensions, HR and management audit. There are also other links to product providers who are introducing their products rather than selling them, for instance, share schemes, personal lease plans etc. These interface links can be web enabled or if the technology does not exist, they can be down loaded into portable files such as Excel which can then be uploaded into payroll, pensions, tax etc.

Key unique features 11.17

The key unique system features of this particular example are:

- ease of administration and effective software;
- fixed, flexible and mixed benefit scheme set up in one administration;
- employee communication simplified;
- employee self-service;
- provision of benefit statements, costs and entitlement;
- centralised reporting and management information;
- total remuneration statements;
- employee directory and other added value options;
- report generation, available by product/providers selected and premiums payable;
- adding joiners and deleting leavers;
- mid-term adjustments;
- authorising change requests;

- generating monthly payroll file

- on-line support including users, guide, troubleshooting systems and frequently asked questions;

- secrecy function enables user to hide/show the confidential information when using the systems;

- HR links gives access to the employee handbook/schedule for easy maintenance;

- all forms can easily be obtained from the system;

- value indicators on products easy to use and effective.

From an employee perspective the key unique features are:

- the ability at any time of the year to log in and see selections;

- stakeholder information allows employees to keep track as frequently as required;

- total remuneration feature shows an individual's 'financial worth' to the company;

- links such as shares schemes show share price and worth of any options/share schemes/private holdings;

- form filling is minimum;

- employees can see salary moving up and down in line with the benefits chosen;

Being web based, an additional option that could be developed is to offer a series of products not directly linked to the scheme and available on an introduced basis. This can be accessed and chosen at any time rather than as a once-a-year basis only.

Key issues   11.18

Although this type of system offers many advantages there are several areas that will require close attention. These areas are summarised below.

Security   11.19

As the Internet is open to anyone with a PC and connection to the Internet, any data held on the Internet is open to all unless it is made secure. Similarly, any network connected to the back of the server

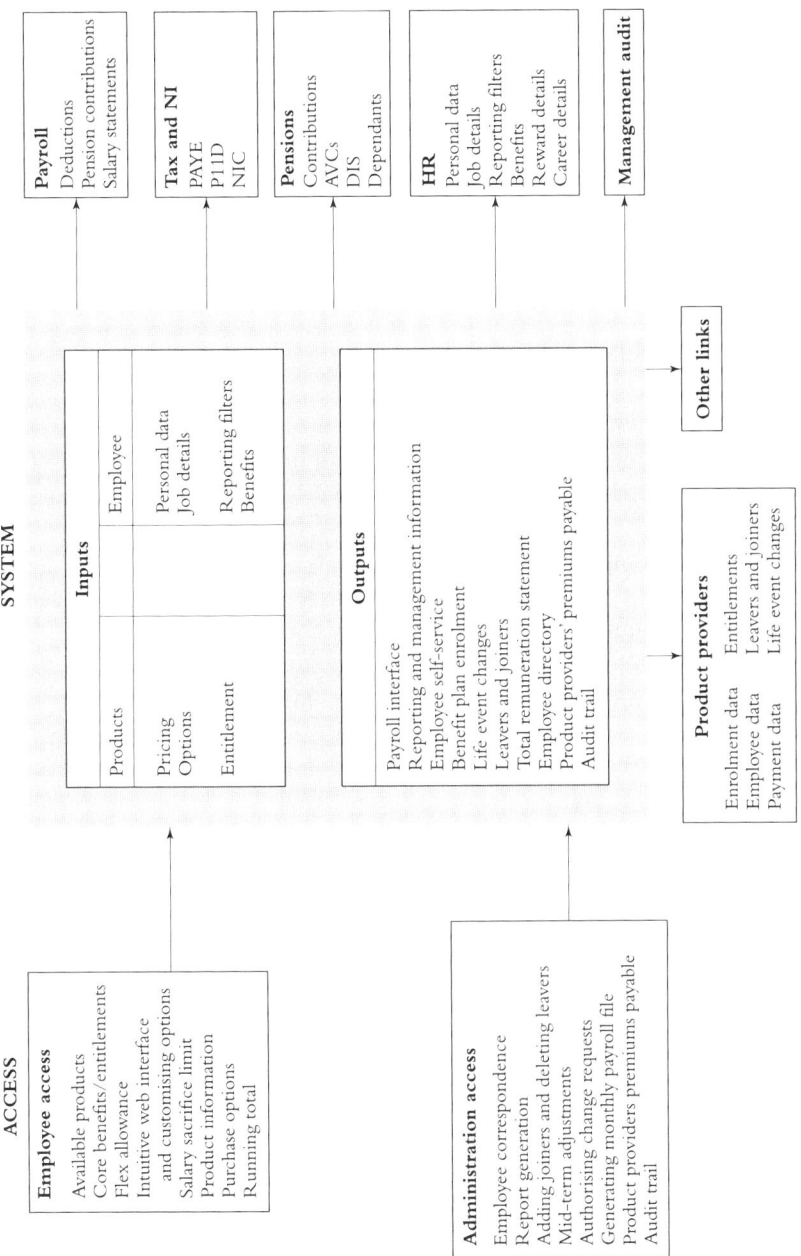

Figure 2: Web-based flexible benefits scheme – process chart

hosting an Internet application is open and accessible to a user on the Internet unless protection is in place.

The frequency of hackers and attacks on company networks (commercial, malicious and frivolous) is already high and on the increase in order to gain confidential data, to damage that data and cause embarrassment to companies. Organisations are also required by the *Data Protection Act 1998* to ensure the security of data.

There are, therefore, two areas that companies need to protect when looking at web hosting:

● internal data, networks and applications; and

● external data and information.

Data can be co-hosted on servers, ie the hosting company can share several different companies application and data over one server or each company can have its own server/s.

Security is provided by 'Firewalls', which is a software to control access to the systems, routers which are hardware control, and the segregation of data either on the main server or separate servers.

Ideally, the company should use different firewalls and router segregation between separate, servers. If using a third part to host the system, then separation of their data from other companies would by the use of separate server/s and in secure locations from that hosted on behalf of other companies.

Reliability 11.20

As data is on the Internet it is potentially accessible 24 hours a day and 7 days a week. There is a growing expectation to be able to access records at any time. This compares to most internal systems which are only in general use 8:00 am to 6:00 pm, Monday to Friday. This 24/7 working does not allow down time to carry out backups, correct problems, replace and upgrade hardware and carry out normal house-keeping.

When specifying a provider, companies should stipulate levels of 'up time', however the higher they are, the higher the cost. This can be achieved by using multiple servers, building in greater levels of redundancy and mirroring data. This helps in response to time but also allows one server to be taken down for maintenance, backups etc and guarantee core hours of access.

Support of the hardware and system can be managed via the hosting company to ensure the servers are backed up, that they are running and performing as expected and provide maintenance, and monitoring in a proactive way, or the organisation can be responsible for support themselves. In the second case, it would be more reactive, dependent on noticing the service was not available and then repairing the fault.

Companies also need to consider the stability of the hosting service provider, many of the smaller companies appear and disappear overnight, and have no concern over service levels. However, the size of the company is not necessarily a guarantee of continued existence. The bigger five are BT, WorldCom, Cable & Wireless, EasyNet and Energis. At lease two of these have 'question marks' over their longer-term survival.

Speed of service   **11.21**

The speed of access to the systems and the number of concurrent employees and administrators able to access the systems depends on the size and speed of the network link. Speed is also dependent on the power and number of the processors and servers in relation to the number of users. Both are key to the perception of employees in relation to the success of the scheme.

Selecting the right mix   **11.22**

Companies have a matrix of choice where they can pitch their requirements in relation to what they want and the demands of their scheme. As the data is highly confidential, if authorised access or publication occurs, a strong level of security is recommended to protect the data on the Internet and protect internal network.

This is particularly so where the Internet front-end application has to connect back in to the internal network and systems to access live data. Organisations need not only Internet security, but also enhanced internal security.

Companies need multiple servers to facilitate maintenance and provide a guaranteed level of service during the normal working day. This will grow if they extend access outside of normal hours on a guaranteed basis. They will also need a managed service to monitor for, and respond to, faults.

Access bandwidth needs to acceptable from day one but can grow with demand. The structure needed must not only allow for the initial requirements, but be configured in such a way as to adaptable to meet future growth and demand.

Choice of system 11.23

The choice of system to administer the flexible benefits scheme depends on a multitude of variables. The feasibility study will have given some indication as to the most appropriate method for the organisation based on balancing cost, complexity/simplicity usability and ease of implementation.

Other factors may also influence the choice of administration system such as employee access to PCs, existing technology and resources required to manage a complete set up.

For some organisations who already have an existing and well advanced integrated HR payroll and benefits system the best alternative may be to design an in-house process that links these all together. This link may be paperbased, electronically linked or reliant on exchange of down-loaded information.

For other organisations where the existing technology for payroll and HR would be completely swamped by any new technology for the flexible benefits scheme, it may be prudent to scale down the level of technology required for the flexible benefits scheme to allow the existing ones to catch up. On the other hand, the organisation may decided that the flexible benefit scheme offers an ideal opportunity to modernise, streamline and rationalise the antiquated HR, payroll and P11D systems.

Because each organisation is different and each flexible benefit scheme has its own unique requirements, it is virtually impossible to compare one generic type of system with another. A paper-based system may be simple and cheap to install but in the long run costs more because of the resources required to handle the various pieces of information than a web-based product.

The best way of choosing an administration system is to first of all evaluate what already exists and then compare it to the ideal solution for the new flexible benefits scheme. The process then becomes one of bridging the gap and then justifying the cost, resources and time required for each individual component in relation to the value it adds to the scheme.

Administration audit   11.24

Any form of administration system needs to be audited on a regular basis to ensure maximum efficiency and cost effectiveness. There also needs to be a regular review of compliance, quality control and service standards. The audit is also an opportunity to benchmark costs.

The following are examples of those areas in a flexible benefits scheme that are usually audited:

- **Membership data/calculation procedures:**
  - [ ] active/leavers/joiners;
  - [ ] calculation events – leavers, joiners, refunds, benefits, quotations, pensions and AVC protections;
  - [ ] event categorisation and record keeping.
- **Member communications and service standards:**
  - [ ] member correspondence for all classes of beneficiary;
  - [ ] benefit statements;
  - [ ] system integration with work processing;
  - [ ] service standards.
- **Scheme management control procedures:**
  - [ ] payments, receipts, authorisations;
  - [ ] scheme accounting and contribution remittance;
  - [ ] cash flow management;
  - [ ] monthly control routines;
  - [ ] scheme control documents.
- **Reporting to employer senior management:**
  - [ ] service standards;
  - [ ] reporting formats and content.
- **Systems:**
  - [ ] review existing capability and potential;

☐ update and audit trail routines and write backs;

☐ security routines and disaster recovery arrangements;

☐ interface routines;

☐ letters and spreadsheet integration.

- **Annual update procedures:**

☐ pre-update planning;

☐ data capture and reconciliation;

☐ benefit statement production;

☐ accounts/valuation data.

- **Departmental and external interfaces:**

☐ review interfaces between pensions, payroll, HR, accounts department and benefit providers.

- **General in-house operations:**

☐ internal cost evaluation;

☐ cost benchmarking – market costs;

☐ structure, staff, training.

12 — Outsourcing Flexible Benefits

This section includes:

- Introduction
- Reasons for outsourcing
- Key aspects of outsourcing
- Selecting an outsourcer
- Outsourcing contracts
- Application service providers
- Generic site outsourcing
- Pitfalls of outsourcing

Introduction   12.1

A key to successful growth of a business is its ability to understand where its strengths lie, what are its core competencies on which to focus attention, and consequently which functions can more efficiently be outsourced. This has been the traditional approach to outsourcing, and in some respects is as relevant today as it was years ago.

What has changed is the growing awareness that outsourcing is more than just a means of achieving business efficiency. It can be used to create strategic advantage; companies can gain access to expertise or competence not available in-house, which in turn can provide an entry into new markets; benefits of scale can be achieved; cost control can be improved.

Outsourcing also gives companies continuous access to new technology, ideas and designs without the burden of up-front investment and risk.

As developments have made businesses increasingly sophisticated, and margins are being fought on tighter boundaries, outsourcers are playing a key role in adding value to the business.

While the benefits are clear, there are many factors to take into account along the route:

- Which are the key elements to outsource?
- How to build the best relationship between people in the organisation and its supplier?
- How to measure the success of the operation?

All or part of a flexible benefits scheme can be outsourced. For instance, the organisation may choose only to outsource the project management of the design and implantation of the scheme. At the opposite end of the scale they may chose to outsource the whole of the scheme including designing, implementation, management, administration and ongoing modifications.

Reasons for outsourcing 12.2

There are two basic reasons why an organisation may wish to outsource some or all of the flexible benefits schemes. The first is a strategic reason, as summarised above and the second is tactical.

Tactical reasons include lack of resource, lack of expertise and systems. Very often the choice of outsourcing is a mix of the two.

The decision to outsource any function is a complex one, but the strategic drivers are perhaps more varied than they were in the early days of outsourcing. There is, for example, growing recognition that outsourcing can play a strategic role in an organisation's HR development objectives.

Outsourcing and market expansion 12.3

A key reasons for some companies to consider outsourcing is that they seek access to expertise or competence not available in-house. For companies trying to improve their competitive HR edge, such expertise may be crucial to success of failure.

This is particularly true as the use of Internet increases and e-HR becomes commonplace. For example, the company can create their own flexible benefit scheme but then choose to outsource the administration element, perhaps by outsourcing IT systems, web management or product management.

This kind of outsourcing is particularly attractive when seeking to enter new ways of working or to operate through new communication channels, because of the added flexibility it allows.

Companies experimenting with e-HR will not know whether a particular service will be successful or not.

By outsourcing some aspects of the new scheme they can avoid massive up-front investment on a risky venture.

By calling on the expertise already gained by others, they can also expect to launch the new scheme more quickly and effectively than would perhaps otherwise be possible. Speed can be an issue if there is a narrow window of opportunity. If the project proves successful, the option remains to bring the outsourced elements in-house at a future date.

Branding issues   12.4

When considering whether outsourced services are appropriate to a new scheme, one key issue concerns the branding of the way in which the service seeks to differentiate itself. Because the experience that the employee has plays a key part of the service, if quality and the particular style of the interaction are to be prime differentiates, then it may be preferable to keep the service in-house.

Outsourcing is still possible, but ensuring the uniqueness of the experience of the employee becomes more difficult. However, for other services where cost is the key differentiation for the service offered, outsourcing could well be an appropriate option.

Variations on the theme may be worth considering, where the company uses its own staff to manage the scheme, but the physical system itself is an outsourced facility. Alternatively, if the outsourced service is merely a support function, or price is the key differentiation for the service offered, then total outsourcing could well be an appropriate option.

Contractual aspects 12.5

Regardless of whether the company outsources part or all of the flexible benefit scheme, it will still have compliance and legal obligations as previously covered in **CHAPTER 8** above. Even if the outsourcer, for instance, is responsible for generating Inland Revenue reports (such as P11D) the company will still be ultimately responsible for its accuracy and completion in time. Any contracts between the company and the outsourcers will clearly define these and set levels of accountability, which may even trigger penalties.

The pricing mechanism must also be transparent in that it is understood, auditable and the occasions for any changes in pricing are specified. It should be possible to adapt the service to meet changing needs without excessive costs being incurred. This is particularly vital when a new flexible scheme is being established and there are some uncertainties as to exact service requirements, such as levels of employee demand.

The growth of outsourcing and ongoing developments in the way it is used are encouraging companies to think more creatively about how they interact with their employees. Rather than simply paying a specialist to process; a joint venture agreement could enable both parties to share the risks and rewards of managing the flexible benefit scheme.

Other strategic drivers for outsourcing 12.6

Even when there are not plans to expand the scheme or develop new product and service offerings, there are other sound reasons behind the decision to out-source some scheme functions.

First, outsourcing can allow an organisation to achieve benefits of scale that are otherwise unobtainable. For example, the organisation will never be able to achieve the same economies of scale in purchasing certain benefits as a specialist service provider. Large-scale investment to reduce manual tasks may not be worthwhile for an individual organisation, but is possible for specialists in a particular service. The outsourcing investment and resulting economies of scale can lead not only to reduced manual input and lower costs, but also to the potential for a higher-quality service.

Outsourcing can also make strategic sense for organisations seeking to improve cost control. Costs can largely be agreed up-front at the start of the outsourcing contract, whether that be for three or up to five years. There is less certainty, however, that real cost savings can be achieved, at least immediately. This is because the outsourcer will need to make a profit itself and because the service may attract other costs that, depending on particular services, may not be fully recoverable. There may also be start-up costs which may be borne up-front, or recovered over the life of the contract.

Only the final analysis will show whether an overall cost saving has been achieved by the end of the outsourcing agreement. However, along the way there is the advantage that related in-house investment would have been reduced. Savings of investments in non-core functions can be applied elsewhere in the company, potentially in areas of greater strategic importance, to generate positive returns.

Some organisations may opt for outsourcing primarily because it supports their business philosophy of 'sticking to the knitting'. The business focuses creativity energy on what it does best, leaving the rest to experts in those particular fields.

This approach is particularly relevant to the outsourcing of flexible benefits. It tends to mean that organisations, guided by the outsourcer, will focus on the 'must haves' in the service and be less distracted by the 'nice to have' elements. By taking the standard service components they can most effectively tap into the desired economies of scale. For instance, the company may use a desktop outsource service provider, who they will trust to provide the right standard of technology to meet their requirements. They state their needs and the outsourcer provides the appropriate solutions, based on their expertise. When flexible benefit services are provided in-house, there can be a tendency for technology to be updated too frequently. Unnecessary updates result in unnecessary costs.

The key strategic questions 12.7

Whether the whole scheme or other services are under consideration, before the decision to outsource can be taken, fundamental questions must be asked.

First – is outsourcing compatible with the organisation's strategic objectives? Outsourcing by definition closes some options, since it leads to dismantling of existing in-house capability or the decision not to introduce some internal capability. Since outsourcing contracts typically run for three to five years, the future direction of the business has to be considered over that whole time span.

Second – a company considering outsourcing must ask whether it has superior operational capability in that area. If not, then outsourcing could give it access to superior service provision. If it does, then the organisation must consider whether the function is so fundamental to the business that it needs to be retained in-house, or whether, it is peripheral to core activities and need not be retained as an internal service. If there appear to be no cost advantages from outsourcing, however, that would suggest little benefit from such a move.

Business risks must also be considered. If the service is being offered by an outsourcer who could be the target of a takeover, then outsourcing could increase business risks. Others could gain access to confidential business information. At an operational level, any risks from outsourcing must again be assessed.

One problem with this assessment can be that many businesses do not themselves know how well a particularly service or function is performing in-house since they do not have the relevant management information. In such situations, outsourcing the service becomes far riskier, since service levels cannot be established from a basis of factual data.

Regulatory implications of outsourcing are also becoming increasingly relevant for flexible benefits. These have been covered in detail in CHAPTER 8 and **12.13** BELOW, but it is important to note that responsibility still lies with the company and not the outsourcer.

No decision on outsourcing can be made without considering all of these issues. However, if buying in services from an outsourcer fits with the overall company strategy, it can prove to be a valuable element in enabling a successful flexible benefit scheme, whether by accessing new technology or by offering new services through new distribution channels.

Key aspects of outsourcing 12.8

With web-based technology now playing a major role in scheme administration and member communication, any outsourced service must add value to the administration process through innovated communication solutions.

Depending on the companies needs, the outsourcer will work as their reward and benefits department, dealing directly with employees and members via dedicated scheme helplines. Alternatively, they will operate behind the scenes, providing back office support while the company continues to be the main point of contact.

Importantly, whichever option is preferred they must ensure that the service achieves maximum possible integration with the organisation's H R and payroll systems.

Internet and Intranet solutions are playing an increasingly dominant role in the provision of administration services (see **11.16** above). The outsourcer must use these new technologies to the advantage of the organisation. These services must meet the challenges faced by organisations looking to provide first class administration to scheme members, combined with rapid access to a wider range of reward and benefits information.

With the day-to-day administration outsourced, the company is more readily able to focus on reward, benefits and communication policies without the worry of maintaining computer systems or resolving staff issues. The quality and frequency of reporting to management and trustees can also be enhanced. In most cases, outsourcing is considerably more effective and can offer improved budgetary control of flexible benefits administration expense.

If the organisation is outsourcing they will need to be aware that, while ultimately beneficial, this is a complex process and needs careful management. Time is needed to select the service provider. An experienced administrator will make the process easier and provide much needed assurance and identify any potential difficulties so that they are fully discussed and resolved before implementation.

Selecting an outsourcer   12.9

Before you can select an outsourcing partner the company needs to take one or two steps back. The first stage, long before selection can be made, is to define their requirements and develop a paradigm or matrix against which potential candidates can be measured. Then they need to define their expectations and determine exactly which parts of the scheme they want to outsource. Even with a fully outsourced service, there still needs to be boundaries and parameters where the in-house management meets the outsourcing service.

There is a need for a philosophy alignment with the outsourcer, and to achieve that, it is first necessary to define the company's requirements and expectations. It is important to ask what they are hoping to achieve from outsourcing and to make sure that they are not entering into it simply because everyone is doing it.

There are big differences between certain types of outsourcing companies and their degree of enlightenment, conservatism and approach. At one end of the scale, there are the 'end-to-end' outsourcers who take complete control of all flexible benefit scheme activities. That may work well for firms who are looking for that type of service. But most companies are seeking to retain some control over aspects of their scheme, and are looking for an outsourcing company more sensitive to their individual requirements and better able to offer high levels of flexibility as the relationship develops. That will require a relationship that has milestones but still manages to be continually evolving.

A mature and pragmatic outsourcing company will have the best interests of its clients at heart, even though that approach may reduce its profits in the short term. The outsourcing company should always be seeking to reduce the costs of ownership and cost of support for its customers, even though this may mean that its charges are reduced. This results in greater trust and understanding between the outsourcer and the company.

The outsourcer should also be prepared to assume known risks. When there are rollouts and upgrades, for example, there are bound to be peaks and troughs in the demand for skills and human resources, and a flexible outsourcer will be able to absorb those fluctuations without any extra charges.

The choice of outsourcer can depend on the size of the business and volume of related work that is to be outsourced. Many firms also choose not to outsource those aspects of their scheme that are key to their organisation. They may also choose to avoid an outsourcing company that is working with their main competitors, for fear of security lapses that might compromise their competitive edge.

All those factors and others should be included in the brief given to potential outsourcing partners. The brief for the potential outsourcer should be drafted in such a way that they can understand exactly what is involved and what the company is trying to achieve. All to often, briefs are too vague and companies are, therefore, not receiving the tenders they would want. It is important to include the key scheme drivers and the current cost of support so that the outsourcer can frame the solution that would provide the service that the company needs.

The approach to selection 12.10

The traditional approach to selecting an outsourcer is for a company to send out a request for information (RFI) and then, on the back of the responses, issue invitations to tender (ITT). The problem with this approach is that outsourcing companies often do not have enough information to deliver the right outline for a solution, and the selecting companies also do not receive enough of the right information make an informed choice.

The best way is to meet the principals of the outsourcing firm and establish that there is a cultural and philosophical match. There needs to be a forum and opportunity to discuss expectations and for ideas to be exchanged. The selection process should be interactive.

It is possible to compare several potential outsourcers in terms of track record, size of other clients and the investment in the skills associated with flexible benefits administration. This involves putting together a detailed response to details such as exactly how will the migration from legacy and existing schemes be integrated with the new technology, and process updated, and who will manage which aspect of the transition.

Many companies looking for an outsourcing partner may not themselves be aware of all the services and processes with which they need help, and therefore underestimate their requirements of the RFI. The outsourcing firm should be looking to engage an outsourcing partner at the right place rather than any price, with a viable and workable service level agreement.

When comparing potential outsourcing providers, cost is an obvious first point of contact, but can be the most misleading. Determining exactly what is included in a price, evaluating the extras and working to eliminate any later queries is important. Companies need to be wary of an all-embracing all-inclusive charge, because this often requires them to hand over more control than is healthy.

Despite the attraction of a predictable cost that can be budgeted for, the arrangement may be too prescriptive. Many outsourcing arrangements are determined and driven by the outsourcing firm. For an outsourcing agreement to work, the levels and areas of control need to be carefully agreed.

It is important to make a site visit before final discussions take place. There is no better way of getting a clear picture of the outsourcer at work than to talk to some existing customers, although obviously no company is going to nominate reference sites that are dissatisfied in any way. Companies can sometimes get a better picture by asking the reference sites which outsourcing providers they turned down, or used to work with and do not any more, and why.

The company's own understanding   12.11

Selection of an outsourcer partnership is a two-way street, and organisations may find that some outsourcing companies are reluctant to work with them unless they have a clear understanding of what their organisation wants, and is committed to it.

This is more sensible and less arrogant than it sounds. The mature outsourcing company will not want to undertake a contract with a customer who fails to show commitment to the outsourcing arrangement at a high level. There has to be board level 'buy-in' if the arrangement is to work.

Outsourcing is a process that can be expensive and time consuming. If an organisation is approaching outsourcing expecting it to dramatically reduce support costs and involve little attention from internal staff, then they are going to be disappointed, however good the outsourcing company is.

While outsourcing can reduce support costs through the benefits of economies of scale, this saving is not likely to be enormous. The greater benefit is the freeing of internal skills to focus on core activity, leaving flexible benefit activity to be managed by flexible benefit experts.

The long-term relationship   12.12

Both the organisation and the outsourcing company should expect the selection process to include an outline of the way that the contract will be managed, with regular achievement criteria, review milestones and measures of post-project success.

The outsourcer needs to meet with the organisation in a partnership in which they retain a level of control that suits them, but get the skills and flexibility from their resources. Care should be taken to match consultants at all levels, including skills, experience, attitude and culture so that they fit with the organisation's needs both today and in the future. Anyone in the process of selecting an outsourcer should take care to look for a partner with whom they can improve services to their employees and keep an eye on future technologies, as well as resolving any immediate scheme problems.

The length of the contract and outsourcing partnership is also an issue. Obviously, both parties will be looking for an agreement that lasts for as long as possible, yet neither will want to be locked into a contract that is unprofitable to either party, for any reason. Three to five years is the ideal time for a contact, but if the company wants to continue working with the outsourcing firm when the contract ends, that is the best compliment.

Outsourcing solutions need to keep changing so that they can maintain the lowest cost and deliver the most effective solutions. Organisations should constantly review their options regarding outsourcing, and outsourcing providers should be constantly reviewing the way they deliver their services. The rise in web-based technology and flexible benefit management will reduce the cost of outsourcing and enable more aspects of in-house schemes to be outsourced.

A pragmatic outsourcing partner will understand that there may be scepticism and some resistance within the organisation if the outsourcing company's consultants are contracted and, therefore, become privy to some of the organisation's employee secrets. Whilst the company are looking for an expert outsourcing firm with a thorough understanding of their business, it is almost inevitable that they will also be working with other similar firms. There is a school of thought that organisations should look for those outsourcers already working with their competitors. The fundamental business processes that function across all sectors and businesses are essentially very similarly and it is not difficult for an outsourcing firm to deliver a workable solution to a certain type and size of business one day and then a completely different one the next.

What is important for those selecting an outsourcing partner to remember is that, regardless of whether they are opting for full or partial outsourcing, there should not be any abdication of responsibility. However the term 'partnership' is used, no one should think that either side can give up responsibility to make sure that the flexible benefit scheme runs smoothly, is upgraded with proven and reliable products and technology and that costs are pegged as low as realistically possible.

No one would argue that the outsourcing company should make a profit, provided it is reasonable. Provided the company sees good value as a result of the contract and that best practices are used throughout all the services and operations, there should be no reason why the outsourcing arrangement should not continue for many years, to the mutual benefit of all parties.

Outsourcing contracts 12.13

A well-drafted contract is of prime importance in any outsourcing deal. Outsourcing the management and operation of an organisation's flexible benefit scheme involves legal rights and obligations that are usually varied and complex. Unless these are identified and the scope of the legal rights are responsibilities carefully defined, the relationship between the company and outsourcer contract must be viewed not just as a record of the basic terms, but as an opportunity to anticipate potential areas of difficulty and deal with then in advance.

Preparation 12.14

The importance of adequate preparation cannot be emphasised highly enough. The amount of information that needs to be gathered is such that those managing an outsourcing project must allocate sufficient time and resources. Outside consultants and advisers are often a vital part of this preparatory process, partly for management or strategic reasons, and partly because gathering and structuring for required information can benefit from being subcontracted.

The decision to outsource will not have been taken without considerable information gathering and analysis (flexibility study). However, more detailed work is required once the initial decision to outsource has been taken, for example:

- comprehensive definition of the scope of the services to be outsourced;

- definition of service levels;

- compiling operational procedures, disaster recovery plans, security policies etc;

- drafting the contract itself.

This preparation culminates in a detailed invitation to tender (ITT) for submission to potential outsourcing companies. The hard work invested in preparing the ITT will be amply repaid, because it will help the company select the preferred outsourcer(s) and subsequently to negotiate with them.

Scope   12.15

Most companies are interested in the cost-reduction aspects of out-sourcing (even though other benefits on a technological or organisa-tional level are being increasingly recognised). However, pricing the outsourced services is impossible without a clear scope of the organi-sation's requirements. There are of course many other elements to be taken into account in calculating the total price, but the definition and extent of the services to be provided are critical.

Intellectual property (IPR)   12.16

The company may have developed applications in which it owns intellectual property rights. If the outsourcer needs to use these in providing the services, then the terms of use have to be established (protecting the organisation's IPR) and the potential impact on the total price considered. The outsourcing contract may contemplate the continued development of these applications.

If the outsourcer is to have a role in such continued developments, and the applications have commercial potential, then the outsourcing contract should address the issues of ownership of the IPR in such developments, the methods by which the portions in which the parties share in the proceeds of commercial exploitations, and the responsibil-ity for commercial considerations (along with related issues such as branding).

The outsourcer's need to be able to access the companies data, and in some cases the outsourcer's obligations to update it, must be addressed and related issues (confidentiality, data protection, employees relations etc) considered and provided for in the contract.

Warranties   12.17

Clearly the company will wish to minimise the scope and number of warranties it gives in relation to the assets and contracts transferred. It may argue that the outsourcer should be able to rely on its due diligence, although the price will inevitably reflect any actual or contingent liabilities that the outsourcer has been able to identify. The question of what liabilities are assumed or excluded will usually be determined by the bargaining position of the parties.

However, it would be normal and reasonable to expect that, for example:

- each party indemnifies the other in respect of third-party claims of intellectual property infringement (the outsourcer against claims affecting software supplied by a third party; the company against claims affecting software transferred to the outsourcer);

- the company warrants that the outsourcer will have undisturbed access to their premises for the purposes of carrying out the services in accordance with the contract.

Service level agreements 12.18

Service level agreements (SLAs) are schedules to the outsourcing contract, and should contain detailed descriptions of the services to be provided and the applicable standards or levels of performance. They are central to the contract because they define the outsourcer's obligations and determine responsibility if things go wrong.

As with other aspects of outsourcing, time spent before and during negotiation in defining the services and the required levels of performance will mean that issues are addressed at the outset, rather than when things have gone awry. Since the SLAs describe the outsourcer's responsibilities, the customer will wish to ensure that they are as precise as possible, while the outsourcer will have an interest in making the performance levels as objectively measurable as possible.

SLAs deal with such matters as:

- response times;

- fault reporting; and

- up-time or down-time targets.

Failure to achieve the required service levels usually triggers credits. These credits must be sufficient to incentive the outsourcer but not be excessively punitive since, unless they can be characterised as a reasonable pre-estimate of the customer's loss, they may be held to be unenforceable. This is covered in more detail in **CHAPTER 13**.

Change control   **12.19**

Service level agreements should not be regarded as fixed in stone. Outsourcing arrangements last for a long time and changes are inevitable, whether due to technological developments or to managerial or strategic decisions. Disputes can easily arise over changes and their impact on cost.

Well-drafted changes control clauses contain and direct the process of change and should provide that:

- the parties notify and consult with each other when a change is anticipated;

- neither side can unreasonably block a request for change; and

- the outsourcer is obliged to prepare an adequate detailed statement of the effects of a proposed change on areas such as staffing, service levels, systems integration and, above all, cost.

The company will want the outsourcer to recommend changes without being committed to them until their implications are understood and a price agreed. Equally, the outsourcer will wish to avoid being dictated to by the company without agreement on cost.

Parent company guarantees and performance bonds   **12.20**

Given the duration of outsourcing arrangements, it is not unusual to expect the obligations of the outsourcer (or indeed the company) to be guaranteed by its ultimate holding company. However, the cost of arranging performance bonds can sometimes be prohibitive in a keenly priced contract.

Price   **12.21**

Consideration of the price payable to the outsourcer for the services can be calculated only after all the above elements have been taken into account.

The company will be looking for certainty, and hence for fixed fees. The outsourcer may wish the pricing model to be able to cope with inflationary increases and this has an element of indexation.

Conversely, the company will want to be sure that it benefits fully from the efficiencies that should flow from outsourcing (economies of scale, greater technological focus and direction and general improvements in equipment and software sourcing), as well as from downward price trends (for example in relation to PCs). The company may even wish to impose a contractual requirement that costs are reduced over the duration of the contract, though this aim may be inconsistent with taking advantage of new technologies.

Termination 12.22

Termination of the outsourcing contract puts everything into reverse and it is essential that all the issues addressed above are dealt with from the perspective of termination. Although the circumstances of termination cannot necessarily be foreseen, a framework should be established to provide for the transfer of the scheme as outsourced elements back to the company. This framework is necessary whether the operations are being 're-insourced' or transferred to another outsourcer ('re-outsourced').

Sometimes outsourcing contracts provide for 'early' no-fault termination. However, it should be borne in mind that early terminations affects an outsourcer's anticipated profit levels and can, therefore, be expected to have an impact on price.

Avoiding disputes 12.23

Whatever the complexities of flexible benefit outsourcing, an outsourcing contract should perform the same function as any other contract and regulate the parties responsibilities in a clear and objective fashion. The best way of avoiding expensive disputes in an outsourcing arrangement is undoubtedly to prepare for and negotiate the contract methodically. This will mean that areas of potential disagreement are resolved before and not during the relationship.

Application service providers 12.24

Due to the growing use of third party application providers (referred to in **11.11** above), this aspect of outsourcing warrants further discussion.

Application Service Providers (ASP) are being put forward not only as a radical way of delivering core flexible benefit IT applications, but as the very future of software itself. Since nearly all companies of any size rely on software applications to manage their businesses from e-HR solutions and accountancy management, to word processing and email, the messages emerging from the new ASP market are essential to take on board.

An ASP has two key characteristics:

● it provides standard application software to businesses as a service with agreed levels of usage, usually on a rental basis; and

● it hosts and maintains the application remotely and delivers it to the customer over a network (in particular, internet-style networks).

To use another term, ASP can be seen as a form of outsourcing. It allows companies to use and benefit from the software without having the capital expenditure of the software and resources to run it.

Website hosting is a type of ASP, as are the growing range of HR applications that are concerned with transactional aspects of managing employees over the internet. These include so-called 'portals' – gateways to a company's electronic resources that can be accessed by its own employees, as well as suppliers, customers and partners.

Choosing a supplier   12.25

There are probably more key differentiates to cover the selection of an ASP supplier than most other outsourcers, due to the critical combination of factors such as security, reliability and integrity.

Clearly, there is a gulf in requirement between the simple, hosting of a non-transactional website and that of an system where key employees data is hosted off-site. In the latter case, no amount of legal agreements can compensate for a lack of trust in a very important business relationship.

Financial stability   12.26

With such a young industry, there is a classic tension between being an early adopter in the hope that more risk will result in more reward, or playing it safe to see how others fair.

Both of these factors make if difficult to assess and predict the future ASP market, especially since even large and apparently strongly backed IT concerns can encounter swift and terminal difficulties.

What is certain is that the major professional services organisations such as IBM Global Services and telecom firms will be in the ASP and other ASP markets for a long time, although certain services will be subject to reappraisal. Smaller ASPs that are subsidiaries of larger groups may have access to more resources.

Management team and staff 12.27

For ASPs specialising in flexible benefits, the quality and commitment of company leaders is vital. The best ones will be advising on and providing opportunities to enhance the administration processes by, for example, forming integration paths with the scheme benefit product providers. The operational staff and consultants employed by an ASP should also be open to scrutiny. Access to superior and scarce expertise is a main selling point of ASPs and should be demonstrated.

Single contact 12.28

As many ASPs will have partnerships with other suppliers, it is essential that companies ensure they have a single point of contact and responsibility.

The services component of an ASP is so vital that any vendor that provides support services such as data centres but does not 'own' the customer relationship should not be called an ASP. An ASP must be able to demonstrate expertise in company support and project management.

Partnerships 12.29

Very few ASPs will be able to go it alone, most will form a number of partnerships with other suppliers, particularly in the case of an ASP that is not supplying its own application.

Some ASPs will have their own data centres; others may form relationships with specialists in hosting secure facilities.

The quality of these partnerships must be tested in advance of signing up. Check, for example, whether an ASP has the best tier of support from the software vendor(s) it represents and whether it is certified by the vendors to offer the application it is delivering.

Facilities **12.30**

A visit to the data centre hosting the application can be reassuring. ASPs need to be questioned about their own backup and disaster recovery plans.

References **12.31**

In an immature market such as ASP, references are critical. Does the ASP have existing customers in the UK who are receiving the same services that you are considering? If so, are they happy with the service provided and their relationship with the vendor? It is worth talking to them prior to signing up.

Costs and return on investment **12.32**

It is entirely possible to demonstrate return on investment in a matter of months or even weeks for straightforward applications.

However, in some cases an ASP solution may not save much in the way of direct costs. Indeed, clients of ASPs often stress that cost savings is not the top reason for outsourcing flexible benefits administration systems. Rather, it is the partnership with an expert partner that is valued for its strategic role and the pay off is in terms of improved business processes and efficiency.

A good ASP will help clients assess the less tangible forms of return on investment and highlight which parts of the overall cost could be included or charged as extras, such as consultancy and training.

Because flexible benefits, by their very nature are mostly start-ups, the pricing model for an ASP should be much easier to judge against equivalent in-house start-up costs.

Similarly, outsourcing an existing application is a relatively easy cost to measure, for example:

● What is the total cost of having the ASP host and deliver the application?

● Is there information on comparative costs and benefits between an ASP and non-ASP delivery method?

● Is there an option to rent or buy software and/or hardware?

- Is there an option to own the software and/or hardware at the end of the contract?

Measuring the total cost of ownership of existing in-house IT can be quite difficult, although, it is widely accepted that the lion's share of the cost of maintaining each user-PC is made up of support costs.

Contract and service level agreements   **12.33**

Service level agreements (SLA) are the bedrock of contractual relationships with ASPs. They are usually a legal document that specifies the delivery of the service, and can include:

- speed of implementation;

- guaranteed level of performance (such as response times when users interact with the software);

- guaranteed level of availability (such as 99% during working hours, not all applications need round the clock 'uptime');

- accessibility of application to users (equipment upgrades may be required);

- provision for upgrades to latest software versions;

- level of customer support;

- end-user training;

- penalties for failing to meet guarantees;

- termination agreement.

An in-house IT department is unlikely to have an SLA with its captive user base. So, one benefit of using an ASP is that it can introduce a degree of certainty to IT delivery that simply was not there before.

Finally, a word of caution: since ASP contracts tend to run for a number of years, it is important that the SLA contains some flexibility so that, for example, a growing business can negotiate for extra users within the initial agreement.

Security   **12.34**

Security is among the biggest concerns of companies looking at an ASP alternative. If core employees' data is residing at another organisation, it is essential to ensure that it is protected both within the boundaries of the ASP and in transmission between ASP and organisation.

However, security should be one of an ASP's greatest selling points, since there is little future in any ASP that cannot demonstrate greater security for its client base than it could ever hope to have itself.

For example, the ASP has a secure building containing state-of-the-art technology including scanning, security zoning and 24-hour monitoring of website activity. Also, firewalling (see **11.19** above) and authentication of encryption. Probably the biggest concern is simply that outsiders, albeit employees of the ASP, could have access to sensitive employee data.

Communications   **12.35**

Allied to security, companies that opt for mission critical applications at an ASP will almost certainly want a dedicated leased line or virtual private network (VPN) to carry traffic. Leased lines can be very expensive, depending on distance. So, close proximity to the ASP's data centre is an advantage. VPNs guarantee a secure portion of the public network to a communication link.

The cost of communications must be factored in, as should service levels agreement and quality of partnership between an ASP and communications provider.

The delivery of the application to the user desktop is also important; simple ASP application should be able to deliver a service simply by configuring a browser on a PC. Other applications may need a degree of installation and customisation on the client's premises.

Exit strategy   **12.36**

With any outsourced arrangement it is wise to have a fall-back plan if things go wrong, ie, the ASP goes under, service levels drop to unacceptable levels or applications do not get upgraded, etc.

Generic site outsourcing (GSO)   **12.37**

Of all the new and proposed solutions to outsourcing flexible benefits, GSOs offer one of the more affordable, ease of administration and effective software packages available.

259

Based on tried and tested existing schemes, they offer a generic solution to what has traditionally been a 'tailored only' market. This is based on the fact that 85% of all flexible benefits schemes are identical regardless of application.

GSO is available to employers and employees via their own Intranet and over the Internet. The scheme provides total management of fixed and flexible benefits and administration. It is fully integrated for connecting employees and companies with the information relevant to their roles.

It is flexible enough to encompass a variety of core and flexible benefits as well as additional facilities for providing links to independent sites, such as employee share schemes.

Because they are based on a generic site, the provider has already been running for some time, and issues such as tax and legal requirements have already been addressed. The scheme launch and communication process is also simplified and companies have the option of using material they have already produced or their own. As well as a standard benefit statement, required for the flexible benefits schemes, GSOs can also produce total remuneration statements as an option.

Key unique system features   12.38

These are a selection of the most common system features for a GSO:

- affordable, easy to use administration and effective software;
- fixed, flexible and mixed benefit schemes set up in one administration;
- employee communication simplified;
- employee self-service;
- provision of benefit statements, costs and entitlement;
- centralised reporting and management information;
- payroll interface;
- benefit plan enrolment;
- life event changes;
- leavers and joiners;
- total remuneration statement;

- employee directory;

- report generation, available by product/providers selected and premiums payable;

- adding joiners and deleting leavers;

- mid-term adjustments;

- authorising change requests;

- generating monthly payroll file;

- on-line support including users guide, troubleshooting systems and frequently asked questions;

- secrecy function enabling administrators to hide/show the confidential information when using the system;

- HR links gives access to the employee handbook/schedules for easy maintenance;

- all forms can easily be obtained from the system;

- value indicators easy to use.

Key unique employee features   12.39

Key unique employee features are listed below:

- the ability at any time of the year to log in and see selections;

- stakeholder information allows employees to keep track as frequently as required;

- total remuneration feature shows an individual's 'financial worth' to the company;

- shareholder links shows share price and worth of any options/ share schemes/private holdings;

- form filling is minimum;

- employees can see salary moving up and down in line with the benefits chosen.

Additional service   12.40

GSO usually offers a variety of tailored services so companies can modify the basic GSO Scheme to suit their own needs. These include:

- feasibility studies for introducing the GSO scheme;

- risk modelling and cost analysis;

- complete project and/or partnership management of the design and implementation of new schemes;

- scheme evaluation and strategy development;

- plan design and due diligence;

- analysis and integration of DB and DC pension arrangements into the flexible benefit scheme;

- product mix and selection;

- product provider evaluation and resourcing, including risk re-broking and affinity products;

- management and administration procedures, including tax and legal requirements;

- scheme launch and communication process;

- installation and implementation;

- ongoing management and administration of the scheme (including adding new options).

Links to other sites 12.41

GSO providers often offer the additional advantage of their bulk buying power where they have secured advantageous deals with a variety of benefits providers. These are proactively managed on a quarterly basis with new options being added and those no longer relevant removed. Access is via a direct link with the GSO site. It is a good way of adding value to the scheme.

Features Include:

- accessed via the main system and home intranet page;

- strategic relationship with providers delivering a competitive and unique discount;

- value for money;

- discounts to suit all;

- the ability to add throughout the year;

- Internet based in most cases.

Administration   12.42

The main advantages of GSO are that it will help reduce the administrative burden and effort of administering the scheme. It also improves the service to employees and allows the company to focus on strategic human resources that assist organisations to achieve business goals.

The scheme supports:

- fixed, flexible and mixed benefit scheme set-up and administration;
- employee communication;
- employee self-service;
- product servicing and management;
- providing employees with a statement of their remuneration, benefits costs and entitlements.

The technology supports:

- centralised reporting and management information;
- employee self-service;
- payroll interface;
- benefit plan enrolment;
- life event changes;
- leavers and joiners;
- total remuneration statement;
- employee directory.

This is an Internet/Intranet business service and usually includes, free access to upgrades, helpdesk support and ongoing maintenance of the software. There is usually no requirement for the company to purchase hardware to run the application.

The full functionality of the GSO technology is delivered to two primary roles within the company – employee and administrator. These roles are fully integrated for connecting employee and employer with the information relevant to their roles.

Access and services required by the HR administrators and employees is defined by the flexible benefits project team. The GSO providers will configure the technology to deliver the system required.

Employee access 12.43

For core benefits, employees are able to select additional products through salary sacrifice, up to an employer-defined limit. Employees are also able to manage their own personal data. This includes registering change of address, changing emergency contacts and adding dependants. Giving employees controlled access to information for which they are responsible will reduce call volumes to HR, enhance communication with employees, decrease administrative workloads and significantly improve employee satisfaction.

For flexible benefits, employees have, in addition to all these features, the ability to mix and match their benefit selection up to their predefined 'flex' allowance within the scheme rules.

For both applications, most of the common product options are included:

- pension;
- car;
- cash;
- holidays;
- death in service;
- income protection;
- critical illness;
- private medical;
- dental;
- optical;
- health club membership;
- childcare and retail vouchers;
- travel insurance;
- personal accident;
- car breakdown;

- health screening and financial advice.

Administrator access   12.44

The benefits administrator will help to define how the scheme is set up and the GSO supplier delivers a customised solution to meet the requirement.

Throughout the enrolment cycle, the administrator is able to view activity, status and correspond with employees.

Other functions provided within the administrator role include:

- report generation;

- adding joiners and deleting leavers;

- mid-term adjustments;

- authorising change requests;

- generating the monthly payroll file.

Reporting   12.45

Reports are available by product providers selected and premiums payable. These can be produced by a cost centre, business unit and within any pre-defined timescale. In addition to a number of standard report formats that are available, the GSO provider can build and customise any additional reports required.

Embedded in the application will be a messaging system and audit trail of transactions.

Systems technology   12.46

GSO uses secure socket layer (SSL) technology, system security methods and layers of firewalls to create authenticated and encrypted transactions. This ensures that users access only the information they are authorised to access. This is consistent with the security standards of many leading financial institutions on the web.

The interface is both intuitive and easy to use. The GSO provider usually also provides a comprehensive training programme for the company so that they can quickly get familiar with the application.

Support resources 12.47

The GSO provider will make available a number of online support resources including:

- how to use guides;

- troubleshooting assistance;

- frequently asked questions.

Total remuneration statement 12.48

This statement is available within GSO (it can also be used as a separate, standalone option for the company if required). The total remuneration statement will contain only the information the company wishes to provide to each employee. This will typically be issued on an annual basis. Once the information and layout have been defined, the GSO provider will specify the format of data it requires from the employer and will then aggregate this data and embed it in a statement that is personalised to individual employees listing their overall compensation package, benefit costs and entitlements.

The statement then becomes a reference point for the employee and reinforces to each employee the additional costs the employer incurs on their behalf and each benefit entitlement. Statements can be issued to employees online or in paper format.

Pitfalls of outsourcing 12.49

Outsourcing flexible benefits cannot guarantee increased efficiency for companies, but outsourcers and their clients have learned the key causes of potential problems from experience. Those embarking on a new contract can learn from the lessons of the past.

Regardless of sector or size of company, the key causes of outsourcing failing to live up to expectations tend to fall into the same categories. These are:

- loss of shared vision;

- people problems;

- communication failure;

- pre-contractual mistakes;

- contractual weaknesses;

- lack of understanding of the outsourcing process.

Loss of shared vision 12.50

At the time an outsourcing agreement is made, both parties may have a clear idea of the aims of the contract, its strategic and operational objectives. But once the outsourcing itself gets underway, that shared strategic vision can become blurred and fade away.

One reason that the common aims become lost is the strategic reorganisation that may accompany the contract can significantly change the profile of personnel involved. Those individuals charged with the ongoing management of the relationship between the company and the outsourcer may have little conceptual understanding of the strategic goals behind the agreement. Operational concerns can dominate, potentially pushing strategic initiatives to improve service quality out of the picture.

The result can be that the company does not receive the value it anticipated from the outsourcing agreement. Similarly, the outsourcer becomes frustrated at the lack of opportunity to come to the table with proposals for performance improvement initiatives and its resulting inability to push through strategic process improvements.

To avoid this situation, the company needs to consider how best to manage its relationship with the outsourcer. They should fill that role with an individual who has a strategic understanding of the aims of the outsourcing by splitting between a contract manager responsible for the commercial, ongoing operational issues around the outsourcing contract, and a second relationship manager who handles the strategic side of the contract.

The people factor 12.51

Continuity of personnel is clearly important to maintain the shared vision from agreeing the contract through to implementation and on through the lifetime of the contract. But the vision aside, as in most aspects of business, it is the people who make the difference.

Outsourcing is no different. The chemistry between the outsourcer and the company can have a significant impact on success or failure. This applies both to the assignment of staff to the contract by the outsourcer and to the company staff managing the scheme. There needs to be a harmonious cultural fit. Outsourcers themselves have a responsibility to make sure that they have strong relationships at the most senior levels of the client organisation.

Communication breakdown   12.52

Effective communication between company management, staff and the outsourcer is vital, even before an outsourcing agreement gets under-way. There needs to be top-down communication of the reason behind the outsourcing move, the scope of the outsourcing relationship and its goals.

Failure to communicate effectively the precise parameters of the outsourcing contract and its potential expansion can cause hostility towards the outsourcer on the part of a company's staff. For example, the organisation may outsource part of their flexible benefit scheme function, but keep certain other groups of the flex team within the company. If those groups are not informed exactly where they stand, perhaps that their role is seen as so strategic it must be kept in-house, then they could perceive the outsourcer as a threat, causing uncertainty, suspicion and unwillingness to work productively with the outsourcer. At an operational level, service delivery could be affected.

Beyond the confines of the HR department, users of a flexible benefit scheme should themselves be informed of the aims and parameters of the outsourcing contract. They need to understand that the outsourced service providers now have a precisely defined role, perhaps more tightly drawn than before. As users of the contracted services they need to understand that they cannot expect outsourcers' staff to provide services beyond their remit, but that they can expect service delivery of a high standard as set out in the outsourcing contract.

Pre-contractual issues   12.53

Rushing through pre-contractual stages can prove a short-term economy. Some companies try to rush through the due diligence stage. All are understandably eager to get the contract finalised, but some have done so because they see the outsourcer's due diligence work as a risk to them or as a chance for the outsourcer to change the scope and terms of the deal. However, they can lose out on several counts.

First, service delivery decisions may be based on out-of-date scheme statistics. If there are twice the number of scheme events the company asserted to be the case in the invitation to tender, the outsourcer will clearly find it hard to deliver planned service levels.

A due diligence process that highlights such a high fault level could have led to suggestions of a process or technology change to reduce the probability of that fault arising.

Secondly, due diligence information can lower the cost of the out-sourcing contract, since if a process change reduces errors, that can have the effect of reducing the drain on the outsourcer's resources.

Realising that scopes or transaction volumes have been misjudged six months after signing the outsourcing agreement results in wasted opportunities for service improvements, boosted efficiency and cost control.

Contract flaws   12.54

Effective service definition should extend to including change management processes in the outsourcing contract. One key benefit of outsourcing is the potential that it gives companies to adapt to change, so the mechanism for changing the service delivery must be included in the contract details. Simply providing for mutually agreeable changes to be made to the contract as they occur is too weak a format. A pre-agreed framework should be established to map through the changed management process, addressing commercial and strategic aspects, and avoiding the need for separate negotiations every time a material change is being made to the contract.

Lack of understanding of the outsourcing process   12.55

In the early days of flexible benefit outsourcing, lack of understanding of the outsourcing process and the factors to consider when selecting a service provider may have caused some contracts to fail to meet expectations. Happily for the industry, this is far less of an issue today. Purchasers of such services are more aware of the key issues to consider. External consultancy to advise companies of the appointment of an outsourcer has increased.

Organisations are themselves are being more thorough in their selection process. For example, there has been a noticeable increase in the time taken for potential users to follow up references. In the past, a short phone call to a referral client may have sufficed, but now those on the brink of entering an agreement are more likely to want to spend half a day visiting those clients to talk about their experiences.

Positive lessons for the future of outsourcing   12.56

As with any new business offering, flexible benefit outsourcing has had its teething problems. Everyone has heard stories of disgruntled companies whose expectations have not been met. There are also experiences of satisfied organisations enjoying the advantages that a well-run flexible benefit scheme can bring.

Companies can do much to ensure that they are among the satisfied user groups by conducting the pre-contractual stages properly and by handling the people issues effectively, including communication of the policy. Finally, if both outsourcer and company undertake to maintain the initial shared vision behind the contract, the potential of the contract has a greater chance of being fulfilled.

13 — Installation and Implementation

This chapter includes the following:

- Introduction
- System installation
- Data requirements
- Service standards
- Product quotations and benefit statements
- Starters, leavers and life changes
- Off-line modelling
- Integrating third-party providers and outsourcers
- Timing
- Resources and management
- Quality control
- On-going scheme development
- Modification, improving and fault-finding
- Monitoring and feedback
- Data Protection Act 1998

Introduction   13.1

The final part of designing and implementing a flexible benefit scheme is an accumulation of all the chapters covered in this book. The organisation now needs to assemble all the various different components of the scheme in order to affect enrolment and administer the various options and choices made by the employees.

This part of the project is more about attention to detail than it is about facilitating. The systems, products and various interfaces have been set up and now the task is to organise and process the various pieces of data and their interactions.

This is a very important part of the scheme as it will be the measure, by the users, of its added value.

System installation 13.2

The first task is to install the various elements of hardware that are required to run the scheme. If the organisation is outsourcing the administration, there is still a requirement to ensure that the hardware within the company is compatible. For example, for a generic site offering, the company needs to ensure that the local PC and hardware have sufficient capacity to cope with the web-based technology and information being used.

It is advisable to address these issues early in the design stage to ensure that there are no hidden costs involved in upgrading equipment and if there is any incompatibility. Due to the sensitivity of flexible benefits it is advisable to set up systems well in advance of the launch date of the scheme so the organisation can experiment on an offline basis to familiarise itself with the hardware and identify any problems.

Once the hardware is installed the next task is to load the software required. As with the above this is worth doing well in advance of the launch of the scheme. The best way of testing the system is to take four or five job positions within the organisation, of varying levels, and apply a fictitious choice of flexible benefit products to each.

The software of any scheme should be easily manageable. It is important for the software writer to provide a comprehensive manual of how the various elements have been put together and a trouble-shooting guide. Given the sensitivity of the flexible benefit scheme it is also vital for them to provide a support service.

From the feasibility study and initial research, the project team will have identified what links the flexible benefit scheme requires to areas such as payroll, P11D, pensions etc. As well as insuring that the hardware and software for the flexible benefits scheme is installed properly, the project team needs to ensure that the links with these various databases is also secured and working properly. For instance, the link with payroll not only needs to ensure the correct deduction from gross pay for certain benefits in kind purchased but also the resultant deductions for tax and National Insurance Contributions (NICs). This also needs to trigger employer NICs payments. If these links are automated, it is important to test them several times to ensure the credibility of the link.

If the flexible benefit scheme has been partially or completely out-sourced, then the above still applies but now needs to blend the requirements of the scheme with the capabilities of the outsourced element. For instance, if the organisation has decided on a fully outsourced system it will still need to have robust links with the company's payroll, P11D and pensions databases. It will also need to have good links with product providers and allow access by both employees and administrators.

Disaster recovery 13.3

All good schemes and systems need a contingency plan should all or part of the scheme fail. It is commonplace within flexible benefits, be they in-house or outsourced, to have a disaster recovery programme. The example below is one based on an outsourced flexible benefit scheme.

All data needs to be backed up on a daily basis as part of the scheme security procedure. The information should be held on a duplicate file server which can be immediately made 'live'. Off-site operations should be possible from other locations in the event of a disaster.

All transactions should be recorded via an audit trail facility. It is a regular housekeeping discipline for audit trail reports to be systematically checked at regular intervals and for appropriate sign-off to be undertaken. In the event of file corruption, it should be possible to restore from the audit trail back up, to the 'position' directly before the problem occurred.

Recovery should be achieved within one hour if the on-site back up can be used, and within three to four hours if there is a need to retrieve the system off-site back up tape. If it was unable to function in one office, it should be possible to transfer the data files to an alternative location.

Data requirements   13.4

Referring back to **CHAPTER 11**, there are three basic types of data required to set up a flexible benefits scheme.

Employee Input Data   13.5

As well as the usual HR information such as name, address, date of birth etc, the flexible benefit will also need job details, reporting filters and benefit entitlements.

It is vital that this data is accurate and up to date. Because flexible benefits systems are highly automated, any incorrect information put into the scheme will be magnified because of the administration process. It is better to spend time cleaning up the data during the initial installation process than it is to try and correct it once the scheme is up and running.

Figure 1 illustrates an example of the typical employee data required for implementing a flexible benefit scheme. Very often this information is collated to allow various reporting filters such as geographical location, function, cost centre, division, business unit and/or company name.

Figure 1: Employee data

• Title	• Employee status
• First name	• Percentage of work (if part-time)
• Surname	• Office location
• Address	• Employee manager
• Post code	• Staff number
• Marital status	• Salary, basic
• Date of birth	• Pensionable salary
• Gender	• Job title
• NI number	• Payroll number
• Job grade	• E-mail address
• Start date	• Benefits entitled to

Product input data   3.6

Because, again, of the highly automated nature of flexible benefits, it is important to ensure that the product information is consistent across all groups of employee benefits. For instance, if private medical insurance is quoted on a per-head charge per annum then dental insurance should be the same.

During the design and development stage the project scheme would have discussed with the relevant product providers the type of information they are going to need to set up a benefits file for each employee. As with the data above this information needs to be accurate and clean as well as up to date.

The type of product input data required for a flexible benefit scheme includes:

● Product.

● Pricing.

● Flex options.

● Entitlement.

The flex options and entitlement are usually segregated into grade and respective entitlement and may include additional fields to allow processing of enrolment such as whether they are entitled to dependants cover or not.

Scheme output data   3.7

Again, referring back to the Process Chart illustrated in Figure 1 at **11.5** above, the various outputs that are required from the flexible benefits scheme are outlined. These include interfaces to payroll, tax and NI, pensions, HR, and management and audit. They also include outputs to product providers.

Each of these will require its own data format. The product provider will require enrolment data, employee data and payment data. They will also require entitlements, information on leavers and joiners and life event changes.

Payroll will require information to allow deduction from salary, pension contributions and other salary statement information.

Tax and NI will require information that affects PAYE, P11D and NICs.

Pensions will require information to enable deduction of contributions, Additional Voluntary Contributions (AVCs) calculations, death in service and dependants entitlement.

HR will require summary information on benefits selected and any changes made as well as changes to employees circumstances.

Management and audit will require data to allow costs to be monitored and forecasted as well as quality controlled.

Service standards 13.8

A flexible benefit scheme is no different to any other process or system. It needs to have service standards in order to maintain control and keep the interest of the employees that use it. As each scheme is different it is difficult to set out a prescribed list of services standards but the example in Figure 2 covers a few that are usually included.

Figure 2: Example service standards

Contribution refunds	Refund letter issued (and cheque if appropriate) **within five to ten working days** of notification of exit.
Benefit quotations	Quotation issued **within five working days** of notification of request.
Leavers quotations	Quotations issued **within ten working days** of receipt of relevant information.
Benefit payment	Benefits are calculated and advised to the client on the **same day**.
Life event changes	Quotations available **within ten working days** of receipt of all relevant information.
Management reports	A draft will be available for audit **two or three months** after the year end. The target date for sign-off is two months later.

The schedule in Figure 2 relates to the principal activities in which the scheme provider is involved. Other background tasks include answering enquiries from previous leavers, dealing with enquiries and correspondence with the statutory authorities. These tasks are also regularly monitored and reported on.

Service level agreements for third party providers should include additional elements covering the functionally of their systems and their responsibilities.

These include:

- definition of service and product providers;

- service availability (definitions and operating hours);

- service levels, escalation procedures and contract points (minor, major and critical loss of service, downtime products);

- issue/reissue passwords;

- service requirements;

- remedies under the agreement;

- review meetings.

An example of service agreement can be found in **APPENDIX 1**.

Most flexible benefit schemes would require more than the above and these would be included in the service standards manual.

If all or part of the scheme has been outsourced these service standards will form an important part of the agreement between the provider and the organisation. It is very important when assessing IT requirements that these service standards are examined to ensure that they are feasible and reinforce the overall levels set for the flexible benefits scheme.

Some schemes treat the first year of operation as a pilot and use that period of time to develop a more meaningful and accurate set of service standards. This is a wise step to take especially if the scheme is fairly unique or the organisation has little experience of such a venture. If the service standards that are set are far too strict and cannot be maintained, then the credibility of the scheme will be quickly undermined.

As well as applying to the scheme services directly offered to the employee, service standards should also apply to other parts of the scheme, including the responsibility of third-party providers to maintain hardware and software and to ensure 24-hour coverage. This is usually contained in the contract and linked to non-performance penalties.

Product quotations and benefit statements 13.9

The busiest time for a flexible benefits scheme is during the annual enrolment. They can be literally thousands of different pieces of information being processed by the system at any given time. The installation and implementation stage should ensure that, despite this, quotations and benefit statements are accurate and timely. This means that the systems and support process required to generate them must be near perfect.

The relationship with the benefit provider will be important during this phase and the organisation must ensure that they can respond to employees' requests for quotations and illustrations within the time scales agreed in the service standard.

If, for instance, it takes an employee several weeks to receive a quotation for a simple dental plan, then not only does it bias his or her view towards that particular product but it also undermines the credibility of the scheme itself. This part of the process should have been tested before the launch and any problems rectified.

In a similar vein, benefit statements produced before and after annual enrolment should be accurate and timely. Organisations cannot expect employees to make a choice about their future benefits if they have not received statements about their current ones. They also need to be satisfied that their choices have been processed.

Benefit statements rely on data from other parts of the organisation and it is important to ensure that these to fit into the same service standard regime as the flexible benefits scheme. For instance, if employees are entitled to trade some of their holidays for other benefits then information should have been returned from the relevant departments stating what holidays they have taken and what they have left. This will allow the benefit statement to accurately reflect what their future entitlement is.

Starters, leavers and life changes 13.10

Although never as busy as the enrolment period, starters, leavers and life change events can generate a lot of activity. Systems, to ensure the smooth and timely processing of information from each of these, should have been set up prior to the scheme going 'live'.

Again, if the information is kept up to date and is at hand it will make the processing for each of these events easy. For instance, if an employee is expecting a child and, coupled with maternity entitlement, is looking to change her flexible benefit scheme options; then the scheme should have a clearly defined process set up already to process the changes required.

Off-line modelling   13.11

The best way of ensuring that a flexible benefit scheme will be almost perfect on the day of the launch is to set it up as an 'off-line' model. This not only allows the double testing of information, data and systems but also gives administrators and other relevant staff live training on the scheme.

It is extremely rare for the management of such a complex project to achieve perfect results first time round. If off-line modelling is built into the timing of the project, it will be easy to achieve. However, if the project team is working to a tight deadline and does not allow for any off-line testing of the system, then the launch becomes the first time the system is tested. This may not an ideal situation, particularly if there are 'teething' problems.

The other advantage of designing a flexible benefit scheme with off-line capability is that it will allow the organisation to test out different variations and products for each year as the scheme evolves. If the scheme is linked into the rest of the HR and the payroll systems electronically, it will also allow the organisation to engage in off-line pay review modelling including the effect of changes to the flexible benefits scheme.

Integrating third party providers and outsourcers   13.12

The key objective when integrating third parties and outsourcers, in terms of installation and implementation, is to clearly define lines of responsibility. If the scheme is totally outsourced, this is a lot easier to do and manage. For example, defining who is responsible for the production of data to be fed into generating P11D reports and subsequent filing to the Inland Revenue.

The main vehicle for ensuring a seamless installation and implementation process between the organisation and a provider is the signed contract between them. It should define exactly what the service standards are for the scheme and who is responsible for maintaining them. If the outsourcer is using their own IT and systems to administer the scheme then the onus should be on them to maintain service standards regardless of any faults within their own systems.

If the organisation is providing its own IT systems or hosting an external web-enabled system then they need to ensure continuity of service. For instance, they will need two servers instead of one to host the applications. In the event of one failing, the system can still continue to operate on the other. This, unfortunately, does add costs to the overall scheme, however, it is a small price to pay for ensuring the service standards of the scheme.

Management of data is also an important issue to consider when using third parties or outsourcers. This is particularly relevant when you take into consideration the *Data Protection Act 1998*. The Act stipulates that there must be in place clearly defined rules and regulations that identify who both the data controller and the data processor are. This is a legal requirement in terms of informing appropriate authorities.

The following example is an extract from an agreement between an organisation and a provider covering data transfer and configuration of benefits calculations.

Data transfer and configuration of benefit calculation

☐ On receipt of the membership data, the system providers will prepare a data map and convert the data for installation onto their own system.

☐ They will then verify the data to ensure all of the data has been transferred and then validate the quality of data by running a series of audit reports. Any incomplete data or odd items will be queried with the organisation. They will report on the quality of the data transferred.

☐ Whilst the data is being converted they will also prepare a benefit specification which they will then use as the basis for configuring the system calculation routines.

☐ Once programmed, the system calculations will be subject to primary and secondary testing routines to ensure total accuracy before the system installation is signed off as completed.

Timing

13.13

Many different issues can affect the timing of the launch of the flexible benefits scheme. They could be strategic events that will affect the scheme and or operational.

From a strategic point of view the organisation has to ensure that the launch date is such that it will enhance any other initiatives being carried out by the organisation. For instance, re-enforcing an annual pay review where the organisation is looking to drive through performance-related changes and an improvement in the perceived value of the overall benefits package.

In the feasibility study the organisation may have looked at its ability to handle such a scheme and decided that although flexible benefits was right for the organisation, a 12 to 18 month delay was required to allow the installation of a new payroll system first.

Other strategic reasons for affecting the timing of the introduction of the flexible benefits scheme could include, massive relocation, adverse restructuring or, (from a positive point of view), a timely thank you for the contribution of the employees to the organisation.

From an organisational point of view, timing usually depends on the resources available to handle the workload generated. For instance, the organisations may choose not to launch their flexible benefit scheme on the same day as their pay review because they don't have the resources and systems to cope with the two initiatives at the same time.

Whatever the reasons are for choosing the specific date for the launch of the scheme it needs to allow the various stages of the project to take place. The organisation will need six to nine months (from start to end) to design and implement a flexible benefits scheme. Working backward from the launch date, the project team can plan out the various actions required (see **APPENDIX 1** for an example) and ensure that key tasks are actually completed well before they are required.

The more successful flexible benefit schemes are those that have completed all the necessary actions well before the launch leaving themselves with the 'simple' task of processing employees choices and ensuring their successful processing.

Resources and management 13.14

Up until the installation and implementation stage, it has been the project team that has driven through the various key tasks for the design and development of the scheme. Now the scheme will require a different set of people to manage and administrate it.

Regardless of whether the scheme has been outsourced or not, the organisation will need to appoint someone who has overall responsibility for the future management of the scheme. They will ultimately be responsible for its success or failure. They will manage the evolution of the scheme involving the outsourcer, senior management team, product providers and employees.

Even if the scheme is outsourced, someone will still have to take responsibility for the interface with the organisation. This person is usually the scheme manager and, depending on how much has been outsourced, may only look after the scheme on a part-time basis. If this is the case the same philosophy applies to future developments. They need to plan well in advance and ensure all the various parties work together on the future evolution of the scheme – probably as a project team.

The scheme will also need an administrator (or if larger, several administrators) to carry out the various functions highlighted above. For a large and complex scheme this could very well be a full time job.

The flexible benefits scheme is an evolving entity and should never remain the same for any subsequent year. The same theories and practices that developed within the scheme also apply to the evolution of the scheme, but obviously in a much less time-consuming manner.

The management and administrators of the scheme are also responsible for reporting back to the senior management and various other interested parties on an on-going basis. As such, they should also be responsible for highlighting any untoward trends or problems in the management of the scheme.

Quality control 13.15

As well as the service standards highlighted in **13.7** above, the organisation needs to ensure that the quality control principles of the flexible benefits scheme support and enhance the overall quality control ethos of the organisation.

For instance, if the company is accredited for investors in people then the scheme must fall into the same regime and be subject to the same quality control audit. (See **11.24** for an example of a quality control audit.)

As well as a commercial reason for ensuring compliance and consistency, quality control also reinforces the cultural image the company is trying to portray. For instance, if the company quality control and customer satisfaction policy dictates that employees should answer a phone within three rings then anybody dealing with queries for the flexible benefit scheme should be subject to the same criteria. This in turn means that the project team has to ensure the correct level of resources for the ongoing administration of the scheme in order to meet these standards.

Ongoing scheme development   13.16

As stated in **13.13** above, a flexible benefit scheme is an evolving entity. Each year it should look to introduce new products identified by employee feedback and also discard any of those that are no longer relevant.

This is easier said than done as certain product providers may insist on a two or three year contract to provide certain products. There may also be other complications in terms of underwriting that also make it difficult. For instance, private medical insurance is usually based on previous claims and demographic profile of the work place and so any changes may result in an increase in premiums.

The company needs to ensure that this process is on going and that employees are engaged in it. They need to have continual dialogue with the scheme management with regards to their preferences and how they would like to see the scheme progressing. In a similar fashion, senior management should also be included.

Modification, improving and fault-finding 13.17

It is wise with flexible benefits schemes to allow time and resources for fault-finding modification and improvement to the process. Unfortunately, such is the nature of such schemes that it is not until the scheme goes 'live' that organisations really find what works and what does not. This is why 'off-line' modelling is often used.

If the project team has sought the advice of external consultants who have had experience of implementing similar schemes before or even outsourced the whole of the project, the frequency and seriousness of these faults are going to be lower, however, they still need to be provided for.

Very often, organisations treat the first year as a pilot scheme which then allows them to modify and improve the design and administration of the scheme at a later stage.

Monitoring and feedback   13.18

The final part of installing and implementing a flexible benefits scheme is to ensure that there are systems and procedures in place for monitoring the progress of the various elements. This can then be fed-back to those responsible for the management of the scheme.

A more popular way of gauging the success of the scheme is through employee feedback, questionnaires or focus groups. Counting the number of people who chose to effect a choice is not really an accurate measure of the success of these types of schemes. If somebody chooses not to have any flexible benefits but to stay with their previous benefits, ironically, this is a choice in itself.

Monitoring of Systems and performance is also important, as it will allow the company to improve the process with time. This can make it more efficient and cost effective.

The success of the flexible benefits scheme is whatever the project scheme set out in terms of the objectives for introducing it. For instance, if one of the objectives was to reduce the amount of money spent on recruitment and this is achieved regardless of whether there is a high number of people signing up for the scheme or not, then this scheme will have been successful.

In a similar fashion product providers should be assessed on a continual basis to ensure that they are still delivering the same level of service that they agreed to and have not lost interest. This is particularly important for providers of voluntary benefits who rely solely on the number of employees who sign up. If this number is low they may not put the same effort into the scheme as originally agreed.

The Data Protection Principles 13.19

The *Data Protection Act 1998* (*DPA 1998*) is a complex piece of legislation that all flexible benefit schemes must comply to. Readers are strongly recommended to familiarise themselves with all aspects and requirements but for the sake of illustration, the following summary is provided.

There are eight Data Protection Principles in the Act; sometimes referred to as the Principles of 'good information handling' which data controllers (the organisation and/or outsourcer) are required to comply with.

The Principles apply to all personal data processed by data controllers. This requirement is irrespective of whether they are required to notify and whether or not they have actually notified.

Any data controller is able to claim an exemption from any of the Principles (whether on a transitional or outright basis).

The Principles are set out in *Part I* of *Schedule 1* of *DPA 1998*. *Part II* of *Schedule I* comprises the interpretation provisions that expand upon the First, Second, Fourth, Sixth, Seventh and Eighth Principles.

Schedule 2 of the Act provides conditions for the processing of any personal data relevant for the purposes of the First Principle, whilst *Schedule 3* provides conditions for the processing of sensitive personal data relevant for the purposes of the First Principle over and above those set out in *Schedule 2*. Additional *Schedule 2* conditions are set out in the *Data Protection (Processing of Sensitive Personal Data) Order 2000 (SI 2000 No 417)* (the 'Sensitive Data Order').

Schedule 4 of the Act consists of cases where the Eighth Principle (prohibiting the transfer of personal data outside the European Economic Area) does not apply.

When considering the Principles it is worth remembering the wide scope of the definition of 'processing' in the Act and, in particular, the fact that the term includes 'obtaining' and 'disclosure' of the data.

First Principle – 'Personal data shall be processed fairly and lawfully'.

This introduces the requirement that, as a requisite of fair and lawful processing, personal data shall not be processed unless at least one of the conditions in *Schedule 2* of *DPA 1998* (the conditions for processing) is met and, in the case of the processing of sensitive personal data, at least one of the conditions in *Schedule 3* ('the conditions for processing sensitive data') is also met.

Second Principle – 'Personal data shall be obtained only for one or more specified and lawful purposes, and shall not be further processed in any manner incompatible with that purpose or those purposes'.

Compliance with the Second Principle cannot be established simply by notification of the purpose(s) for which personal data are processed, as was possible under *DPA 1984*. The link between compatibility and notification has now been removed by *DPA 1998*.

It is to be noted that the Commissioner takes a strict view of the concept of compatibility of processing of personal data.

Third Principle – 'Personal data shall be adequate, relevant and not excessive in relation to the purpose or purposes for which they are processed'.

The wide definition of processing should be borne in mind when considering the Third Principle.

In complying with this Principle, data controllers should seek to identify the minimum amount of information that is required in order properly to fulfil their purpose and this will be a question of fact in each case. If it is necessary to hold additional information about certain individuals, such information should only be collected and recorded in those cases.

Fourth Principle – 'Personal data shall be accurate and, where necessary, kept up to date'. Data are inaccurate if they are incorrect or misleading as to any matter of fact. DPA 1998 provides guidance in interpreting this Principle as follows:

This Principle is not to be taken as being contravened because of any inaccuracy in personal data which accurately records information obtained by the data controller from the data subject or a third party in cases where:

- taking account of the purpose for which the data were obtained and further processed, the data controller has taken responsible steps to ensure the accuracy of the data; **and**

- if the data subject has notified the data controller of the data subject's view that the data are inaccurate, the data indicated that fact.

Fifth Principle – 'Personal data processed for any purpose or purposes shall not be kept for longer than is necessary for that purpose or those purposes'.

To comply with this Principle, data controllers will need to review their personal data regularly and to delete the information, which is no longer, required for their purposes.

Sixth Principle – 'Personal data shall be processed in accordance with the rights of the subjects under this Act'.

DPA 1998 provides guidance in interpreting this Principle.

A person will contravene this Principle if, but only if:

- he fails to supply information pursuant to the subject access request under *section 7*; or

- he fails to comply with notices given under the following provisions of the Act:

  ☐ *section 10* (right to prevent processing likely to cause damage or distress);

  ☐ *section 11* (right to prevent processing for the purposes of direct marketing); or

  ☐ *section 12* (rights in relation to automatic decision-taking); or

- he fails to comply with a notice given under *section 12A* of the Act (right to require data controller to rectify, block, erase or destroy inaccurate or incomplete data or cease holding such data in a way incompatible with the data controller's legitimate purpose) in respect of exempt manual data only during the transitional period up to and including 23 October 2007.

Seventh Principle – 'Appropriate technical and organisational measures shall be taken against unauthorised or unlawful processing of personal data and against accidental loss or destruction of, or damage to, personal data'.

The Act gives some further guidance on matters which should be taken into account in deciding whether security measures are 'appropriate'. These are as follows:

- Taking into account the state of technological developments at any time and the cost of implementing any measures, the measures must ensure a level of security appropriate to:

  ☐ the harm that might result from a breach of security; and

  ☐ the nature of the data to be protected.

- The data controller must take reasonable steps to ensure the reliability of staff having access to the personal data.

Eighth Principle – 'Personal data shall not be transferred to a country or territory outside the European Economic Area, unless that country or territory ensures an adequate level of protection of the rights and freedoms of data subjects in relation to the processing of personal data'.

For legal analysis by the Commissioner and a suggested "good practice approach" to assessing adequacy, refer to the guidance published by the Commissioner entitled, 'The Eighth Data Protection Principle and Transborder Data Flows'. For compliance advice on the Eighth Data Protection Principle refer to the guidance entitled, 'International Transfers of Personal Data'.

14 — Cost, Savings and Risks

This chapter includes the following:

- Introduction
- Feasibility study
- Strategy and design
- Pensions
- Tax
- Employment law
- Documentation
- Scheme launch and communication
- Management and administration
- Outsourcing flexible benefits
- Installation and implementation

Introduction

14.1

The cost, savings and risks associated with the design and implementation of a flexible benefits scheme are very much dependant on the mix of all the individual constituents covered in this book. Readers may wish to return to this chapter when they have read about them all.

By targeting benefits to where they are needed by employees it is possible to save the cost of providing unwanted benefits. National Insurance (NI), income tax and VAT savings can be achieved though a more efficient payment structure. Further savings can be made through the additional buying power which the company can enjoy through the use of a third-party provider.

As well as these direct implications there are also indirect cost savings and risks which need to be considered. For instance, an indirect saving could be the decrease in the recruitment budget due to a reduction in turnover, supported, in part, by the introduction of a flexible benefits scheme. An indirect cost could be the upgrading of the process or payroll system to cope with data from the new scheme.

Flexible benefits allow the organisation to restructure their employee benefit whenever necessary without major cost and risk.

The best way to identify cost, savings and risks in a flexible benefits scheme is to analysis each separate section and develop a model to map out the net effect of any changes applied to it. For instance, when choosing the mix of benefit products, a model could show the direct cost of purchase to employer and employee as well as the indirect cost of tax and NI. Changes to the mix of products may affect both these.

The way the scheme is managed itself also has an effect on cost, savings and risk. If, for example, the company is using an external benefits consultant to advise them on the scheme design and implementation and if their services are restricted to that of project manager and expert adviser; the cost is reduced because the organisation is using their own staff to carry out most of the work.

It is fairly difficult to quantify the costs, savings and risk associated with a flexible benefits scheme, however, the following will help to identify the process of identifying how best to manage them.

Feasibility study   14.2

Feasibility study is the most important part of designing and implementing a flexible benefits scheme as it sets the framework for the rest of the project (see further **CHAPTER 4**).

The ultimate objective of the feasibility study is to determine whether the benefits and advantages that the flexible benefits scheme gives to the organisation is worth the investment and the risk.

The direct costs, savings and risks associated with the flexible benefits scheme are covered at **14.11** below, as are indirect cost and risks.

Indirect savings, however, are usually identified as part of the feasibility study. For instance, the company may identify a potential saving of 10%

of its recruitment budget by introducing the new scheme. If this budget is say, £1million the savings will equate to £100,000.

Other indirect savings include rationalisation of different benefit schemes, better targeting of money spent, improved perceived value of reward, and improved performance.

The actual cost of a feasibility study varies from company to company. It is determined, in the main, by how much the company wishes to invest at this early stage in the proceedings. It is also affected by how much external advice is sought. The amount of money invested in the study is proportional to the depth and accuracy of the business case developed.

Current market charges for such a study ranges from about £5,000 up to about £50,000.

The size of the organisation and number of employees is not a major determining factor in this cost. For instance, the company may decide to look at implementing a generic site offering (see **12.37** above) so the feasibility study will be fairly straight forward as the outsourcer will be providing most of the technology and support services. However, if the organisation intends to provide all the IT services, networks, backup and support services, then the feasibility study will require more analysis and resource and, therefore, cost more.

Even if the organisation, based on the feasibility study, decides not to proceed with the flexible benefits scheme, the information gathered as part of the study will still prove valuable in terms of identifying key reward and benefit issues within the organisation. It will also suggest alternative solutions to addressing them.

As a rough guide, it is suggested that the company spend no more than 10% of its overall budgeted fee for the flexible benefits scheme on the feasibility study. If there is no budgeted fee, then the cost of the exercise needs to be based on the anticipated benefits the scheme may bring.

Strategy and design   14.3

Traditionally project management fees have accounted for a large proportion of the design and implementation of a flexible benefits scheme. This can be reduced by restricting external consultancy support to project management and advice, and only using the company's own staff to carry out most of the work required. However, this approach should not be judged only on cost as the use of external consultants will inevitably lead to better overall savings in the scheme and large reductions in costs and risk.

The analysis from the feasibility study and research should give the project team the framework for identifying the financial benefits, costs and risks associated with the flexible benefits scheme. For instance, employee feedback may have identified an unused benefit indicating that the organisation is wasting its investment. It may also have identified – indirectly – that the payroll systems in the organisation are antiquated and, regardless of the flexible benefits scheme, may need replacing. This in turn might suggest that the new flexible benefits scheme could also be widened to include payroll, thus reducing the overall spend for the organisation.

The feasibility study will also have identified some of the major costs associated with the scheme. For instance, if the decision is to outsource some or all of the administration of the scheme then at this stage the company should have some indication of what it may cost. This would be given by third-party providers looking to secure the business. (This is covered in more detail at **14.11** below.)

The basic design and framework for the proposed flexible benefits scheme needs to be thought out carefully to ensure that the best possible tax advantages have been gained. For instance, not only does buying holidays improve the tax situation for the individual it also reduces the NI payable (on the element of salary given up) by the organisation. Of course, there may be indirect costs associated with this as the company may have to provide cover for those individuals when they are on holiday.

The design and development stage offers the organisation the ability to not only provide an increased perceived value, with a little or no increase in direct costs, but a chance for further enhancement though good management of tax and NI.

One of the major cost savings that a flexible benefits scheme can deliver is a better preferential rate through bulk buying and/or re-negotiations. When setting up the new scheme both of these are required anyway. Very often better providers can be found to replace existing ones but the change should only be made if there are greater benefits in doing so.

Further improvements can be obtained if the organisation chooses to use a GSO, where their purchasing power is usually much greater. This is because their negotiating is based on all the employees of all the organisations that use their scheme.

The most cost-advantage products to provide in the flexible benefits scheme are those that are merely introduced by the organisation and do not require payroll deduction. There is no employer contribution because they are paid out of net pay and there is no additional employer NI. However, these may not offer the same advantages as payroll deducted products and benefit in kind and they would certainly not provide the tax advantages afforded to pensions and non-taxable benefits.

Costs   14.4

It is possible to provide a range of flexible benefits to employees at no extra costs to the organisation, however, it is worth modelling the resultant tax and NI effect of the choice to ensure that this the correct situation.

For organisations going through mergers or acquisitions, the strategy and design stage of the scheme is vital. This is where the mix of flexible benefits can reduce both the cost and risk of harmonising different sets of benefits. However, as you will see in **CHAPTER 8**, care needs to be taken that the final product mix is compliant with current legislation and Inland Revenue requirements.

As pensions can have a major effect on the structure and cost of a flexible benefits scheme there is a separate chapter on this subject (see **CHAPTER 6**). It is advisable that any alterations or addition to pension provision within the flexible benefits scheme should be properly costed out and the risk analysed.

For instance if a final salary scheme is included in the scheme and employees are allowed to 'top-up' their existing provision with added years, then the organisation clearly needs to model out what the potential additional risk will be in adding this to the main scheme.

With buying and selling holidays, theoretically speaking, there should be no additional costs to the organisation. In most schemes buying balances out selling. However, the risk is that there will be more people selling holidays than buying holidays and the organisation needs to find the money to pay for this. The rules and regulations of the scheme should ensure minimum risk, however, it is worth putting a provision in the overall funding of the scheme to cover any potential variations.

Usually the cost of private medical insurance is based on the demographic makeup of the work force along with previous record of claims. Although there is a possibility of reducing the overall costs to the organisation of private medical insurance by allowing employees to trade up or down, the resultant decrease in premiums may not be proportional to the benefits they buy.

It is worth, at the outset of the strategy and design stage of obtaining quotations for moving to single core provision with options to buy different levels.

Childcare vouchers and similar products attract favourable treatment by the Inland Revenue with regards to National Insurance contributions (NICs) (see **5.33** above for more details). The company can use these savings to either offset costs elsewhere in the scheme or pass on some form of discount to the employee. It is, however, worth checking the administrative costs as sometimes this can cancel out the savings.

Any form of trading benefits with salary, holidays and bonuses that generates extra NIC costs for an employee will also generate extra NIC premiums payable by the employer. It is suggested that trading benefits for cash is an example where some administrative charge can be made to offset the increased employer premiums payable.

The final point to consider in terms of costs with regards to product selection and mix is the possibility of increased take up of existing benefits. If, via the flexible benefits scheme, there is an increase in those signing up to a contributory benefit (eg pension scheme, PMI etc), then the organisation would need to find funds to pay for their increase in contribution.

Pensions 14.5

Pensions are an element of flexible benefits that can add the most perceived value to an employee's benefits package. However, if not managed properly it can also add the most cost and most risk.

The main consideration for the inclusion of a pension scheme is the risk that it may pose the employer. If the organisation offers a final salary scheme and allows individuals to trade within it, every time a change is made it subsequently changes the risk base of the whole of the scheme. This is a complicated area and professional advice from appropriate consultants is suggested.

There may be costs associated with additional contributions the organisations may have to pay if employees decide to put more money into their pension. This can be limited by stating that the company will only match core contributions and that all flexible benefit contributions are at the expense of the employee. However, this may not be suitable if the company is looking at salary sacrifice or paying employee contributions via the flexible benefit scheme.

The main savings that comes from including pension schemes in a flexible benefits scheme is that it allows pension planning to respond more effectively to the changing needs of the work force. Also, in terms of mergers and acquisition, it helps to facilitate harmonisation of different arrangements as well as rationalisation. Flexible benefits also reduce costs and risk and increases savings in terms of the transition between a defined benefits scheme to defined contribution scheme.

Flexing pensions can also reduce the HR and payroll administration. The flexible benefits scheme and administration can often provide a cheaper more efficient vehicle for front-end management of the pension.

See further **CHAPTER 6**, before considering the cost, savings and risk of including pensions in the flexible benefits scheme.

Tax   14.6

Careful management of the tax and NI treatment of benefits in flexible benefit schemes provides a major saving for both employer and employee. **CHAPTER 7** contains several illustrations to show how the use of trading salary can offset tax and NICs, eg benefit in kind charges for private medical insurance.

Again choice of product can play an important part in terms of added value and management of tax and NICs. For instance, the current Inland Revenue stance of no NICs due on buying personal computers (subject to certain conditions) may provide a favourably priced product for employees.

The only real tax and NIC risks to the organisation are higher take up of benefits in kind and trading down holidays. Those products eligible for tax relief and those that are non-taxable benefits obviously will not be a risk. Certain circumstances may help to offset them.

However, it is the mix of products that is the most important consideration in terms of tax and NIC within a flexible benefits scheme, and this is also where the main risks are associated. If more employees decide to sell holidays than buy, the organisation is going to have a higher NIC bill.

There are special products that do not fit in the usual tax regime, such as share schemes (see **7.22** above) and these should be treated separately. For instance, the savings that a SAYE scheme may afford both employer and employee needs to be offset by the cost of setting up such a scheme. Again, it would be wise to seek professional advice on this specialist subject.

It is strongly recommended that a model is drawn up with the relevant benefits, pricing and tax rules to clearly show what the individual cost, savings and risks are. Changing levels of take up will show how they are affected.

Employment law   14.7

The only direct cost implications arising from employment law issues are those associated with changing the terms and conditions of employment, such as contracts. If the flexible benefits scheme is being used as part of a merger then the cost of any changes required are more to do with the acquisition of the organisation than the implementation of a flexible benefits scheme.

The main issue with employment law is the consequences of not planning properly for the new scheme. There are severe penalties and fines for those organisations that breach any legislation. Claims for unfair treatment and loss of potential benefits can run as high as up to £50,000 if within the jurisdiction of a County court and even higher if the matter is referred to the High Court.

In terms of cost, savings and risks therefore, the main emphasis for employment law is to ensure that all legislation has been accounted for and the scheme rules and regulations have been designed to suit them.

Documentation 14.8

The most important objective, for documentation, is that employees clearly understand what options are available, the consequences of their choices and accept responsibility for them. Good and clear documentation reduces the risk of misunderstanding and future claims. If the documentation does not clearly set out the tax consequences of the mix of products employees choose then at some stage in the future, they may have grounds for compensation.

It is important when putting the documentation together for the scheme that enough time, resource and money is allowed to ensure the messages being developed are sound enough to support the scheme.

How this is then packaged is entirely up to the company. Most organisations that have implemented flexible benefit schemes have tended to produce fairly glossy handbooks. They have left out those items that may change on a continual basis (pricing etc) for inclusion in the preference form. This, by its very nature, can be changed on a more regular basis without additional costs.

The main cost consideration is the choice between paper forms and e-communication (see **9.15** above). One consideration for using it is the savings it brings by not having to use paper.

More organisations are now moving towards total reward statements. On their own they can be quite expensive. However, if the organisation is intending to put in a flexible benefits scheme then the majority of the process and systems required are the same.

It makes commercial sense, therefore, to take the additional step of including them in the design of the scheme. The addition cost of providing them will be more than offset by the improved perceived value that it offers the employees in terms of their total reward package.

Scheme launch and communication 14.9

The scheme launch and communication process is the one area of flexible benefits where the organisation can easily be carried away in terms of costs. As it is at the heart of the success of a flexible benefits scheme it is also fundamental to achieving the savings and reducing the risks associated with the scheme. The message must always remain far more important than the vehicle used to deliver it.

In its simplest form the scheme launch and communication can be based on issuing communications via paper and group presentations. Although cost effective the indirect costs of extra time and resources can make it impractical.

An element of cost needs to be included to account for both time and materials required communicating the scheme pre and post launch. For instance manpower to organise and run the launch.

Again the use of technology will influence the overall cost of the scheme launch and communication. It may actually reduce the amount of manpower because employees have interactive access to information via the web.

If the organisation already has its own Intranet site and has decided to administer the scheme themselves then the cost associated with the scheme launch and communication will include updating their site to suit.

Independent financial counselling is an important aspect of communicating flexible benefits because of the impact of individual choice. As an ethical backstop it allows the organisation to ensure that employees have sought, at the very least, independent advice before making any decisions.

The cost of this provision is based on either a fee or a commission basis. My preference is for a fee-based service to employees as this is the less controversial way of providing independent financial advisers. The organisation can save cost by merely referring employees to the IFA, but this must be carefully managed.

Management and administration 14.10

Traditionally, the management and administration of a flexible benefits scheme has been the most complex, time consuming and expensive part of a flexible benefits scheme. However, the effective use of technology now offers the opportunity to elevate historical and administrative problems.

Costs, savings and risks associated with the management and administration of the scheme depends firstly on whether the organisation intends to run the scheme in-house or outsourced (cost savings and risk for this option are covered in **14.11** below).

Regardless of choice, the basic process for in-house administration of the flexible benefits scheme is the same. It requires the management of input, calculations and output to various databases within the organisation (this is covered in more detail in **CHAPTER 11**).

The simplest and cheapest way of administering a scheme in-house is to use simple spreadsheets. However, this would be far too complicated, time consuming and leave itself open to inaccuracies. The option for the organisation, therefore, is either to buy in a bespoke system that integrates with existing databases (payroll, HR, P11D etc), or rebuild existing databases and put in new links.

The cost of bespoke systems differs widely dependent on the organisation's needs and suppliers used. As a guide, a bespoke flexible benefit administration system could cost between £60,000 and £100,000 (for a company with 500 employees over two sites). These costs include up-front consultation to install the systems along with ongoing support and training.

There are, of course, systems that are cheaper than this, however, it is possible that the indirect costs of running them and the risks that they pose in terms of incorrect management of the flexible benefits scheme does not really make them viable.

For larger organisations that already have a fairly integrated and sophisticated HR system (one that already includes some sort of benefits management), there is the option of rebuilding them to meet the needs of the new scheme. It is difficult to quote any indicative prices for this as each system is different, however, it is more likely to be cheaper than the alternatives above.

If the decision is to use a web-based administration system then the cost is not much different from those outlined above. This is because they would include additional costs to set up the interface between the organisation and the web provider.

A standard interface system consisting of two application servers, two web servers, two routers and two firewalls could cost in the region of £85,000. It is more common in terms of web-based administration systems for an external body to host the application – in which case there will be no need to invest in this hardware. However, there will be a hosting fee which can be typically as much as £20,000 to £40,000 pa (based on 500 employees at two sites).

As well as the direct cost of the administration process for the flexible benefits scheme there may also be some indirect costs associated. For instance, the payroll system may have to be updated to cope with a shadow salary or the P11D system may have to be automated further to cope with an increase in activity.

As well as the hardware costs and third party costs referred to above there will also be additional costs for the organisation in terms of staff required to run the scheme. Even if parts of the scheme are outsourced the company will still need a person to manage the relationship with the third-party provider.

Typically for a scheme of 500 employees the company will require one full time administrator if they are to manage the whole of the administration in-house. Probably, only a part-time co-ordinator will be required if parts of the process were outsourced.

Outsourcing flexible benefits   14.11

The decision to outsource the management and administration of a flexible benefits scheme is not based solely on reducing costs. The main reason why most organisations outsource this type of scheme is to allow them to concentrate on their core competencies rather than use valuable time and resources in managing a system that they are not experienced in.

Outsourcing also gives companies continuous access to new technology ideas and designs without the burden of up-front and continual investment and risk.

CHAPTER 12 covers this subject in more detail and outlines the risks that organisations need to consider when selecting an appropriate provider.

It is becoming more common for organisations to outsource the whole of the management of their flexible schemes to a third-party provider. The installation fees for a totally outsourced solution vary dependant on supplier and requirements. For a company employing 500 staff across two sites, the fee could be between £50,000 and £100,000. This is based on a total bespoke service. In addition to an installation fee there will be an ongoing administration of between £50 and £75 per employee pa.

Again, this is not an easy market to define in terms of costs and there are providers that can offer a full outsourcing at cheaper values. However, care needs to be taken about the level of service that they provide and how they have managed the associated risks detailed in this book associated with flexible benefits.

Although these figures may seem a lot to pay for outsourcing a flexible benefits scheme this cost is not too far from what companies would have to pay if they were running the scheme in-house. It is worth carrying out at a cost comparison between insourcing and outsourcing the scheme to ensure that the organisation has a benchmark by which to measure all prospective providers.

A new area of flexible benefit outsourcing is generic site outsourcing (GSO). This is based on tried and tested existing schemes that offer a generic solution to what has traditionally been a tailored–only market. See **12.37** above for more information on this type of outsourcing.

The basic principle is based on providers that have set up a flexible benefit scheme for their own employees and clients. Their scheme is designed in such a way that it can be easily modified without having to completely rebuild it. The benefit is that the organisation does not need to pay up-front fees for a tailored product and can benefit from the additional buying power that the GSO provider has earned by including the total number of employees managed by the scheme.

In comparison to the costs above, a typical GSO would cost in the region of £40,000 to design and install for a company employing 500 over one or two sites. Because GSOs use web-based technology, the only technical requirement is that the company's desktop computers have enough memory and configuration to be able to open up their intranet site.

Ongoing administration costs run at about £40 per employee pa. The organisation benefits for the advantages of networking with all the other companies that are included in the scheme and preferential rates negotiated with suppliers.

The main disadvantage of GSOs is that the company is reliant on the integrity and the efficiency of the provider to maintain a high level of operating standards. This is applied to any form of outsourcing.

Installation and implementation 14.12

The main costs associated with installation and implementation are manpower and resources. The organisation needs to build in some provision for the time it will take them to install whatever systems they have chosen and to load data.

The costs of the systems installation, in terms of hardware and software, are usually included in the providers fees (covered in **12.21**). However, the organisation should also budget for the time their own in-house IT and systems people will need to manage the installation of the new flexible benefits scheme.

The service standards developed for the scheme are vital in ensuring reduction in risks and running costs. It is worth spending some time developing these and ensuring that they do not inadvertently add to the running costs of the scheme by demanding over and above the supplier's normal terms.

The process for issuing quotations and benefit statements should be treated in a similar vein. There should be little costs for these as the quotations will be supplied by the benefit product provider as part of their overall package, and the benefit statements generated auto-matically from the systems used to administer the flexible benefits scheme. There may, however, be some time cost involved in dealing with starters, leavers and life changes and this should be budgeted into the overall costings of the scheme.

Off-line modelling is the best way of ensuring that the new flexible benefits scheme is running correctly before launching it to employees. It is worth the investment in time and effort to do this properly as it will save costs at a later stage (correcting the system) and reduce risks. If the organisation is outsourcing all, or part, of the administration of the scheme it is worth insisting that the providers are not paid until the successful completion of off-line trials and associated modifications.

When it comes to integrating the flexible benefits scheme with third parties and outsourcers the most important element to look at is the interaction with the other databases associated with the scheme. This includes P11D reports, payroll, Inland Revenue requirements etc. With these the risks are consequential. For instance, inaccurate data may mean spending more time at a later date to correct the chain of events that they trigger. There could also be significant ramifications if data is submitted to the Inland Revenue that is incorrect and has to be corrected at a later stage. This very often involves rebates, and in severe cases, fines.

The scheme should have contingency plans and disaster recovery plans to ensure continuity in the event of the failure of one or two or more components of the administration system. This may necessitate extra hardware, software or resources, but worth including to ensure minimum disruption and risks. Again, the price of these should be included in the overall contract fee if outsourcing part or the entire scheme.

Timing is an important factor in terms of controlling cash flow of the organisation. It is worth analysing the effect of the new scheme to ensure that it is not putting undue strain on the amount of money being paid out by the organisation. As well as negotiating a favourable financial deal from any outsourcers it is worth negotiating staggered payments to them to ease the pressure on the organisation.

Resources and management of the scheme has already been discussed, however, an element of their time needs to be included for the installation and implementation of the scheme.

15 — Key Criteria for Success

This chapter includes the following:

- Introduction
- Feasibility study
- Strategy and design
- Pensions
- Tax
- Employment law issues
- Documentation
- Communication
- Management and administration
- Outsourcing flexible benefits
- Implementation
- Costs, savings and risks

Introduction

The number of flexible benefits schemes in the UK has doubled over the last four years and, according to a variety of surveys, is set to increase over the next decade.

There are very good reasons for having a flexible benefits scheme, including harmonisation, improving the perceived value of benefits and improving communication generally. Flexible benefits can bring great advantages to your organisation if they can identify and meet employee needs and expectations. At the same time, it can form a valuable part of gathering information.

The key to the successful choice and implementation of a flexible benefits scheme is to establish a clear strategy linked to the overall objectives of the business. Once the strategy is determined, there must be a structured framework for its implementation. This must be based on clear communication, not just the benefits themselves, but also the message which management wishes to send to employees.

Key criteria

● Establish a clear strategy linked to the overall business objectives.

● Ensure a structured framework for implementation.

● Base strategy and implementation on clear communication.

● Deal with infrastructure issues as soon as possible.

● Introduce the initiative at an even pace

Feasibility study   15.2

An extensive feasibility study is advisable as a flexible benefits scheme is not always the right choice for an organisation. This is especially true if a substantial business case cannot be made to support it, the organisation's culture is not ready for such a change or there is no way of communicating such a concept.

Key criteria

● Ensure the new scheme will support and enhance the reward strategy.

● Develop a pragmatic and robust set of flexible benefit scheme principles.

● Ensure the market driven issues are clearly understood.

● Ensure the HR issues are clearly understood and how flexible benefits can help to address them.

● Put together the basic product selection and mix.

● Concentrate on analysing the administration, outsourcing, IT and infrastructure issues.

● Identify, as far as possible, the financial benefits, costs and risks for scheme.

● Base all assumptions on quantifiable research.

Strategy and design   15.3

If the decision is made to introduce a flexible benefit scheme into the company, the main measure of success will be its positive impact on both the individual and organisation. It is important, therefore, to ensure that the new flexible scheme, can deliver tangible Human Resource results. Benefit design must be complementary with reward policies and must not only support but also enhance the company's pay and motivation strategy.

Key criteria

- Establish the project management team as soon as possible.

- Decide on key tasks and timescales.

- Analyse feedback from feasibility study and base strategy and design on it.

- Base product selection on quantifiable data and not individual desires.

- Ensure an effective and robust link between trading salary, bonus and flexible benefit scheme.

- Develop a good set of rules, regulations and limits to control the scheme.

- Consider Inland Revenue and Employment Law ramifications.

- Ensure that whatever strategy and design is put together can be supported by the administration, IT and internal structure.

- Ensure that whatever strategy is developed it can be communicated effectively.

Pensions   15.4

There is a growing recognition among employees, of the importance of a pension and the need to provide for their own retirement. This increase in pension awareness may prompt many individuals to find ways of improving their company private pension. A flexible benefits package, with pensions as one of the menu items, can help them do this.

Components of pension schemes, such as additional voluntary contributions (AVCs) and death benefits, are already relatively prevalent in flexible benefit schemes. Pensions themselves figure less however their importance, as part of the flexible benefits menu, is growing.

One reason that pensions may not be included in the case of final salary schemes is that their inclusion can be complex. However, this complexity, which can be more apparent than real, is not insurmountable. There are ways of flexing pensions without complexity, before deciding if, and how, to include pensions in the scheme. However, there are some ethical tax and legal implications that need to be understood by employers and employees.

Key criteria

- Only include pensions in flexible benefits scheme if there is an existing pensions strategy.

- Consider a variety of different options to assess which is best in terms of both employer and employee requirements, tax and affordability.

- At the very least, use additional voluntary contributions and other pension vehicles to provide the option of topping up pensions.

- Also consider using salary sacrifice where applicable.

- Make sure that the design of the pensions element of the flexible benefits scheme does not inadvertently contravene any Inland Revenue requirements, in particular contribution limits and earnings cap.

Tax   15.5

The correct management of tax in a flexible benefits scheme is not only a legislative requirement, but also an important part of maximising the benefits the scheme delivers and minimising the costs. However, It is only effective if carefully planned during the design and strategy stage of the project and then effectively communicated.

Because each individual has their own unique tax situation, the tax implications of a flexible benefits scheme need to be delivered in such a way that each individual can calculate what the best mix is for them.

> **Key criteria**
>
> • Clearly understand the current employees and employers position on tax.
>
> • For each product selected, define precisely its tax treatment.
>
> • Analyse the result of mixing benefits together in conjunction with the use of salary and bonuses to fund choices.
>
> • Use modelling to ensure the best mix.
>
> • Develop a clear, simple, effective communication strategy specifically for tax.

Employment law issues   15.6

The subject of employment law is very complex and the consequences of not meeting legal and statutory requirements can be severe. It is strongly recommended that when setting up the project team that an employment lawyer is included to ensure compliance and good practice.

Because flexible benefits have a long-term effect on both the employer and the employee, it is important to think ahead in terms of the legal consequences concerning the flexible benefits scheme.

> **Key criteria**
>
> • Analyse existing terms and conditions of employment to see where changes may be required to accommodate new scheme.
>
> • Determine how best to change conditions of employment.
>
> • Ensure that indirect discrimination has not been built in to the design and strategy of the scheme.
>
> • Consider impact of the employment legislation and equal opportunities on the scheme.
>
> • For business transfers, ensure that all the requirements of TUPE (*SI 1981 No 1794*) are carried through into the scheme design.

Documentation   15.7

To a large degree the success or failure of the flexible benefits scheme can hinge on the quality of the company's communications. Scheme documentation is an integral part of these communications and by getting the documentation right a company will go a long way towards successfully promoting the scheme and ensuring its effective installation.

The most important issue, however, is that employees clearly understand what options are available, the consequences of their choice and that they accept responsibility for them. This means that education is more important than promotion.

Key criteria

• Design a documentation plan of action based on pre-installation, installation and post-installation requirements.

• Plan out how the organisation intends to announce the scheme.

• Use the employee handbook as the main guide for the design of the scheme.

• Design a preference form so that product and scheme information can be easily changed.

• Try, if possible, to use total reward statements to enhance the overall perceived value of the scheme.

• Ensure pension documentation is changed to suit the scheme.

• Ensure that the preparation of all documentation meets current legal requirements.

• If using e-communication as the main vehicle for documentation, ensure that the message remains far more important than the medium used.

Communication   15.8

Communication of the scheme must be unique in brand and style. It needs to be proactive, based on internal marketing rather than just issuing information.

Employee counselling on a structured basis is becoming increasingly important with increase in choice of benefits available to the employee to ensure individuals make informed decisions. As well as enhancing the perception that the employer is behaving ethically and responsibly, employee counselling also reinforces the communication process.

Key criteria

- Base the communication strategy on a unique design, brand and style.

- Use proactive communication.

- Decide what needs communicating and to whom, and what media the organisation is going to use to communicate it.

- Use the most respected communicators and avoid those who are negative.

- Ensure timing is chosen to give the flexible benefits scheme the best possible hearing.

- Take into consideration all the communication difficulties that might occur, for instance 'Chinese whispers', and plan for them.

Management and administration 15.9

Establishing the right administration structure and processes (in particular IT systems) required to support the new scheme is vital. The simplest way forward is to use existing, processes and incorporate the new scheme. However, this may not be feasible, in which case it may be necessary to budget for a new system or consider outsourcing.

Key criteria

- Decide at an early stage whether the administration of the flexible benefits scheme is to be in-house or outsourced.

- Agree basic administration functions and process as soon as possible.

- Ensure that all input, calculations, processing and outputs are identified before embarking on the overall design of the scheme.

- Ensure all organisational requirements are also catered for. ➤

- Ensure design of administration and management integrate easily with other systems such as payroll, P11D etc.

- Allow plenty of time to install and test the system.

- If using web-based administration systems, ensure that the organisation has budgeted for security and interfacing.

Outsourcing flexible benefits   15.10

Outsourcing is more than just a means of achieving business efficiency. It can be used to create strategic advantage – companies can gain access to expertise or competence not available in-house which in turn can provide an entry into new markets – benefits of scale can be achieved and cost control can be improved.

Outsourcing also gives companies continuous access to new technology, ideas and designs without the burden of up-front investment and risk.

While the benefits are clear, there are many factors to take into account along the route – which are the key elements to outsource, how to build a better relationship between people in the organisation and its supplier and how to measure the success of the operation?

Key criteria

- Ensure there are clearly defined reasons for outsourcing and that any alternative has been compared to the ability of the organisation to run the scheme in-house.

- Ensure any selection of outsourced elements are managed correctly. Use RFIs (requests for information) and ITTs (invitations to tender) to select the most appropriate provider.

- Ensure that whatever contracts are drawn up that they are well drafted and the organisation's legal tax and financial obligations will not be compromised (eg *Data Protection Act 1998*).

- Ensure a good but practical set of service level agreements.

- Ensure the outsourcer provides a good set of guarantees and performance bonds, in particular, include clauses on non-performance.

- When using application service providers make absolutely sure that all eventualities have been catered for.

- If using generic site outsourcing make absolutely sure that the organisation is represented on their client user monthly management meetings.

Implementation   15.11

The final part of installing a flexible benefits scheme is to assemble all the various components, covered above, in order to enrol and administer employees' choices.

Attention to detail is key as it will be the ultimate measure of value by its users.

Key criteria

- Define data requirements as soon as possible ensuring that it is up to date and clean.

- Try to install systems as soon as possible to ensure that there is ample time for commissioning and testing.

- Double check service standards set to make sure that they are realistic and that they are being adhered to.

- Set up an off-line model to allow extensive testing.

- Ensure that all third-party providers and/or outsourcers are included in the overall installation and implementation planning.

- Ensure that the timing is best suited to members of the scheme and administration.

- Ensure that there is enough resource and management to carry the project through.

- Make absolutely sure that all the requirements of the *Data Protection Act 1998* are met.

Costs, savings and risks   15.12

Can flexible benefits achieve cost savings? In the short run, the answer is no; but in the long run, flexible benefits can result in substantial cost savings. By targeting benefits to where they are needed by employees, it is possible to save the cost of providing unwanted benefits. National Insurance, income tax and VAT savings can be achieved through more effective payment structures. Further savings can be made through the additional buying power which employers and their employee benefit advisers have.

However, there is risk and loss associated with achieving the aims of the scheme. These must be clearly identified and managed.

Key criteria

- Quantify all potential savings first.

- Include indirect as well as direct savings.

- For each element, ensure that all items and eventualities have been costed.

- Use a good model to analyse the risk associated with each element of the scheme.

- Remember that a flexible benefit scheme is a long-term project with long-term rewards.

Appendix 1 — Example of Typical Documents

This appendix includes the following:

- Typical project brief
- Internal fact find
- IT assessment
- Compensation benchmarking
- Benefits audit
- Setting up an employee survey
- Employee survey
- Communications audit
- Key tasks: flexible benefits project
- Timescale: flexible benefits project
- Employee handbook
- Preference form
- Third party service level agreement

Typical project brief   1A.1

This typical project brief is based on a fictitious organisation (the organisation) and is designed to give you a practical overview of the types of issues and solutions involved with the design and implementation of a flexible benefits scheme.

Scheme principles   1A.2

There are five important principles that will underpin the success of this flexible benefits scheme:

The introduction of the flexible benefits scheme should have a positive impact on both the individual and the organisation. It should deliver tangible HR results that support and enhance the company's pay and motivation strategy.

It is vital to establish the right administration structure and process (in particular, IT systems) to support the new scheme. If this is not feasible, the introduction of new systems or outsourcing may have to be considered.

Communication of the scheme must be unique in brand and style. It needs to be proactive and based on internal marketing rather than just issuing information.

Employee counselling on a structured basis is becoming increasingly important, with the increase in choice of benefits available to employees to ensure individuals make informed decisions. It enhances the perception that the employer is behaving ethically and responsibly.

The key to a successful choice and implementation of a flexible benefits scheme is to establish a clear strategy linked to the overall objectives of the business. There must be a structured framework for its implementation based on clear communication, not just to employees themselves, but also the message which management wishes to send.

The organisation's background   1A.3

The organisation operates nine manufacturing and distribution units across the United Kingdom – six are divisions, whilst the remaining three are subsidiaries. Their overriding strategy is to provide targeted products to their key customer group in each of their locations.

The organisation's main future strategy is to grow the business through further development of their existing portfolio and acquisition of similar companies.

They employ 1,500 staff across the UK with an additional 500 concession workers. The split between full and part-time workers is currently 60/40, but the trend is moving more towards 70/30. Their Headquarters has a different profile.

Staff turnover is about 50% pa, however, they also have 75% stability. The high levels of turnover are at the lower end of their employment band. There are two main bands, in terms of length of service: less than two years and above ten years. There are a large number of single and middle aged people.

Recruitment is described as a 'nightmare', especially at mid- to junior-management level. This is further aggravated by the lack of turnover at mid-management level, which is creating a lack of inertia within the group of staff the organisation considers to be the main catalyst for change.

In line with their competition and most other organisations in the UK, the organisation is looking for a better link between contribution and reward. They believe one of the most important and influential parts will be employee benefits, particularly in improving the perceived value of the overall reward scheme.

They have already given quite a lot of thought towards moving to a total reward system over the next few years. They also believe that there is continual erosion of the benefits that they provide and this issue needs to be addressed.

Benefits strategy   1A.4

From discussions with the organisation, we have drawn up the following assumptions about their desired benefits strategy.

The need to both support their developing performance management culture and to attract and retain the required staff has necessitated a comprehensive review of the organisation's approach to reward and recognition.

They have identified a poor fit between current policies and changing needs during the recent restructuring programme. Staff and managers alike may be dissatisfied by the current policies and systems which have been in operation for some time and appear to no longer meet their current and future organisational needs.

Their ability to measure and incentivise the performance and behaviour that they wish to encourage amongst various staff groups will be essential if they are to achieve their corporate objectives.

Benefits scheme objectives   1A.5

The objectives of the benefits scheme are as follows:

- Review, design and implement a benefits strategy, which is designed to meet the future needs of the organisation.

- Be key to attracting and retaining the people needed to deliver the new business strategy – delivering skills needed, when needed, and in the locations where needed.

- Be key to driving individual, team and organisational performance.

- Underpin and support the development of the desired culture and behaviours needed to achieve corporate objectives.

- Be an integrated resolution to a range of urgent business-driven reward issues, which have resulted from the need to review and update reward strategy in line with recent and planned changes.

Envisaged benefits scheme principles   1A.6

The envisaged principles of the benefits scheme are:

- Movement from passive pay and benefits administration to active reward management aligned with strategic goals.

- To support changes in working methods, traditions and attitudes.

- To ensure coherent direction to reward management avoiding mixed messages and one-off, uncoordinated initiatives.

- To create the conditions for greater staff motivation.

- To underpin the business needs relating to recruitment and retention.

- To provide value for money.

- Perceived fairness.

- Flexibility.

Current benefits provision: 1A.7

The main benefit provision is the Money Purchase Pension Scheme (MP) with an additional 'Stakeholder' Scheme (primarily for part-time workers). There is three times death-in-service provision.

In addition to this, there are other benefits, which include:

- permanent health insurance;

- private medical insurance;
- holidays (20 days, with up to 5 days extra for length of service);
- share option scheme;
- company car scheme.

Basic framework and process 1A.8

A basic framework and process for the proposed flexible benefits scheme has not yet been decided but for the purposes of illustration, we will use a GSO flexible benefit product.

Based on the four basic principles outlined above, the basic process for the intended flexible benefit scheme will be:

- Employer designs and presents a menu of benefits, including prices.
- Employer sets rules and regulations governing the scheme and limits on entitlements. This will include voluntary benefits.
- Employees seek advice from a professional advisor on the appropriate mix of benefits and the consequences of their choices.
- Employees select preferred combination of benefits to meet their needs.
- Employees' preferences are approved by the employer, except in special circumstances.
- The employees' selection is then made, for the duration of the period of flexible benefit, subject to lifestyle changes.

Feasibility study 1A.9

An extensive feasibility study will be undertaken to ensure that the introduction of a flexible benefits scheme is the right choice for the organisation. The main objective is to build a substantial business case for its introduction, ensure the culture is ready for such a concept and determine the best way of communicating the new scheme.

Other feasibility indicators include assessing whether flexible benefits will improve HR competitive edge and support/enhance the existing reward and motivation policy. The study also needs to establish if the organisation's infrastructure should be modified to support the new scheme and what the total cost for the initiative will be.

The main elements will be as follows:

- Determine if the concept of a flexible benefits scheme will support and enhance the organisation's mission statement and key priorities.

- Establish the market driven reasons for introducing the new scheme.

- Examine the HR issues of introducing the new scheme.

- Examine the communication issues of introducing the new scheme.

- Determine the product mix for the new scheme.

- Evaluate the administration and outsourcing options for the new scheme.

- Establish who will be involved in the new scheme. Evaluate required expertise and experience to deliver project and select right mix of external consultants and internal staff.

Project team   1A.10

In order for the organisation to maintain ownership and control of the flexible benefits scheme and to minimise costs, it is proposed that a joint project team is formed between the consultants and the organisation. The role of the consultants will be to provide the project's management skills and specialist advice. The process of setting up this project team will be as follows:

- Evaluate required expertise and experience to complete the project, concentrating on a good mix of internal and external consultants.

- Agree basic responsibilities and action.

- Establish expectations from directors and key staff for the success of the project.

- Establish outcomes to be measured and milestones.

- Produce project model/blue print and timescales.

Research   1A.11

The success for the design and implementation of the organisation's flexible benefits scheme will depend on the quality of information and statistics gathered at the commencement of the project. We have assumed, for the basis of this project that the following will have been carried out:

- Competitive benchmarking for key job groups, including benefits: determine how competitive each pivotal job role is against industry and local norms.

- Employee satisfaction survey: identify preferences, key concerns and communication issues from the perspective of employees.

- Current benefits review: identify all benefits provided, their respective costs, take-up and effectiveness/competitiveness.

- Communications audit: identify current strategy, policies and structure to determine key issues and how best to manage communication of new initiatives developed.

- Administration: ensure the new scheme achieves maximum possible integration with the organisations HR and payroll systems.

- Systems and Infrastructure: ensure IT, infrastructure and resources can support any new initiatives developed.

- Evaluation against best practice: measure overall performance against industry norms.

Strategy and design   1A.12

The design of the scheme needs to be innovative to mirror the developing culture of the organisation and create a set of benefits above and beyond those offered by the organisation's competitors.

To ensure the ownership of the scheme by the organisation, that the new scheme meets the expectations of all concerned and offers value for money, we believe the following strategy and design should be followed:

- Identify current situation and identify benefits most wanted by employees. This will be via the research carried out in **1A.11** above.

- Analyse current providers of existing benefits to determine how they will fit in with the new scheme.

- Evaluate information gathered from above and agree overall scheme strategy.

- Select products to be included in scheme menu.

- Agree rules and regulations and set limits on entitlements.

- Plan, design and due diligence.

- Complete design, administration procedures, communication process and tax and legal requirements.

- Gain Inland Revenue endorsement for the scheme.

- Design and implement launch, concentrating on effective communication to all staff.

- Ongoing management and administration of the scheme.

- Review options to add additional benefits at a later date.

- Quality control policies and procedures.

Scheme launch 1A.13

A flexible benefits scheme should be uniquely branded based on internal marketing. The vision and mission set must be meaningful and based on the desired outcomes relevant to the organisation.

Information gathered from employee feedback and previous history will be used to develop a communication strategy that will ensure employees have a clear understanding of the new strategy; how it affects them individually and their part (responsibility) in making it work for both them and the organisation.

This is an important part of ensuring that the critical success factor (identified as obtaining workforce buy in and acceptance) works.

The design and launch of the benefits scheme should concentrate on effective communication to all staff and others involved. To achieve this, we will carry out the following:

- Obtain top team endorsement for the scheme.

- Identify current communication strategy and develop an appropriate strategy for benefits.

- Ensure that all personnel involved in the communication process have received comprehensive training in communication skills and possesses adequate knowledge.

- Agree a format for communication, which could include:

    ☐ group presentations;

    ☐ New scheme handbook;

☐   individual counselling and helplines;

☐   newsletters, e-mail, etc.

The design of an Intranet-based handbook and preference form would be done in conjunction with the organisation's IT team.

Employee financial counselling   1A.14

Employee benefit packages are complex and often involve choices to be made at different stages of an employee's career. Traditionally, employees have taken 'core' benefits for granted because, to all intents and purposes, they were out of their control and their perceived benefits long term.

By introducing a flexible benefit scheme, the organisation will be moving the emphasis of ownership for control and management of benefits from the employer to the employee. Because of this and to ensure that the perceived advantages of a flexible benefit scheme are reinforced, education through employee financial counselling, on a structured basis, will be vital.

- Agree format of financial counselling surgeries.

- Set up individual consultations to allow employees to enter the scheme in the most appropriate manner, eg make an informed decision about the initial mix of benefit they require.

- Agree and set up a regular review process for employees. eg agree frequency and level of support.

- Agree parameters for extraordinary consultations, eg changes in lifestyle, such as bereavement.

- Agree format, frequency for annual surgeries to update staff on scheme changes, changes in legislation etc.

Systems and infrastructure   1A.15

The system and infrastructure chosen to run the organisations flexible benefits scheme will be based on the consultants GSO product, 'Choices'.

Choices' main advantages are that it will help reduce the administrative burden and effort of administering the scheme. It will also improve the service to employees and allow the organisation to focus on strategic human resources that assist organisations achieve business goals.

Choices supports:

- fixed, flexible and mixed benefit scheme set-up and administration;

- employee communication;

- employee self-service;

- product servicing and management;

- providing employees with a statement of their remuneration, benefits costs and entitlements.

Choices will manage both fixed and flexible benefits administration for the organisation.

The technology supports:

- centralised reporting and management information;

- employee self-service;

- payroll interface;

- benefit plan enrolment;

- life event changes;

- leavers and joiners;

- total remuneration statement;

- employee directory.

This is an Internet/Intranet Business Service. It includes free access to upgrades, helpdesk support and ongoing maintenance of the software. There is no requirement for the organisation to purchase hardware to run the application.

The full functionality of Choices' technology will be delivered to two primary roles within the company – employee and administrator. These roles are fully integrated for connecting employee and employer with the information relevant to their roles.

Access and services required by the HR administrators and employees will be defined by the project team. The consultants will configure the technology to deliver the system required. The following guidelines will be used.

Employee access   1A.16

For core benefits, employees will be able to select additional products through salary sacrifice, up to an employer-defined limit. Employees will also be able to manage their own personal data. This includes registering change of address, changing emergency contacts and adding dependants. Giving employees controlled access to information, for which they are responsible, will reduce call volumes to HR, enhance communication with employees, decrease administrative workloads and significantly improve employee satisfaction.

For flexible benefits, employees will have, in addition to all these features, the ability to mix and match their benefit selection up to their predefined 'flex' allowance within the scheme rules.

For both applications, most of the common product options are included: pension, car, cash, holidays, death in service, income protection, critical illness, private medical, dental, optical, health club membership, childcare and retail vouchers, travel insurance, personal accident, car breakdown, health screening and financial advice.

Administrator access   1A.17

The benefits administrator will help to define how the scheme is set up and Choices will deliver a customised solution to meet the requirement.

Throughout the enrolment cycle, the administrator will be able to view activity, status and correspond with employees.

Other functions provided within the administrator role include:

- report generation;
- adding joiners and deleting leavers;
- mid-term adjustments;
- authorising change requests;
- generating the monthly payroll file.

Reports are available by product providers selected and premiums payable. These can be produced by cost centre, business unit and any pre-defined timescale. In addition to a number of standard report formats that are available, Choices can build and customise any additional reports required.

Embedded in the application will be a messaging system and audit trail of transactions.

Choices uses secure socket layer (SSL) technology, system security methods and layers of firewalls to create authenticated and encrypted transactions. This ensures that users access only the information they are authorised to access. This is consistent with the security standards of many leading financial institutions on the web.

The interface is both intuitive and easy to use. Choices will also provide a comprehensive training programme for the organisation so that they can quickly get familiar with the application. The organisation will have the option of onsite training at the organisation's office or at one of the consultant's regional offices.

Choices will make available a number of online support resources including:

- how-to-use guides;

- troubleshooting assistance;

- frequently asked questions.

Total remuneration statement 1A.18

This statement is available within the Choices product (it can also be used as a separate, stand-alone option for the organisation). The total remuneration statement will contain only the information the organisation wishes to provide to each employee. This will typically be issued on an annual basis. Once the information and layout have been defined, THE CONSULTANTS will specify the format of data it requires from the employer and will then aggregate this data and embed it in a statement that is personalised to individual employees listing their overall compensation package, benefit costs and entitlements.

The statement then becomes a reference point for the employee and reinforces to each employee the additional costs the employer incurs on their behalf and each benefit entitlement. Statements can be issued to employees online or in paper format.

Management and administration 1A.19

The management and administration of a flexible benefit scheme is more a co-ordination of resources, rather than a process. This is due, in the main, to the assumption that each individual benefit provider will provide individual case-by-case administration (including projections, registration, on-going support, etc) that is interlinked with the scheme's main systems.

The organisation already has IT systems in place covering payroll and benefits. This system is linked/integrated and can cope with a 'shadow salary'.

In setting up a flexible benefit scheme, the following areas will need to be reviewed:

- Define and set service standards for all parts of the scheme.
- Design and issue Administration Manual covering working practices, methods of transmission of data, etc.
- Define and set up management accounting system.
- Define and set up employee flexible benefits records.
- Ensure smooth processing of payments to benefits providers from the organisation and, where relevant, individual employees.
- Define parameters to measure effectiveness of scheme and monitoring.
- Assess the organisation's database to manage and monitor above, modify to suit.
- Arrange administration training for the organisation's personnel.

Installation and implementation 1A.20

The joint organisation/the consultant's team will oversee the installation of the new scheme. This will include obtaining, collating and reviewing all information and data needed to set up and run the project.

An installation plan will be drawn up covering actions required, who will be responsible for them and what timescales will be involved. In addition to points already covered in this proposal, these will include:

- Establishing targets and agreed reporting times for the team.

- Gathering basic data for prospective members.

- Agreeing data requirements, in particular for Choices.

- Loading and validating data, in particular for Choices.

- Co-ordinating with payroll and benefit providers to discuss working practices, future transmission of data, contribution data, etc.

- Set parameters regarding quotations, etc.

- Define new entrant data 'forms'.

- Define leaver and change 'forms.

Quality control 1A.21

Quality control and customer care is the hallmark of any good flexible benefit scheme. Because of the multitude of variables involved, a quality control and code of practice will be developed in conjunction with the organisation.

Adding new options 1A.22

The scheme will be designed to allow the addition of new benefits such as discount vouchers, risk benefits etc over the next few years as the scheme picks up.

Timescales 1A.23

The average timescale for the design and implementation of the flexible benefits scheme covering these numbers of employees and sites is between six to nine months. It is possible to achieve a launch date in a shorter period of time but it usually necessitates an element of compromise in both product selection and communication.

The concept for the scheme and perhaps some of the products can be launched/communicated earlier.

We would require further discussion with the organisation to produce a more detailed project chart with time scales.

Fees 1A.24

The consultant is able to provide a comprehensive list of services and can accommodate a whole range of different fee bases ranging from time cost for all services to a fixed fee for regular services and time cost for tailored and occasional services.

Because of the nature of most of their projects and the difficulty in determining exactly what external resources and timescales would be involved, their proposals are usually based on a time cost.

Once they have a clearer idea of the project key tasks and timescales, it may be possible to offer a finite day rate as well as hourly charges.

Invoicing for projects is usually on defined phases, for example:

1. Set up project.
2. Feasibility study.
3. Research and benchmarking.
4. Strategy and design.
5. Scheme launch.
6. Employee financial counselling.
7. Management and administration.
8. Installation and implementation.
9. Quality control.

A capped fee is usually agreed with the organisation at the commencement of each phase. This will only be exceeded with the consent of the organisation.

Quality management policy

Financial Services Act 1986 1A.25

The activities of the consultant are regulated under the *Financial Services Act 1986* and the company operates subject to the rules of the

Securities and Investments Board (SIB). Additionally, the company is subject to the rules of the Personal Investment Authority (PIA).

The company must, at all times, act in such a way as to comply with the SIB Principles and the Rules of PIA which are incorporated in the company's compliance rules as outlined in the company's Compliance Manual. The company complies properly with any restrictions or prohibition as to its business which may be imposed under PIA's rules.

All employees are expected to make themselves familiar with the contents of the Compliance Manual and to abide by it at all times. Breach of the company's compliance rules is a serious offence that may, in some circumstances, lead to dismissal.

Members of staff are individually authorised to give investment advice to clients only for specified investment categories. Consultants may not give advice except in those areas in which they are authorised.

Group compliance policy statement   1A.26

It is the policy of the consultant to observe high standards of integrity and fair dealing and to act with due skill, care and diligence in the conduct of business.

To those ends, all Group companies:

- comply with both the spirit and the letter of all relevant laws, codes, rules, regulations and standards of good market practice in each jurisdiction where they conduct business; and

- ensure that any irregularities which arise are promptly resolved in a manner which minimises financial loss and protects the good name and reputation of the Group.

Client or member complaints   1A.27

All staff are aware that the complaint must be referred to a main board or Regional Director (the Complaint Owner) who is senior to the person involved in the complaint and the complaint acknowledged within seven business days of receipt.

The Complaint Owner would then undertake to investigate the complaint within two weeks (our maximum period is two months for more complex cases) and to write to the complainant confirming the results of the investigation within the next seven business days.

Customer care policy   1A.28

There are a number of different levels to the Customer Care and general quality standards. These are summarised into the following areas;

- **Quality Personnel** – The consultant has for a long time regarded quality and therefore professionalism as paramount. This is a necessity if the services and advice we provide is to be relied upon. Those services are dependent on the individuals providing them and we must, therefore, value and invest in them.

- **Technical and Professional Quality** – We work to strict standards and procedures to control accuracy and quality of service in relation to the control and security of client assets, and administration technical service standards, etc.

- **Procedural Instruction Manual** – Our Procedural Instruction Manual is issued to all staff (along with a separate Compliance Manual). The first Procedural Instruction Manual was prepared as long ago as September 1983 and has been updated at ever increasing intervals since then.

  The Procedural Instructions (PIs) contained within are added to and currently number seventy-eight. They range from general procedures like chasing of debts, and computer viruses, to specific processes like advice on pension transfers and trustee liability insurance.

  All PIs are, therefore, issued on the basis of improving the efficiency and quality of advice given. Failure to follow a PI is a compliance failure and is itself a disciplinary action.

- **Compliance** – Compliance is used in a number of contexts and different ways. First, it is 'Compliance with either the *Financial Services Act 1986* or with Personal Investment Authority (PIA) rules'. Second, it is 'following the official rules imposed by legislation, external regulation, of the consultant.

- **Office Procedures** – We have clear standards for logging all incoming work (via use of computerised workflow system) and subsequent monitoring of progress and completion against performance standards. Maintenance and organisation of records, and creation of audit trails are also documented and all areas are regularly reviewed by our own internal technical manager as well as by the consultant's auditors.

Internal fact find   1A.29

Listed below is the relevant company information required for the internal fact-find process.

Company information:

- Company cultures.
- HR key issues, policies and strategy.
- Reward issues, policies and strategy.
- HR structure, capabilities and capacities.
- Plans for harmonisation, mergers, change etc.

Communication:

- Communication strategy.
- Communication stakeholders.
- Informal, eg social, verbal etc.
- Formal, eg newsletter, e-mail, team briefs, focus groups etc.

Employee information:

- Demographics – location/catchment.
- Age/sex.
- Length of service.
- Dependants.
- Turnover statistics and exit interviews.

Employee feedback and surveys:

- Results of surveys/focus groups, etc to date.
- Informal assessment of employee perception of current reward.
- Trade union and/or employee representation.

Administration:

- Brief on process and systems for:
  - ☐ Payroll.
  - ☐ Pension.

☐ P11D.

☐ HR data base.

Employment law and tax:

- Tax advisors and local IR office.

- Copy of standard contract of employment.

Competitive benchmarking:

- Grades and job description.

- Companies that you would like to add to target list for bench-marking.

Existing benefits audit:

- Details of statutory and non-statutory benefits (including employee share schemes etc).

- Costs.

- Levels of take up.

- Details of providers.

- Details of current contracts.

- Holiday entitlement and take up.

IT – Assessment   1A.30

One of the main areas we assess when considering the design and implementation of any flexible benefit scheme is the infrastructure required to process the various transactions created. The flowchart in **CHAPTER 11.5** illustrates a typical scheme and flow of transactions.

Every scheme is unique, and so there are no fixed formulas for designing the required infrastructure. However, we know from our experience, simplicity and modification of existing process is by far the best option.

In the first instance, we need to understand, in basic terms, what systems you already have. We may come back to you later for more detail if required. Any comments you or your team may have would also be appreciated.

The questions below are not based on system requirements for a flexible benefits scheme but to establish what would be required to 'blend' the processes required into your existing infrastructure.

1. Do you have an integrated IT system/database for HR, pensions, PAYE/P11D/NI and payroll?

2. If the above are all separate; who are the providers and what are the systems?

3. If the above are all separate; how are they linked?

4. Are there are future plans for replacement or modification of any of the above?

5. Can your payroll database cope with shadow (contractual as opposed to actual) salary calculations? (Perhaps you may have had a PRP or similar bonus scheme in the past).

6. Is there a facility in your database(s) for electronic transactions with external providers?

7. Do you issue any form of benefit statements?

8. Do you show/refer to employee benefits on your pay slips?

9. What type of management report do you prepare, relating to the above and the flowchart in **CHAPTER 11.5**.

10. Are there any special requirements with regard to the *Data Protection Act 1998* or any of the above?

11. Do you have/what are the general service standards for the above?

Compensation benchmarking   1A.31

In the UK today the major human resources' issue that is holding back individual company growth is the ability to attract and retain good employees. In certain parts of the country record low levels of unemployment coupled with increased flexibility have led to a saturated labour market.

As we move into the new millennium, companies will have to compete not only with organisations within their own industries but those with similar processes and skill sets. This will mean that employers will have to modify their strategies to ensure they offer competitive reward packages and effective recruitment marketing campaigns.

The first and most important step in the above is to ensure that the current compensation policy and strategy is the most appropriate for recruiting and retaining employees to ensure a growth in the business. This is done through compensation benchmarking.

The basic framework for a typical project, agreed at a meeting between the consultant and their client, would include:

- objectives, assumptions and expectations;

- identifying appropriate markets;

- data capture;

- data selection;

- interpreting results.

The process of compensation benchmarking involves:

- review and analysis of job descriptions to determine target markets and data required;

- analysis of competition and similar process companies to determine target market;

- gathering competitive data via existing clients and national database;

- collating data gathered, reviewing responses and consolidating data;

- analysing data, producing statistics and presenting findings and recommendations.

Benefits audit   1A.32

An example of a benefits audit is illustrated below.

CORPORATE DETAILS	
Company Name	**Example Ltd**
Address	
Contact and Position	
Telephone Number	

Fax Number	
Nature of Business	
VAT Status	
Number of Employees	Full Time:
	Part Time:
	Contract:
Background of Company (including ownership and influence of parent)	
Company Employee Culture	
Locations in UK	

COMPANY CARS

Number of vehicles in fleet?	
What proportion are 'perk' vehicles?	
Do you have formal vehicle policy?	YES/NO
	If YES please supply copy
Are your vehicles 'banded'?	YES/NO
If so, what are the bands and what is the basis for their calculations?	
Do you provide *'second cars'*?	YES/NO
How are the vehicles acquired?	☐ Outright Purchase
	☐ Hire Purchase
	☐ Contract Hire
	☐ Contract Purchase
	☐ Leasing
	☐ Finance Leasing

What is the replacement cycle?	Number of miles
	Number of years
Do you provide a fuel card?	YES/NO
Do you pay for private petrol?	YES/NO
What preparations have been made for the tax change in 1994?	
HOLIDAYS	
What is the normal leave allowance for all staff?	
Do senior staff have longer holiday entitlement?	YES/NO
What would the minimum acceptable annual leave be?	
What would the maximum acceptable annual leave be?	
How much does the annual leave cost the company?	
DENTAL/OPTICAL	
Do you provide a staff dental plan?	YES/NO
Who is the provider?	
What is the annual cost of the dental plan?	
Do you provide a staff optical plan?	YES/NO
Who is the provider?	
What is the annual cost of the optical plan?	
How many staff use VDU equipment?	
Do you have a formal eye screening policy?	YES/NO
LVs/CANTEEN	
Do you provide luncheon vouchers?	YES/NO
To what value?	
Total annual cost?	
How often are these reviewed?	
Do you provide a canteen?	NO/some sites/all sites
Does the canteen receive any corporate subsidy?	YES/NO
What is the total annual cost of subsidised canteen?	

CRÈCHE	
CRÈCHE	
Do you provide crèche facilities for your staff?	YES/NO
Do you provide childcare vouchers for your staff?	YES/NO
Are there other employers in your area that provide crèche facilities?	YES/NO
What proportion of your staff have children under four years old?	

PENSIONS	
The following documents should be obtained where applicable:	
	1. Copy of scheme booklet.
	2. Copy of latest scheme accounts.
	3. Copy of last actuarial valuation.
	4. Copy of any pension claims used in contracts of employment or offer letters.
	5. Staff data.
The following information is required:	
Type of scheme	FS/MP/PP
How invested?	
How administered?	
How many benefit categories?	
Summary of contribution/benefit structures	
How are eligibility conditions applied in practice?	
Level of scheme take-up and company attitude	
Company's view on private arrangements to non joiners	
Has recent legislation been acted on? (Pensions Act, including LPI, MNT's, etc.)	
LAB provision for non joiners	
LAB Insurer	
Claims History	
Company aims in making pension provision	
Problems experienced	

PHI	
COMPANY'S CONTRACTUAL LONG TERM DISABILITY OBLIGATION	
(Obtain copy of Contract Clause/Staff Handbook)	
Eligibility	
PHI benefit structure	
Basic benefit	
Employer's pension contribution cover	
Employer's National Insurance contributions cover	
Salary definition	
Deferred period	
Cessation age	
Current insurer	
Claims/premiums history	
Current unit rate	
Guarantee period	
Problems (including underwriting and claims)	
EMPLOYEE SHARE OWNERSHIP PLANS (ESOPs)	
Name of company which has established the ESOP	
Who are the beneficiaries under the ESOP?	
Copy of Trust Deed, if available	YES/NO
PROFIT RELATED PAY (PRP)	
Name of employment unit which established the scheme	
What is the relationship of the employment unit with the corporate structure?	
Who are the participants?	
What are the Scheme Rules for eligibility?	
What is the profit period?	
Copy of the Scheme Rules?	YES/NO
SUBSIDISED LOANS	
Are all employees eligible for subsidised loans?	
If not, which group of employees is eligible?	

Are loans available for any purpose?	
If not, state the purpose for which such loans are given?	
Is it an interest free loan?	YES/NO
If interest is charged, what is the rate charged?	
Which lender provides the loan arrangements?	
Does the company receive any preferential rate or arrangements from the lender?	
EMPLOYEE SHARE SCHEMES	
What Employee Share Schemes are available?	
Approved Profit Sharing Scheme	☐
Savings Related Share Option Scheme	☐
Approved Selective Share Option Scheme	☐
Employee Share Ownership Plan	☐
APPROVED PROFIT SHARING SCHEME	
Provide details of Profit Sharing Schemes (including PRP if appropriate)	
GROUP MEDICAL INSURANCE	
Details of the eligibility conditions for the scheme	
Has this eligibility changed over the last three years?	
Do members join during the year or only at renewal?	
Do you have a high turnover of staff?	YES/NO
Membership details 2001/2002 – Opening and closing membership is required together with a note of when there were substantial reductions in membership during the year (ie when did these reductions take place?).	
2001 – Opening and closing membership details	
2000/2001 – Opening and closing membership details	

Premium details: 2001/2002 2000/2001 1999/2000	
When was the first year of insurance with your current insurer?	
Details of large claims as follows: Year Condition Still on Scheme? Back at Work? Cost	 YES/NO YES/NO YES/NO
Are there any large future claims that have not yet been submitted, and if so, please give details?	
Do you exercise any claims control, and if so, what are they?	
Membership profile detailing the numbers under the Single, Married Family and Single Parent categories, both under 16 and over 65	
Problems	

Setting up an employee satisfaction survey

Typical process chart   1A.33

Once appointed to carry out a benefit review, the following procedure is usually adopted. It would be normal to agree a timetable with a client for completion of the following actions.

Note that it is necessary to be fairly flexible in what is actually included and the format of the communication exercise that goes with it.

IDENTIFY AREAS TO INCLUDE	
Review clients' benefits.	Benefits here could be taken in its widest sense. A fact find is completed to aid this process.

Produce a summary of benefits.	This is intended to be an overview summary, not in great detail. The purpose is to ensure that no misunderstandings over benefits exist at the outset of the project.
Agree a summary of benefits with the client.	The client should 'sign off' the summary as correct.
Agree benefits to include in survey project.	

QUESTIONNAIRE

Produce a first draft for discussion.	A standard is as a template that usually can be used as a first draft.
Review and produce advance draft.	
Discuss and amend advance draft with client.	
Test advance draft with pilot group of employees.	This should be issued with the final draft communication material. This exercise should identify any ambiguities for other misunderstandings that can arise.
Make final amendments, taking account of input from pilot group.	
Provide quality final copy for client to print.	Clients can print the questionnaire in their own house style using their own facilities but we can arrange for printing (or photocopying if wanted by the client) at an extra cost.

METHODS OF ISSUING

Identify current staff communication channels.	This can vary significantly from client to client dependent upon industry, culture, etc.
Agree preferred method of distributing questionnaires.	Generally it is best to have a method whereby people receive a briefing and the questionnaire to complete on the spot.

Agree method of collection.	It is important that whatever method of collection is used it can be shown to offer confidentiality to individual respondents.
Draft communication material.	Communication material should be worded to avoid raising false expectations.
Revise draft communication material.	
Produce final draft communication material taking account of group response.	
Provide quality final copy of communication material for client to print.	
REPORTING	
Agree information required on format of report.	This should be identified at the early stages of the project, by the time that questionnaire design has reached an advanced stage.
Receive response from client.	
Input responses – see systems required below.	Input is expected to be carried out by local secretarial staff but we can provide at extra cost.
Output statistical analysis of results.	
Draft report incorporating results.	
Issue and discuss first draft report.	This discussion will normally identify further statistical analysis that the client wants from the database of information.
Issue final report.	

Example employee survey   1A.34

An example of an employee survey in the form of a questionnaire is illustrated below.

Confidential questionnaire

None of the individual information provided will be seen by anyone else in your company. The company will only receive an independent statistical summary of the results overall.

To help us analyse the statistics from the exercise, please provide the following information:

Sex:
☐ Male ☐ Female

Which age band do you fall into?
☐ 16–24 ☐ 25–30 ☐ 35–44 ☐ 45–54 ☐ 55+

What is your current marital status?
☐ Single ☐ Co-habiting ☐ Married ☐ Separated ☐ Divorced

Do you have dependants?
☐ None ☐ Children ☐ Adult (eg elderly parents)

How long have you been employed by Example Ltd?
☐ Under 1 year ☐ 1–2 years ☐ 2–5 years ☐ 5–10 years ☐ 10 years+

Please indicate by ticking in the appropriate box your view of the statements made below.

Strongly Disagree   *Strongly Agree*

PENSIONS

Membership of some form of pension plan is of great importance to me.
☐ ☐ ☐ ☐ ☐ ☐ ☐

344

None of the individual information provided will be seen by anyone else in your company. The company will only receive an independent statistical summary of the results overall.

Are you a member of the Example Ltd pension scheme?   ☐ Yes   ☐ No

	Strongly Disagree					Strongly Agree

If I were not a member of the Example Ltd pension scheme I would have to make significant payments to a private arrangement

☐ ☐ ☐ ☐ ☐ ☐

I don't need to make any extra pension provisions as the Example Ltd pension scheme will provide a big enough pension to meet my needs

☐ ☐ ☐ ☐ ☐ ☐

DISABILITY

A guaranteed income while unable to work is important to me.

☐ ☐ ☐ ☐ ☐ ☐

I think Social Security benefits would look after me adequately.

☐ ☐ ☐ ☐ ☐ ☐

MEDICAL

It is very important to me to know that I am insured to receive private medical treatment.

☐ ☐ ☐ ☐ ☐ ☐

None of the individual information provided will be seen by anyone else in your company. The company will only receive an independent statistical summary of the results overall.

It is very important to me to know that my family and dependants are insured to receive private medical treatment. ☐ ☐ ☐ ☐ ☐

I would value the ability to receive enhanced medical cover at the expense of other benefits. ☐ ☐ ☐ ☐ ☐

My partner is receiving this cover from somewhere else (their employer, a private insurance, etc). ☐ Yes ☐ No

HOLIDAYS

Strongly Disagree   *Strongly Agree*

I should be able to 'buy' extra days holiday at the expense of other benefits. ☐ ☐ ☐ ☐ ☐

I should be able to cash in part of my Holiday allowance to enhance other benefits. ☐ ☐ ☐ ☐ ☐

The Company may fee that it should insist on a minimum and maximum number of days' holiday between which flexibility is allowed.

What should these be? Min_____days Max_____days

None of the individual information provided will be seen by anyone else in your company. The company will only receive an independent statistical summary of the results overall.

COMPANY CARS

Do you current receive either a company car or a car allowance in lieu?   ☐ Don't qualify   ☐ Car   ☐ Allowance

If you qualify for the Car or Allowance, please answer the following questions:

	Strongly Disagree				Strongly Agree
I would like to have a higher value car/allowance at the expense of other benefits.	☐	☐	☐	☐	☐
If financially neutral, I prefer the concept of personal ownership of my car to use of a company car.	☐	☐	☐	☐	☐

DEATH BENEFITS

The provision of a lump sum to be paid to my dependants in the event of my premature death is important enough to me that I would want private insurance if the company did not provide it.	☐	☐	☐	☐	☐
I should be able to influence the level of cover provided by Example Ltd.	☐	☐	☐	☐	☐

347

None of the individual information provided will be seen by anyone else in your company. The company will only receive an independent statistical summary of the results overall.

DENTAL

I would be ready to pay towards to cost of insurance for me to receive private dental treatment. ☐ ☐ ☐ ☐

I would be ready to pay towards the cost of insurance for my family to receive private dental treatment. ☐ ☐ ☐ ☐

OPTICAL

I would be ready to pay towards the cost of private optical services for myself. ☐ ☐ ☐ ☐

I would be ready to pay towards the cost of private optical services for my family. ☐ ☐ ☐ ☐

LUNCHEON VOUCHERS/CANTEEN

Do you currently receive Luncheon Vouchers from the company? ☐ Don't qualify ☐ Yes ☐ No

How often do you use the company canteen? ☐ Daily ☐ Weekly ☐ Monthly ☐ Never

If you receive Luncheon Vouchers, please answer the following questions:

None of the individual information provided will be seen by anyone else in your company. The company will only receive an independent statistical summary of the results overall.

	Strongly Disagree				*Strongly Agree*
I should be able to cash in the cost of these Luncheon Vouchers to enhance other benefits.	☐	☐	☐	☐	☐
The company should not subsidise the canteen but use the money saved to subsidise other benefits.	☐	☐	☐	☐	☐

CRÈCHE

Do you currently have access to a company-provided or subsidised crèche? ☐ Yes ☐ No

If you do have access to a company crèche, please answer the following questions:

How often do you use the crèche? ☐ Daily ☐ Weekly ☐ Monthly ☐ Never

	Strongly Disagree				*Strongly Agree*
The company should not subsidise the crèche but use the money saved to subsidise other benefits.	☐	☐	☐	☐	☐

OTHER BENEFITS

Do you currently receive or are you a member of any of the following?

Employee Share Ownership ☐ Don't qualify ☐ Yes ☐ No

None of the individual information provided will be seen by anyone else in your company. The company will only receive an independent statistical summary of the results overall.

Profit Related Pay	☐ Yes	☐ No	☐ Don't qualify	
Subsidised Loans	☐ Yes	☐ No	☐ Don't qualify	
Employee Share Scheme	☐ Yes	☐ No	☐ Don't qualify	
Approved Profit Sharing Scheme	☐ Yes	☐ No	☐ Don't qualify	
Share Option Schemes	☐ Yes	☐ No	☐ Don't qualify	

If the answer is yes to any of the above, please answer the following questions:

	Strongly Disagree				*Strongly Agree*
I should be able to buy any of the extra benefits listed above at the expense of other benefits.	☐	☐	☐	☐	☐
I should be able to cash in part of any of the benefits listed above to enhance other benefits.	☐	☐	☐	☐	☐

Prioritise first five benefits – mark with an 'X' any benefits that don't interest you.

There are a number of benefits currently available to you or that could be made available to you. In the boxes below enter a number to put the difference benefits into order with the one you consider most important as 1, 2 being the benefit of next interest, and so on.

☐ Holiday flexibility.   ☐ Continued income in ill health.

None of the individual information provided will be seen by anyone else in your company. The company will only receive an independent statistical summary of the results overall.

☐ Assistance with childcare (crèche etc).

☐ Private optical services.

☐ Private dental insurance.

☐ Profit related pay.

☐ Employee share schemes

☐ Subsidised loan.

☐ Private medical insurance.

☐ Company car/allowance scheme.

☐ Voluntary personal accident scheme.

☐ Employee share ownership plan.

☐ A lump sum payment to my dependants should I die prematurely.

Are there any other benefits that you would include in the above list?

If so, how high up the list would you put it (out of 15)?

Benefit: Placing ☐

Benefit: Placing ☐

Communication audit 1A.35

The audit is intended to be a framework to help to establish the expectations, outcomes, strategies and actions required to implement an effective Communication Plan.

Establish context and concept of changes:

- Company history.
- Forces of change.
- Business strategy and plan for change.
- HR change strategy.
- Pay and reward strategy.
- Benefits strategy.
- Communication strategy.

Benefits change strategy:

- Benefits and surveys.
- Reasons for change– harmonisation, cost reduction, simplification, etc.
- Establish basic change process.
- Establish development and implementation of new benefits regime.
- Establish expectations of change.
- Establish milestones and measurements.

Communication strategy;

- Establishing existing communication strategy including branding.
- Establishing pay and reward and benefits communication strategy (eg selling or educating).
- Determine current climate and culture of organisation, eg cynical, modern, etc.
- Establish numbers and grades.
- Establish location and demographic mix.
- Establish extent of 'tailoring'.

Communication process and resources:

- What needs communicating?

- Who needs communicating to?

- What medal should be used?

- Who will communicate?

- Timescales.

- Training needs.

Key tasks: Flexible benefits project   1A.36

Listed below are the necessary key tasks that must be carried out. A flow chart indicating timescales for these tasks is illustrated at **1A.37** below.

1. **Project team:**

   1. Set up joint client/consultant project team.

   2. Agree basic responsibilities and actions.

   3. Establish expectations from directors.

   4. Establish outcomes to be measured and milestones.

   5. Produce basic project chart with timescales.

2. **Research:**

   1. Carry out and evaluate internal fact find.

   2. Evaluate employee feedback.

   3. Carry out and evaluate benefits audit.

   4. Evaluate competitive benchmarking of pay and benefits.

   5. Based on the above, determine basic strategy and structure for proposed flexible benefit scheme.

   6. Evaluate proposals against 'best practice'.

3. **Strategy and design:**

   1. Identify current situation regarding the total reward system.

   2. Identify benefits most wanted by employees.

   3. Analyse current providers of existing benefits to determine how they will fit in with the new scheme.

4. Agree scheme branding, logo etc.

5. Evaluate information gathered from above and agree overall scheme strategy.

6. Select products to be included in scheme menu.

7. Agree rules and regulations and set limits on entitlements.

8. Research and consolidate tax and National Insurance implications. Gain inland approval of scheme.

9. Plan, design and due diligence.

10. Complete design, administration procedures, communication process and tax and legal requirements.

11. Design scheme manual, members' booklet and preference form.

12. Ongoing management and administration of the scheme.

13. Review options to add additional benefits at a later date.

14. Obtain top team endorsement and support for project.

4. Scheme launch/communication:

1. Identify current communication strategy and develop an appropriate strategy for employee benefits.

2. Ensure that all personnel involved in the launch of the scheme have received comprehensive training in communication skills and possess adequate product and process knowledge.

3. Agree format for launch, (eg group presentations, new scheme handbook, individual counselling and helplines, newsletters, e-mail, etc).

4. Establish feed back and monitoring systems (eg surveys, focus groups, team briefs etc).

5. Employee financial counselling:

1. Agree format of group presentations for launch.

2. Agree and set up a regular review process for employees, eg agree frequency and level of support.

3. Agree parameters for extraordinary consultations, eg changes in lifestyle, such as bereavement.

4. Agree format, frequency for annual group presentations to update staff on scheme changes, changes in legislation etc.

     5.   Set up individual consultations to allow employees to enter the scheme in the most appropriate manner, eg make an informed decision about the initial mix of benefit they require.

6.   Systems and infrastructure:

     1.   Set up administrator access and parameters.

     2.   Set up employee – self service and access.

     3.   Set up payroll interface and shadow salary.

     4.   Set up benefit plan enrolment.

     5.   Set up life event changes.

     6.   Set up leavers and joiners protocol.

     7.   Set up total remuneration statements.

     8.   Set up employee directory.

     9.   Set up links with product providers.

    10.   Set up audit trail.

    11.   Set up interface with Tax, NI, pensions and HR.

    12.   Set up reporting and management information.

    13.   Set up on-line support resources.

7.   Management and administration:

     1.   Define and set service standards for all parts of the scheme.

     2.   Design and issue Administration Manual covering working practices, methods of transmission of data, etc.

     3.   Define and set up management accounting system.

     4.   Define and set up employee flexible benefits records.

     5.   Ensure smooth processing of payments to benefits providers from client and, where relevant, individual employees.

     6.   Define parameters to measure effectiveness of scheme and monitoring.

     7.   Assess client database to manage and monitor above, modify to suit.

     8.   Arrange administrating training for client personnel.

8. Installation and implementation:

1. Validate existing data and system (eg age, gender, addresses, length of service etc).

2. Obtain, collate and review all information and data needed to set up and run the project.

3. Input employee data into system.

4. Input product data into system.

5. Establishing targets and agreed reporting times for the team.

6. Loading and validating data.

7. Establish electronic links between payroll and benefits provider.

8. Co-ordination with payroll and benefit providers to discuss working practices, future transmission of data, contribution data, etc.

9. Set parameters regarding quotations, etc.

10. Define new entrant data 'forms'.

11. Define leaver and change 'forms'.

12. Test and validate new system.

13. Train administration staff.

9. Quality control:

1. Because of the multitude of variables involved, a quality control and code of practice will be developed in conjunction with the Client.

10. Time scales:

1. Need to produce a more detailed project chart with time scales. Post launch questionnaire and feedback will also be required

Timescales: Flexible benefits project   1A.37

The following flowchart lists the recommended timescales for the key tasks listed at **1A.36** above.

Year	2002						2003									
Month	July	Aug	Sept	Oct	Nov	Dec	Jan	Feb	Mar	Apr	May	June	July	Aug	Sept	Oct
Project team	X															
Research	X															
Strategy & design			X													
Scheme launch/communication				X												
Employee financial counselling										X						
Systems & infrastructure				X												
Management & administration				X												
Installation & implementation						X										
Quality control														X		
Timescales	X															
Project team	X															
1.1	X															

Year	2002						2003									
Month	July	Aug	Sept	Oct	Nov	Dec	Jan	Feb	Mar	Apr	May	June	July	Aug	Sept	Oct
1.2	X															
1.3	X															
1.4	X															
1.5	X															
Research																
2.1	X															
2.2	X															
2.3	X															
2.4	X															
2.5		X														
2.6		X														
Strategy & design																
3.1			X													
3.2			X													
3.3				X												

Year	2002						2003									
Month	July	Aug	Sept	Oct	Nov	Dec	Jan	Feb	Mar	Apr	May	June	July	Aug	Sept	Oct
3.4				X												
3.5				X												
3.6				X												
3.7				X												
3.8					X											
3.9						X										
3.10							X									
3.11						X										
3.12																
3.13						X										
3.14																
Scheme launch communication				X												
4.1				X												
4.2							X									

Year	2002						2003									
Month	July	Aug	Sept	Oct	Nov	Dec	Jan	Feb	Mar	Apr	May	June	July	Aug	Sept	Oct
4.3							X									
4.4										X						
Employee financial counselling																
5.1										X						
5.2										X						
5.3										X						
5.4										X						
5.5											X					
Systems & infrastructure																
6.1				X												
6.2				X												
6.3				X												
6.4				X												
6.5				X												

Year	2002						2003									
Month	July	Aug	Sept	Oct	Nov	Dec	Jan	Feb	Mar	Apr	May	June	July	Aug	Sept	Oct
6.6				X												
6.7				X												
6.8				X	X											
6.9					X											
6.10					X											
6.12						X										
6.13						X										
Management & administration				X												
7.1							X									X
7.2							X									X
7.3								X								
7.4																
7.5																
7.6																X

Year	2002						2003									
Month	July	Aug	Sept	Oct	Nov	Dec	Jan	Feb	Mar	Apr	May	June	July	Aug	Sept	Oct
7.7				X												
7.8						X			X							
Installation & implementation																
8.1						X										
8.2																
8.3											X					
8.4																X
8.5						X										
8.6								X								
8.7						X										
8.8								X								
8.9								X								
8.10								X								
8.11								X								

Year	2002						2003									
Month	July	Aug	Sept	Oct	Nov	Dec	Jan	Feb	Mar	Apr	May	June	July	Aug	Sept	Oct
8.12									X							
8.13									X							
Quality control 9.1														X		
Timescales 10.1	X															

363

Employee handbook

Introduction 1A.38

The company's flexible benefits scheme gives you the opportunity to adjust your benefits package to suit your own individual circumstances.

The Company has traditionally provided you with a comprehensive range of employee benefits through your terms and conditions of employment. However, as part of the new strategy of offering a more personal response to your specific needs, and adapting to your changing lifestyles, flexible benefits are the way forward.

Your remuneration package has a total value, made up of salary and benefits. Each benefit within the total package has its own value and Flexible benefits can be arranged in the best way to suit your personal circumstances.

Flexible benefits:

- Private Medical Insurance (single – for those currently not eligible, married, family cover and single parent).

- Critical illness cover.

- Personal accident/disability insurance.

- Trade up/down holidays (up to five days – pro rata for part time).

- Medical screening (for those currently not eligible).

- Additional Voluntary Contributions (AVCs).

- Dental care plan.

Other benefits are called 'core' benefits. These benefits cannot be flexed. This means that the company has a duty of care to provide these, as a minimum level, for everyone. The core benefits within the scheme are listed below.

Core benefits:

- Pension (final salary/money purchase – whichever is applicable).

- Single cover private medical insurance (for those currently eligible).

- Medical screening (for those currently eligible).

- 20 days holiday (not including the privilege day or any extra days awarded for long service).

- Company car (provided by the company as a requirement of the job).

In addition to these core and flexible benefits, the company will be acting as an 'introducer' to a personal car lease plan provider. The provision and contract of this service is independent (ie a private arrangement between employee and the car lease plan company).

Flexible Benefits also allows you to exchange 20% of your shadow salary as defined below, in order to put together a chosen benefits package. This means that you can pay for additional benefits, either through deductions from salary and/or by trading-in other benefits.

Your shadow salary is your current gross contractual salary excluding any bonus payments, car allowance or overtime.

If you currently have a car allowance, or are able choose to take a car allowance at a future date, you can use this allowance to purchase benefits from the flexible benefits scheme in addition to the 20% of your shadow salary.

It is your personal responsibility to read the terms and conditions of any flexible benefits which you want to utilise. If you are in any doubt we recommend that you seek independent financial advice.

You may choose not to change the mix of your core and flexible benefits at all, and that's fine. However, if you do wish to take advantage of the new adaptability that flexible benefits offers, having decided what you would like to alter, you will need to complete a **Preference Form** (see **A1.39** below). This will have to be signed and returned to the HR Department before any changes can be processed.

You should note that it is not possible to exchange benefits and/or holidays for cash payments.

Once you have finalised your choices, completed and returned your Preference Form, your new benefits package will take effect from the next annual review date and will be set for the term of one year, unless you experience a 'lifestyle change'. There are details on 'lifestyle changes' later on in this handbook.

How will flexible benefits work?

Having read and understood the employee handbook, look at your Preference Form, which you will be able to personalise by filling in your remuneration details.

If you do not want to alter any of your benefits, you can leave them exactly as they are. Please tick the appropriate box on your Preference Form. If the HR Department does not receive a completed Preference Form from you, your benefits package will stay the same.

How do I choose?

Read this booklet carefully and consider how much you really value the benefits which you receive at present. (These will be specified on your benefits statement.) Are there some that you value more than others? Are there some that you feel you do not really appreciate at present? Would you appreciate more of some benefits, and less of others?

This is your starting point. Obviously, you will probably want to discuss your thoughts with your partner or family. They may be affected by some of the benefit changes. To help you decide, use the Preference Form, so that you can 'try out' and evaluate various exchange options.

When you have come to your decision, you must enter this on your personal Preference Form. If you choose to change your annual leave entitlement, your Line Manager must also sign your Preference Form; this is so that the necessary arrangements for cover can be put in place.

Flexible benefits – terms and conditions

You will find the terms and conditions relating to your decisions at the back of this booklet. You must read these and the declaration on the Preference Form carefully before you sign. We also advise you to keep a copy of your Preference Form.

What happens next?

The HR Department will issue you with a personal benefits statement. You will then need to use/refer to this in order to fill out your Preference Form. Once you have selected the benefits you want send the completed Preference Form to the HR Department. HR will send you an acknowledgement of the decisions you have made.

In order to ensure that your preferred option choices comply with the statutory requirements for your particular circumstances, the company must approve everyone's selection individually. In addition, any new legislation may alter the implications of the choices that you have made.

Your options will then take effect from 1 January, following their confirmation.

Thereafter, you will have the opportunity to reassess your options annually, except in the case of lifestyle changes, where you may be able to alter your selection earlier.

A step by step guide to choosing your benefits

1. Read the employee handbook carefully.

2. Check your details on your personal benefits statement, and let the HR Department know if there are any errors, before choosing your options.

3. Fill in your own details on the personalised Preference Form.

4. Make use of the Preference Form to test out different options.

5. Let your Line Manager know of any changes to annual leave (cross refer to the page on holidays buying and selling).

6. Read the declaration on the Preference Form.

7. Sign the Preference Form for your choices, and the declaration on the form.

8. Return your signed form to the HR Department by the stated date.

You will hen be sent an acknowledgement confirming your choices and the date from which they will become effective.

Taxation

You must be aware of the tax and National Insurance implications when you make your decision about your Flexible benefits.

Non-taxable benefit

Some of the core and flexible benefits are non-taxable and, therefore, particularly cost effective. These are Additional Voluntary Contributions (AVCs) and medical screening.

Taxable benefits in kind

Some other benefits within the scheme are treated as 'benefits-in-kind', for tax purposes. This means a taxable value is assigned to the benefit purchased on your behalf by the company, which may then reduce your PAYE tax coding. These benefits are private medical insurance and company car.

Voluntary benefits

Voluntary benefits deducted from net salary after tax are not taxable. Basically, you have already paid tax on your salary, and so will not have to pay again on any voluntary benefits that you may choose.

When you consider the choice between a benefit in kind and a voluntary benefit, you must weigh up the different tax implications. The benefit in kind options would reduce your PAYE tax coding, and thereby increase the amount of income tax payable, whereas the voluntary benefit is deducted from your net salary without affecting your tax position.

The voluntary benefits within the flexible benefits scheme are personal accident insurance, critical illness insurance and the dental care plan.

Personal lease plan

The personal lease plan is a private contract between yourself and the provider, which will not affect your PAYE tax and National Insurance.

Lifestyle changes

During the course of your employment with the company there may well be changes in your personal or family circumstances. The circumstances which would constitute 'lifestyle changes' are:

- marriage;
- birth or adoption of a child;

- death of a partner or dependant;
- divorce or permanent separation.

It is recognised that these events may result in changes to your benefit requirements. Therefore, if you do experience a lifestyle change between annual scheme review dates, you are permitted to make appropriate changes to your benefits package.

Terms and conditions

'Partner' is the person with whom you cohabit, at the same permanent address. 'Family' includes your partner and any immediate dependants. Either yourself, or your partner, must be the parent or legal guardian of any dependants. Dependants must be under the age of 18.

Maternity Leave

When an employee returns from maternity/paternity leave they will be given the opportunity to revise their chosen benefits on the birth of his or her baby. If an employee is on maternity leave at the annual enrolment date she will be eligible to enrol when she returns to work.

Core benefits

These are the benefits that most employees receive. These cannot be exchanged.

Pension benefits

The final salary pension scheme is a 1/60th scheme. You contribute 5% of basic salary.

There will be no new joiners to the Final Salary scheme from 1 January 2001. The Company is introducing a new Money Purchase Plan from 1 January 2001 (Employee contribution 4%). Details of the new scheme are available from the Pensions Department.

Private medical insurance

Private medical insurance may already be available to you as a benefit. For some, this will be as single cover with a £100 excess charge, others will be members of the senior scheme and will also be entitled to cover for family members with no excess charge. No changes will be made to these benefits for existing employees

Company cars

If you have a company car as a requirement of your job, this is a core benefit. Some staff are eligible for a choice of a car or car allowance. If you have chosen to have a company car instead of a car allowance, you will be required to retain it until the end of the lease period. You will then have the option to choose a car allowance or another benefit.

Medical screening

Some staff are eligible for medical screening and for these employees this will remain a core benefit.

Holidays

Currently your core entitlement is 20 days (not including the privilege day or any extra days awarded for long service).

Flexible benefits

Additional Voluntary Contributions (AVCs)

This benefit is only available to you if you are a member of one of the company's two pension schemes.

AVCs are a tax-efficient way of building up savings within a pension scheme to provide you with larger pension benefits at retirement.

'How much can I pay into AVCs?'

You may contribute a maximum of 15% of your taxable earnings in any year (less any regular contribution which you are required to make into one of these pension schemes). The amount that you will be able to contribute by way of AVCs will, therefore, be the maximum permitted less any contributions that you are already making to the scheme.

You need to be aware however, that your choices under this scheme may affect your taxable earnings.

'How often may I change the amount of my AVCs?'

Once you have decided on your AVCS, and they have been accepted, you can change the amount that you contribute at any time, subject to the limits described above. You can do this by contacting the Pensions and Trusts Department.

'How will AVCs affect my tax position?'

AVCs currently qualify for tax relief at your highest marginal rate. The amount of National Insurance contributions you pay will not be affected.

'What can my AVCs buy me?'

AVCs paid into the company's pension schemes may only be used to buy a pension for yourself and/or your spouse/dependants when you retire. Please contact the Pensions and Trusts Department should you have any queries concerning AVCs.

Your choice of other benefits may affect the amount of AVCs you can pay.

Questions to consider

- Will the pension I receive from the company's pension scheme, together with any accrued rights I am entitled to under other pension schemes, be enough?

- Will I want to retire early?

- Do I have any other source of income (eg spouse's pension, investments)?

Should you need help with these questions or any others you should obtain independent financial advice.

Holidays

You may choose to increase your current holiday entitlement by buying additional holidays. You can buy up to five days extra.

You may sell some of your holiday entitlement and put the value into your flexible benefits allowance to go towards payment for another benefit which you would value more at the moment, for example, AVCs. **You cannot sell holiday to convert to cash to increase salary.**

'How many days holiday may I sell each year?'

You may sell up to a maximum of five days holiday each year. All employees must take a minimum of 20 days holiday per year.

'How do I know how much one day's holiday is worth?'

The cost of one day's holiday is calculated as 1/260th of your shadow salary if you are working a five-day week. If you work less than a five-day week the calculation will be pro rata. This excludes any bonus payments or other allowances.

'What if something crops up, and I want to change my mind?'

Once you have decided to sell your holiday, on approval of your Line Manager, you are not able to change your mind until the review date.

If you reduce your holiday entitlement and take other benefits, your tax position may be affected.

If you increase your holiday entitlement and take less salary, you may affect the amount of AVCs you are entitled to make and you may also affect your pension benefit entitlements.

Questions to consider

- Do you need extra holiday due to health, family commitments or an extended holiday?

- Do you always use your full holiday entitlement, and wish you had more?

- Do you find at the end of the year that you have not used your entitlement and, therefore, lose out?

- Do you often carry over holiday from one year to the next?

Critical illness cover

Critical illness cover provides a tax-free cash sum if you are diagnosed as suffering from a specified critical illness, whilst an employee of the company. Benefits are provided through an insurance policy, and you may specify the level of cover, which you require.

Flexible benefit options are available in units of £10,000, up to a maximum benefit of £250,000 (or four times your annual salary).

'How often, and by how much, am I allowed to increase the amount of cover?'

You may increase your cover by up to two units of £10,000 at each annual review date and if you experience a 'lifestyle' change within that period, without certification of health.

'So I do not need to have a medical?'

No, however, there is a pre-existing condition exclusion, that applies from the date that cover, or increase in cover, is put into effect. If you choose to take cover of £100,000 or more, you will need to complete a medical declaration.

'Is my spouse or partner automatically covered also?'

Cover may be extended to include your spouse or partner. The level of this cover must not exceed your own, or £50,000 if less. The same table of premium rates would apply for your partner as yourself, with the cost being based on the appropriate age and sex.

'What are the costs involved?'

The current costs are shown on your personal Preference Form. You may not be required to provide any medical evidence. However, if you are not actively at work on the day in which you take out the cover, it will only become effective on your return to work (with the consent of your Doctor or medical adviser).

'What are the Terms associated with Critical Illness Cover?'

No benefit will be paid for any pre-existing condition that you may have suffered prior to start of cover, or increase in cover. The benefit will be payable after the diagnosis of a critical illness for the first time. **Cover includes such critical illness as Alzheimer's disease, blindness, cancer, coronary artery surgery, heart attack etc.**

Critical illness cover is deducted from your net pay, therefore, you pay no additional tax.

Questions to consider

- If I became critically ill, do I have other ways of creating income to support my family and myself until I become fit to work again?

- If I were to become permanently unable to work, would I have any other ways of creating income to support my family and myself?

Personal accident/disability insurance

Personal accident/disability insurance offers you important cover to protect your family and yourself from the possibly disastrous consequences of an accident, by providing tax-free benefits at a low cost.

You are offered a wide range of cash benefits to cover disabling injuries, accidental death and hospital/coma benefits which might arise from an accident.

There is no medical examination, and you are guaranteed acceptance so long as you are a full-time employee.

'How much cover will I have?'

You can choose the number of units that you can afford, and need. Details of costs and cover can be found on your Preference form.

'Can I include my partner and family?'

Yes, you may include your partner and family under the family option, which costs extra.

'Is there any age limit to being accepted for the personal accident insurance?'

The plan is available to all members of staff up to 62 years of age. Acceptance is guaranteed and there are no medicals necessary.

'Are there any limitations on how I would be able to spend the money?'

Accident victims are free to spend their money in whatever way they choose, for example, on home improvements to make mobility easier, or on extra medical care to help them recover from the accident as soon as possible.

Personal accident/disability insurance is deducted from your net salary, therefore, you will incur no additional income tax.

Questions to consider

- Do you have eligible dependants who require cover?

- Would you or your dependants suffer financial problems if you or they had a serious accident or died?

- Would you suffer long-term financial hardship as a result of permanent disability?

- Would extra finance be required to adjust to a new way of living, due to disability?

- Do you have dependants who would need financial support if you were unable to continue working for an extended period?

Please note that personal accident/disability insurance is not a substitute for critical illness cover – if in any doubt please seek independent financial advice.

Private medical insurance

The company has two private medical insurance (PMI) schemes. One is for senior staff, and the other scheme is for employees with over two years' service.

The senior scheme provides private medical insurance for members and their families (where appropriate). It covers the cost of outpatient and inpatient treatment received as private care, up to defined limits. No excess fee is charged to the member.

If you are in the senior scheme you must retain single cover, you may however, use the difference between the value of the single cover and your current level of cover to buy other benefits. You can, of course, choose to keep your existing benefit.

The other scheme provides single basic cover for those with over two years' service. This is a core benefit. There is an excess fee chargeable of £100.

There is a range of options in terms of whom the cover may apply to. These are:

• cover for yourself and your partner;

• cover for yourself, your partner and children; or

• cover for yourself and your children.

'What level of cover is available to me under PMI?'

There are a range of options and terms of cover available. These are shown on the Preference Form and they are not dependent on your age or state of health.

'I am not currently covered by PMI – what are my options?'

You can buy the single basic cover with the £100 excess.

'What if my circumstances change, will I be able to change my cover?'

Once you have selected the level of cover, and this has been accepted by the company, you would normally only be able to change at the annual review. Of course, if you do experience a lifestyle change this would mean that your cover could be reassessed.

'What happens if I want to leave the scheme, may I rejoin it at a later date?'

If you do decide to leave the scheme at any time, and then want to rejoin, you may be asked to supply evidence of good health. In this case, treatment for any pre-existing conditions, diagnosed within the last five years, will not be covered.

'*If I leave the company, how long will my benefits be operative for?'*

Any benefits taken will cease at the end of the month in which you leave the Company.

PMI is treated as a benefit in kind – so your PAYE tax coding will be affected.

Questions to consider

- Is the availability of prompt medical attention important to you and your dependants?

- Do you or they have eligible dependants who require cover?

- Do they typically have extensive medical expenses that are not covered by health insurance?

- Does your partner have cover available to them, or your family?

- Would delayed medical treatment seriously affect your own or your family's health?

Medical screening

You may be entitled to either an Executive or Standard medical screen. If so, this must be retained as a core benefit. The medical screenings are available at medical centres in your area.

If you are not already receiving this benefit, or if you wish to enhance your existing core benefit, you can use your flexible benefits allowance to purchase an annual medical screen at the centre of your choice, shown on the Preference Form. Details of how to contact these clinics can be obtained from the HR department.

'*What are the different options available to me?'*

You can take advantage of the following options:

- an Executive Health Assessment, which is carried out by an experienced doctor;

- a Standard Well Person Screen, carried out by an experienced doctor;

- a Basic Well Person Screen which is carried out by an experienced nurse.

'How much will the various options cost me?'

Please refer to your personal Preference Form to see the cost of purchasing an annual medical screen.

'How do I go about organising my medical screening?'

When you have chosen the particular type of screening you would prefer, you can make your own appointment with the centre or clinic of your choice. This means that the company does not see any of your test results, ensuring complete confidentiality.

'What happens if I need further tests, after the first consultation?'

If this were to happen, you would either stand the cost yourself, or retrieve the cost through your own medical insurance or PMI if you have chosen this as a benefit.

'If I have selected this option and then leave the company before the screening, what would happen?'

In these circumstances payments made would not be refunded.

Medical screening is a non taxable benefit. If you choose this option you may affect the amount of AVCs you are entitled to make and may also affect your pension entitlements. If in any doubt you should contact an independent financial adviser.

Question to consider

- Do you have concerns over your health, which maybe you have put off dealing with?

The Company encourages all employees to be aware of their medical welfare.

Dental care plans

Most people use the NHS for dental treatment. However, over the last five years there has been a trend towards private care. There has been a substantial increase in the cost of dental care. NHS patients now have to fund 80% of fees up to a maximum of £348. Although many parts of the country remain well serviced by the NHS, 30% of all treatment is carried out privately.

Private charges vary from dentist to dentist.

'What sort of cover do the plans offer?'

Flexible Benefits offers two different plans, providing cover depending on which plan you chose, ranging from accident and emergency cover, to a significant contribution to even the most expensive private medical fees. The choice is yours. Please refer to the dental care plan brochure for the details. **All reimbursements are made in accordance with a benefit schedule available from the HR Department, with separate annual limits for both routine and accident and emergency treatment.**

'Can I choose whether or not I use the National Health Service?'

Yes, you have a free choice of dentist, either NHS – the Plus option ,or private – the Premium option, and no dental checks are required for acceptance to any of the schemes.

'How soon can cover start, and what about any problems that I may have already?'

Cover is effective from the next annual review date, and all necessary treatment, including an existing course of treatment, is covered from day one. All pre-existing conditions are covered, except for oral cancer.

'Is there a limit to the number of claims you can make, say, in a year?'

There is no limit to the frequency of claims – any number can be submitted. Reimbursement is available within the guidelines set out in the particular plan's benefit schedule. There is a simple claims procedure, and a prompt claims payment service.

'Would we be covered whilst travelling abroad and, for example, if we were injured?'

Cover is worldwide, and takes into account accident and sports injuries.

Dental insurance is deducted from your net salary; you will pay no further income tax if you decide to take this option.

Important: if you chose to opt out of this benefit at a later stage you will not be able to re-join.

With the Plus scheme, most, if not all, NHS charges are reimbursed up to an annual limit of £600.00. The Premium scheme contributes towards private charges up to an annual limit of £950.00.

Questions to consider

- Do you require dental cover?

- Does your partner or spouse have dental cover available to them?

- If you do have cover already, does it provide the kind of cover you require?

Personal lease plan

The Company will act as an 'introducer' to a personal car lease plan provider. The provision and contract of this service is independent (ie a private arrangement between employee and the car lease plan company). The company will not act as guarantor or pick up the cost of any default.

The personal lease plan allows you to finance a new car for yourself or a member of your family, and you are not tied to a specific dealer, make or model of vehicle. You are able to lease the car at an agreed guaranteed purchase price, and enjoy the security and peace of mind of owning a fully maintained and serviced vehicle.

'Couldn't I get the same sort of deal from any motor dealer?'

Unlike various plans from specific dealers, this scheme allows you to take advantage of a competitive reliable finance scheme to purchase **any** make or model of car.

'How do I go about this?'

First, choose the make and model of car that you or your family member wants. Next, decide whether you want to keep the car for two or three years, taking into account the annual mileage you are likely to do. The monthly repayments are then calculated to cover the difference between the 'on the road' price (minus any deposit you choose to pay), and the 'option to purchase' price (see below).

'May I use my current car as part exchange?'

Yes, you can use your current car as part exchange. Its value can be used as all, or part, of a deposit.

'What happens at the end of the lease period?'

At the end of the agreement you would have a variety of options to choose from:

You can return the car, choose another one, and start another agreement. You could purchase the car outright – this would be at the 'option to purchase' price previously agreed. Finally, you can simply return the car and walk away.

Questions to consider

- Do you need to purchase more than one vehicle? Under the personal lease plan you can have as many vehicles as you like for your partner or children.

- Do you need reliable, well maintained transport?

Rules and regulations

- For new permanent staff there will be a two-week period, immediately following their start date, in which they may opt into the scheme.

- There will be a fixed date for registration at the commencement of the scheme.

- The date for annual review of the scheme will be 1 January.

- Wherever relevant, the financial value of a flexible option will be based on annual shadow gross salary.

- You can forego up to 20% of your annual shadow salary in order to provide flexible benefits.

- There is no option to 'cash in' unused benefits at the end of the scheme period.

- All options exercised must fall within statutory limits imposed from time to time by the Government.

- The company will set core benefits from time to time.

- Participants will not be able to exchange core benefits, as defined in the employee handbook, for additional salary.

- Each option will have its own individual specifications, cost, and rules and regulations.

- Employees wishing to participate in the scheme must sign a Preference Form indicating the benefits that they would like the company to consider providing for them for the duration of the scheme year and that they acknowledge that certain benefits (indicated in the handbook) will involve deductions for income tax and National Insurance contributions.

- Flexible Benefits, and any subsequent changes to them, will only be accepted on an authorised Preference Form obtainable from the HR department. Qualified personnel, to ensure that the choices fall within the scheme rules and are acceptable to the company, will then check this.

- Options may only be altered annually, on the annual review date, except in the case of 'lifestyle changes'.

- All choices and/or changes will be confirmed to the employee by means of a signed acknowledgement. This could include changes brought about by changes in legislation.

- If an employee takes maternity leave, their return to work will constitute a lifestyle change.

- Terms such as 'partner', 'dependant', 'family' etc, are clearly defined in the section on lifestyle changes, and must be strictly adhered to.

- Unless otherwise specified, all Flexible benefits will cease immediately an employee leaves the company.

- There will be no refund for unused benefits once selected and approved.

Preference Form

An example of a typical preference form is illustrated below.

Flexible Benefits – Typical **Preference Form**

Full Name:	Fred Bloggs	Department:	Communications
Employee Number:	123456	NI Number:	AB654861A

YOU WILL NEED TO REFER TO THE FLEXIBLE BENEFITS EMPLOYEE HANDBOOK AND YOUR PERSONAL STATEMENT OF CURRENT BENEFITS BEFORE AND WHILST YOU ARE CALCULATING YOUR OPTIONS BELOW.

YOU MUST ALSO ENSURE THAT THE FINAL BALANCE OF YOUR SELECTION (SEE SECTION 11) IS EQUAL TO ZERO BEFORE SUBMITTING YOUR FORM. THE BEST WAY OF DOING THIS IS BY COMPLETING SECTION 3 LAST.

FIGURES BELOW ARE FOR ILLUSTRATION ONLY AND MAY DIFFER ACCORDING TO YOUR PERSONAL TAX CIRCUMSTANCES.

Section 1   Tax details

In order to help you understand the effects of taxation on your Flexible Benefits, there is a simple illustration built into this preference form that shows you the approximate affect of tax on your selection. (Please note that this does not include National Insurance.)

If you pay tax at 22% please enter 22 in this box, if you pay tax at 40% please enter 40 in the box. (Most people will start paying tax at 40% when taxable income exceeds £32,785.)

	%
	40

383

Section 2   Salary details

Your current shadow salary **(Fig. 1)**

		£40,000.00

Section 3   Flexible benefits allowance (complete this section last)

From the benefits you are already entitled to, if applicable, you may exchange **(Fig. 5)**.

		£4,326.00

If you are entitled to a car allowance and the balance of your Flexible Benefits is above zero, you can transfer any surplus back into your car allowance by entering the amount here.

		£

(NB Must be less than your total car allowance – Fig. 3)

Do you wish to use some of your Salary to add to your basic Flexible Benefits allowance?

	0.00

If you do, please enter the amount (in £s) here (up to a maximum of 20% of your shadow salary).

2.13 %	£853.60

Total Flexible Benefits allowance (combination of the three boxes above)

The balance of your Flexible Benefits allowance is now

		£5,179.60 £0.00

Section 4   Additional Voluntary Contributions

Do you wish to alter your current Additional Voluntary Contributions (AVCs)?

If you do please enter the total % you now wish to contribute here.

A maximum of 10% of shadow salary for Group A members or 9% for Group C members.

10 %	£4,000.00

If you are altering your AVCs and are already making contributions enter your current contribution details here **(Fig. 2)**.

	%	£
	5	2,000.00

Total change in costs of AVCs selected: £ **2,000.00**

Notional change in net amount added to/deducted from pay: £ 2,000.00

The balance of your Flexible Benefits allowance is now £0.00

Section 5   Holidays

Do you wish to trade up or trade down some of your holiday entitlement? A maximum of five days to the nearest half-day can be traded (pro rata for part time employees).

	Days	£
Trade down (decrease holidays).	0	0.00
Trade up (increase holidays).	0	0.00

*For maximum entitlement see **Fig. 6***

Total balance from holidays traded: £ 0.00

Notional net amount added to/deducted from pay: £ 0.00

The balance of your Flexible Benefits allowance is now £0.00

385

Section 6 Critical Illness Protection

Do you want Critical Illness cover?

From the table below, select the amount of cover required at your age (eg if you are 43 years old and require £40,000 of cover, the cost would be £109.60 per annum).

Age (age next birthday)	Male (£s) (per £10,000 benefit)	Female (£s) (per £10,000 benefit)
Up to 25	6.60	4.10
26 to 30	7.20	8.70
31 to 35	10.10	16.40
36 to 40	14.50	28.30
41 to 45	27.40	45.60
46 to 50	53.70	69.00
51 to 55	95.80	93.60
56 to 60	169.80	138.20
61 to 65	282.80	191.80

Age	Gender	Amount of cover	Cost (£s)
43	male	40,000	191.80
			0

Please confirm your choice:

Your partner's choice:

Total cost of Critical Illness cover selected:

£ 191.80

Net amount deducted from pay: 191.80

The balance of your Flexible Benefits allowance is now: £0.00

Section 7   Personal Accident/Disability Cover

Do you want Personal Accident/Disability cover?

From the table below, select the number of units or amount of cover required (eg if you require 6 units of cover on the family protection basis, the cost would be £156 for the first year and £187.20 in the second year).

NB Personal accident / disability cover must be effected for minimum of two years

Units	Accidental death Amount of cover (£s)		Disability Amount of cover (£s)		Personal protection Cost (£s)		Family protection Cost (£s)	
	Year 1	Year 2	Year 1	Year 2	Year 1	Year 2	Year 1	Year 2
1	7,500	15,000	15,000	25,000	Free	15.60	15.60	31.20
2	15,000	30,000	30,000	50,000	15.60	31.20	31.20	62.40
3	22,500	45,000	45,000	75,000	31.20	46.80	62.40	93.60
4	30,000	60,000	60,000	100,000	46.80	62.40	93.60	124.80
5	37,500	75,000	75,000	125,000	62.40	78.00	124.80	156.00
6	45,000	90,000	90,000	150,000	78.00	93.60	156.00	187.20
7	52,500	105,000	105,000	175,000	93.60	109.20	187.20	218.40
8	60,000	120,000	120,000	220,000	109.20	124.80	218.40	249.60

| 8 | 67,500 | 135,000 | 135,000 | 225,000 | 124.80 | 140.40 | 249.60 | 280.80 |
| 9 | 75,000 | 150,000 | 150,000 | 250,000 | 140.40 | 156.00 | 280.80 | 312.00 |

No of units	Personal or Family protection
6	Family

Please confirm your choice:

Total cost of Personal Accident/Disability cover (year 1 of 2): £ 156.00

Net amount deducted from pay: 156.00

The balance of your Flexible Benefits allowance is now £0.00

Section 8   Private Medical Insurance

*Single basic cover for Private Medical Insurance is already provided for some staff as a core benefit. You may wish to continue with your current level of cover, however, Flexible Benefits allows you to exchange the difference between your core single cover and your current level of cover (this value is referred to in **Fig. 4**). If you do not already receive PMI as part of your package, you can choose to buy cover as shown in the table below or you can choose to upgrade from basic to executive cover.*

A: Already entitled to Executive cover PMI (for senior staff)

B: Already entitled to Basic single cover PMI (staff with more than two years' service)

C: Not entitled to PMI

Level	Cost (£s)		
	A	B	C
Single Basic★			205.00
Single Executive★★		205.00	410.00
Married Executive★★	405.00	610.00	815.00

388

	726.00	931.00	1136.00
Family Executive**			
Single Parent Executive**	324.00	529.00	734.00

*Single Basic cover carries an excess of £100 per annum for any claim

**Executive cover carries no excess charges

Group	Level
C	Single parent Exec

Please confirm your choice:

Total cost of private medical insurance cover selected: £ 734.00

Net amount deducted from pay: £0.00

The balance of your Flexible Benefits allowance is now

Section 9   Medical Screening

For those not already entitled to Medical Screening this option offers two levels of screening.

Option	Cost (£s)	
	Finsbury Circus	Saxon Clinic
Basic Well Person (nurse based)	70.00	
Standard Well Woman (by doctor)	130.00	123.00
Standard Well Man (by doctor)	130.00	149.00
Executive (by doctor)	258.00	236.00

Option	Location
Standard Well Woman	Finsbury Circus

Please confirm your choice:

389

Total cost of Medical Screening selected: £ 0.00

Net amount deducted from pay: 0.00

The balance of your Flexible Benefits allowance is now £0.00

Section 10   Dental Plan

This option offers either NHS cover (Plus) or private dental cover (Premier).

Option	Cost (£s)
Plus	61.20
Premier	97.80

Please confirm your choice:

Option
Premier

Total cost of Dental Plan cover selected: £ 97.80

Net amount deducted from pay: 97.80

The balance of your Flexible Benefits allowance is now £0.00

Section 11   Total costs of options selected and resultant Flexible Benefits balance

This is a summary of the options you have chosen, their costs and the resultant balance for your Flexible Benefits allowance.

Benefit	Costs (£s)
Benefits already entitled to	4,326.00
Car allowance surplus	0.00

Additional salary	853.60
Total Costs of Additional Voluntary Pensions selected	–4,000.00
Total balance from holidays traded	0.00
Total Cost of Critical Illness cover selected	–191.80
Total cost of Personal Accident/Disability cover selected	–156.00
Total Cost of Private Medical Insurance cover selected	–734.00
Total Cost of Medical Screening selected	0.00
Total Cost of Dental Plan cover selected	–97.80
The balance of your Flexible Benefits allowance is now	*0.00*

	£
The total cost of the benefits you have chosen is:	5,179.60
The approximate change to your net salary will be:	2,379.60

Section 12   Confirmation of Flexible Benefits selected

This section is your confirmation that you wish to select the options above as your preference for this year.

If you do not wish to change any of your benefits pleases put an 'X' in this box

Please return your completed form to HR by 1 October latest. If you make no return, your benefits will remain unchanged. I authorise XXXX to make the necessary adjustments to my salary and benefits in accordance with the preferences I have indicated above.

I hereby confirm that I have read and understand the Employee Handbook explaining the Flexible Benefits scheme. I also confirm that I have considered and understand the tax and National Insurance implications of my choices, after taking professional advice which I felt appropriate Consequently, I hereby indemnify XXXX from any liability or responsibility in the exercise of my choices.

I understand that the choices I have made, if agreed with XXXX, will constitute a change to my terms and conditions of employment in so far as I have elected to take, or not to take, benefits which were previously part of my compensation and benefits package.

I further understand that XXXX reserves the right to alter Flexible Benefits or any of its constituent parts at any time.

Signed _____   Date _____
Fred Bloggs

Signed _____   Date _____
Line Manager
(Only required when changing your holidays)

Signed _____   Effective Date _____
Acknowledge and authorised by HR Department

Signed _____   Date _____
Finance Department

Third-party service level agreement

Definition 1A.40

The system is defined as an application, with supporting services, which is installed, maintained and controlled by Third Party Administrator (TPA) in its own nominated data centre or (where agreed with the Licensee (Company), on the server of the Licensee).

It performs the following functions:

● flexible benefits administration;

● self-service enrolment and renewals (where the duration of the agreement with the Licensee is more than one year);

● standard benefit reporting (unless any specific reporting requirements are agreed with TPA in writing).

It does *not* include those services that are hosted outside of their facilities, such as the products provided by external parties and the communications equipment that is outside of the hosting environment used by them.

Specifically, TPA cannot be responsible or liable for any loss of service due to network connectivity disruption on the Internet, or any devices attached to it, out of TPA's control.

The components that comprise the system application is as follows:

● the 'live' web server(s) that acts as an interface for the TPA;

● the system application;

● the 'live' database server(s) which holds the information used by the system application; and

● the system application.

Service availability 1A.41

TPA undertakes to provide the system during operating hours (see (b) below) with an availability of 95%. For the avoidance of doubt it will be available 24 hours a day, 365 days a year, but will be subject to a minimum guarantee of availability of 80%. This figure will be calculated as an average availability percentage calculated over each calendar month.

However, where there are any restrictions on the provision of the services which are out of the control of TPA, such restrictions shall not be taken into account when calculating the 95% availability of the sysytem:

(1) Definition of system availability – for the purposes of this Agreement 'available' shall mean that the system is contactable, running and able to process legitimate requests from each Licensed Employee so entitled to access the Customer Benefits Scheme.

(2) Operating hours – the helpdesk service will be available Monday to Friday from 8 am to 6 pm with the exception of bank and public holidays in England.

(3) Severity levels, escalation procedures and contact points – the following severity levels exist within this Agreement:

- **Minor loss of service (severity level A)** – this occurs when a particular element or component of the system, including but not limited to, a product or service is inaccessible ('Minor Loss') and, in TPA's opinion, this inaccessibility has no impact on the rest of it. Several of these losses may occur from the same source or at the same time.

- **Major loss of service (severity level B)** – this occurs when a major system component or element of the system such as the Licensed Employee update system is inaccessible by the Licensee ('Major Loss') and such a Major Loss affects more than 50% of the Licensed Employees and which may affect other system components of it.

- **Critical loss of service (severity level C)** – this occurs when the whole of the Customer Benefits Scheme becomes unavailable for a length of time greater than that where a fail-over situation will correct the problem; fail-over being in this instance the initiation of an automatic recovery of the system and measured for the purpose of this Agreement as five minutes ('Critical Loss'). Severity level C includes Licensed Employees being unable to access the system.

Escalation procedures are as follows:

- TPA's initial acknowledgement and initial response to a Minor, Major or Critical Loss will be as set out in the table below.

- In the case of Major or Critical Loss of service, if the problem has not been resolved within 24 hours of notification by Licensee, TPA will appoint a crisis manager to co-ordinate the system recovery and will advise the Licensee of the Severity level allocated to the Major or Critical Loss. Thereafter he will report regularly to the Licensee between 8 am to 6 pm, Monday to Friday as to the expected time to recovery.

Severity level	Initial acknow-ledgement	Initial response	Feedback periods	Reso-lution time
Minor A	Within one hour of notifica-tion.	24 hours of notifica-tion.	Daily Mon to Fri	30 days
Major B	Within ten minutes of notifica-tion.	Two hours of notifica-tion.	Every two hours during helpdesk hours	7 days
Critical C	Immediate on notification (if notification is made during helpdesk hours).	One hour of notifica-tion.	Every hour during helpdesk hours.	1 day

Contact with TPA should be made to their help desk via email helpdesk@thethirdpartyprovider.com in the first instance with a clear description of the problem, a contact name and email address and telephone number if appropriate.

In the case of Major Loss or Critical Loss the help desk may be telephoned directly on the published number between 8 am and 6 pm excluding Saturdays and Sundays, and public holidays and bank holidays in England.

The help desk will be available on a schedule aligned with the service availability.

A problem reference number will be issued and progress will be relayed through email by the help desk unless this method is deemed inappropriate by the help desk.

A schedule of contact names and numbers will be provided by the third-party provider to the Licensee prior to the implementation date and will be updated from time to time as appropriate.

A list of Frequently Asked Questions (FAQs) will be available online 24 hours a day, 7 days a week.

(4) Emergency Downtime Procedure – should an unforeseen emergency occur where the Customer Benefits Scheme would have to be taken offline, TPA shall notify the relevant contacts at the Licensee by telephone in the first instance with notification of the extent of the emergency and an outlook as to the duration of the downtime required. All subsequent notification will occur through the use of email.

Issue/reissue of passwords 1A.42

TPA will be responsible for reissuing passwords to the Licensee's employees. This will be managed electronically – employees will request a new password by email and TPA will issue the new password by email. Email requests will be monitored daily (within business days) and passwords reissued by email within four hours of receipt of request.

Service measurement 1A.43

Service measurement will be based upon the system availability figures produced jointly between TPA and the hosting facility at the end of each calendar month.

These figures will include the average system uptime plus any instances of system unavailability during the preceding month.

Any incident that has an impact on availability in the previous month will have an incident report completed and circulated to TPA and the company's nominees. This report will include the nature of the incident, the cause, and the nature of the resolution.

Remedies under the Agreement 1A.44

In the event of non-delivery of the terms of the Service Level Agreement, TPA will undertake to reimburse the company with an amount equivalent to two times the pro-rata license fee.

Regular review meetings   **1A.45**

Regular review meetings will be held with the designated primary contact of the company and the TPA assigned account manager. The meetings will be scheduled as follows:

First month:	Weekly
Months 2/3:	Monthly
Months 4 onwards:	Quarterly

The client will have the right to call an extraordinary meeting at any time having given seven days' notice.

Appendix 2 — List of providers

This appendix lists the contacts details of the following providers:

- Jardine Lloyd Thompson – Reward consulting services
- Jardine Lloyd Thompson – Generic site offering
- Vebnet – Third-party provider
- Norwich Union Healthcare – Health care insurance
- National Dental Plan – Dental plan insurance
- Denplan – Dental plan insurance
- Leapfrog Childcare Vouchers – Childcare vouchers
- Accor Services (UK) – Childcare vouchers
- Incorpore Corporate Fitness Network – Sports and leisure clubs
- Safeway – Gift vouchers
- Automobile Association (AA) – Motor assistance

Third-party providers

Jardine Lloyd Thompson

Reward consulting services

- *Project management* – from complete 'turnkey' projects, such as flexible benefits, to advice only.
- *Strategic reward* – helping clients to identify future business issues and developing reward policies and strategies to suit.

- *Research* – a variety of tools and techniques for gathering information that also contributes to the communication process.

- *Administration services* – from simple advice to the provision of outsourced administration for a variety of process including flexible benefits, pensions administration, scheme accounting and pensioner payroll services.

- *Communication* – unique blend of consultancy and support services designed to improve the appreciation and understanding of reward.

- *Flexible benefits* – feasibility, design, strategy, communication and implementation.

- *Employee share schemes and benefits trusts* – feasibility, design, strategy, communication and implementation. This includes corporate issues and associated technical considerations.

For further information contact Philip Hutchinson.
Tel: 0161 957 8087
Email: Philip_Hutchinson@JLTGroup.com.

Jardine Lloyd Thompson

Choices

Choices offers a generic solution to what has traditionally been a "tailored only" market.

Choices Tailored offers a variety of tailored services so clients can modify **Choices** to suit their own needs. This covers everything from feasibility studies to full outsourcing.

For further information contact Philip Hutchinson
Tel: 0161 957 8087
Email: Philip_Hutchinson@JLTGroup.com

Vebnet Limited

Third-party provider

The company offers technology solutions for the administration of both fixed and flexible employee benefit programmes.

Vebnet has launched its first product called FIX&FLEX and is promoting this product to mid market companies with 100–5,000 employees. FIX&FLEX supports online and paper-based enrolment, for flex schemes, in which employees have the opportunity to mix and match their benefit selection up to the allowance the employer has defined and within the rules of the scheme. Therefore, employees are able to purchase additional benefits that are relevant to their lifestyle, and which traditionally have not been offered by their employers. Throughout the enrolment cycle, the benefit administrator can view the status of enrolment, track and manage activity to ensure the process remains on schedule. A comprehensive reporting suite exists which allows the administrator to run reports covering product take-up, premiums payable and employee/employer cost reports. Reports can be produced using multiple display and filter options and can be created in HTML or saved as an Excel spreadsheet.

For further information contact Gerry O'Neill CEO, Vebnet Limited, CBC House, 24 Canning Street, Edinburgh EH3 8EG.
Tel: 0131 272 2708
Mobile: 07990 584096
Fax: 0131 272 2800
Email: gerry@vebnet.com
Website: www.vebnet.com

Private medical insurance

Norwich Union Healthcare

Norwich Union Healthcare offers a range of Private Medical Insurance, Income Protection and Cash Plan products. Listed below are a number of products that are particularly suited to corporate clients:

- **Company Fair + Square First/Club** – Fair + Square First and Club are comprehensive private medical insurance (PMI) products which offers the individual the choice between using the NHS and benefiting from money back or opting for private treatment.

- **Company Express Care** – Express Care is a comprehensive PMI plan providing prompt access to specialists (via the General Practitioner) for eligible out-patient, day-patient and in-patient consultations, diagnosis or treatment. It also provides up to 90 days emergency overseas cover.

- **Company Trust Care** – Trust Care is a comprehensive product providing most of the benefits of Express Care, except overseas cover, but using private facilities available in NHS/Trust Partnership hospitals.

- **Company Cash Plan** – A range of plans offering up to 100% money back towards routine medical expenses such as dental and optical check-ups.

- **Group Income Protection** –Group Income Protection is an income protection scheme taken out by employers to ensure their workforce still receive a regular income, should most types of illness and injury prevent them from working.

For further information contact Norwich Union Healthcare, Chilworth House, Hampshire Corporate,Park, Templars way, Eastleigh, Hampshire SO53 3RY.
Tel: 023 8037 2277
Fax: 023 8037 2459
Email: healthcare@norwich-union.co.uk
Website: www.norwichunion.com/healthcare

Note: For security and administration, calls and e-mails to and from Norwich Union may be monitored and/or recorded.

Dental healthcare

National Dental Plan (NDP)

- Free choice of dentist – either NHS or private.

- No dental checks.

- All pre-existing conditions covered (except oral cancer).

- Immediate cover – all treatment, including an existing course of treatment, is covered from day one.

- Simple claims procedure and prompt claims payment.

- No limit to frequency of claims – any number of claims may be submitted, although reimbursement is available within the limits and regulations set out in the plan benefit schedule.

- Worldwide cover.

- Cover for accident and sports injury, including contact sports.

For further information contact National Dental Plan Ltd, Ibex House, Minories, London, EC3N 1DY.
Tel: 020 7480 7201
Fax: 020 7481 2842
Email: ndp@nationaldental.co.uk
Website: www.ndp@nationaldental.co.uk

Denplan

Denplan offers employees dental plans with cash-back benefits. The plans are simple and allow employees to receive immediate cover for their dental treatment. Employees can also choose the level of cover to suit their needs. The dental plans are geared towards the reimbursement of dental costs incurred by the average UK adult. The focus is on preventative dentistry, supported by an encouragement to attend a dentist on a regular basis. This means Denplan offers an opportunity to add value to benefits packages from £3.50 per person per month. Three levels of cover cater for occasions when employees experience a dental accident or emergency, and include plans that provide cover for their regular dental care. Denplan can provide cover for employees at home and abroad and offer the choice of visiting any dentist, whether NHS or private.
Tel: 0800 169 3279
E-mail: corporatesales@denplan.co.uk

Childcare vouchers

Leapfrog Childcare Vouchers

The Leapfrog Childcare Voucher Scheme provides for employers and employees to obtain National Insurance savings through their childcare costs.

- Employees order the required amount of vouchers.

- The information is sent to Leapfrog accompanied by payment.

- Vouchers are issued direct to employees.

- Employees pass on the voucher as payment to their Childcare Provider.

- Vouchers are reimbursed to the Childcare Provider via Bacs or Cheque.

One of the most significant aspects of the voucher scheme is that vouchers can be used for children up to the age of 16 and employees can, as a parent or guardian, choose where they want to use the vouchers. This is particularly important if their child is already settled in a routine with one Childcare Provider.

For further information:
Free Phone: 0800 783 7624
Email: Vouchers@leapfrogdaynurseries.co.uk
Website: www.leapfrogdaynurseries.co.uk

Childcare vouchers

Accor Services (UK)

Accor Services offers a range of advanced services designed to make it easier for employers to offer family-friendly policies cost-effectively. The Group has strong relationships with other bodies in the childcare sector and is acknowledged as a leader in the field of worklife benefits.

In addition to Childcare Vouchers, Accor Services' product portfolio includes:

Family life solutions

For advice and support on all elder care, disabled care and childcare related issues.

Employee advisory resource (EAR)

The UK's leading provider of employee assistance programmes improving workplace productivity.

Eyecare vouchers

To enable employers to discharge their legal obligation to provide eye care.

Clean Way vouchers

To provide employees with a simple effective way to have working clothes dry cleaned.

Luncheon vouchers

To enable employers to provide a flexible meal benefit.

For further information contact the Sales Information Line on: 020 7887 1246.

Health club membership

Incorpore Corporate Fitness Network

The Incorpore Corporate Fitness Network has been created to provide employees with access to corporate membership rates at health clubs all over the UK. This gives employees the freedom of choice to select the most convenient and desirable health club suitable to their needs, whether close to the office or home the employee is still eligible for that health clubs lowest corporate membership rate. The network, endorsed by both the Fitness Industry Association (FIA) and the International Health Racquet and Sportsclub Association (IHRSA) is contracted with over 1,500 health clubs in the UK and Ireland and membership also includes access to their hotel network.

Incorpore also provide advice and assistance to employees searching for lifestyle, health and wellness information from nutritional advice to stress management and smoking cessation programmes. In the new Incorpore ACTIVE website section, members can find information, competitions and promotions on a whole host of related lifestyle, health and fitness issues and products.

The cost of the Incorpore benefit to your staff is based on a per person year basis and is dependent upon the total number of employees.

For further information contact Glenn Rankin, Managing Director.
Tel: 01444 411411
Email: inf@incorpore.co.uk
Website: http://www.incorpore.co.uk

Gift vouchers

Safeway

Gift vouchers can be used to motivate, recruit or used as an incentive in order to promote staff performance or as part of a bonus scheme.

As a flexible benefit Safeway Gift Vouchers can provide employees with a monthly discount on their shopping budget. Alternatively, a savings scheme could be implemented where staff save through their salary during the year and receive a lump sum including the discount entitlement as a saving or in additional vouchers.

For further information contact the Sales Team.
Tel: 0800 953 0169 (freephone)
Tel: 01704 516340 (standard rate)
Fax: 01704 516345
Email: sales@safewayvouchers.co.uk

Motor assistance

Automobile Association (AA)

Vehicle-Based Personal Membership can now be tailor made to fit in with Flex Schemes and a number of large companies now incorporate this into their schemes. The plan is flexible in approach, allowing for existing AA members to transfer their existing personal memberships at renewal.

All four levels of Breakdown Cover are available: Roadside; Relay; Homestart and Relay Plus. Each plan is adjusted to fit into the requirements of the various flex schemes.

For further information contact Third-Party Sales Support, AA Membership, Fanum House, Dog Kennel Lane, Halesowen, West Midlands B63 3BT.
Tel: 08705 444222
Fax: 0121 501 7861

Index

410

412

413

Get ahead

with www.pensionsPro.com

pensionsPro Premium
All the primary materials and legal references you need. Includes legislation, cases, pensions law reference, IR materials, article citator and lots more.

pensionsPro Essentials
Guidance on running schemes and an invaluable on-screen form filler containing all the Revenue forms. Includes a complete service for pension scheme administration and IR12.

pensionsPro Legal Documents
All the legal documents you need for setting up a scheme, running a scheme and dealing with a scheme transfer.

See how much time and money you could save.
Visit www.pensionsPro.com for your *FREE 7-day trial*.

Check out the website for details of prices –
we think you will be pleasantly surprised. Alternatively, call our sales team on 020 8686 9141 ext. 5233 or email sales@pensionspro.com.

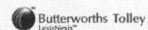